OLD INDUSTRIAL CITIES SEEKING NEW ROAD OF INDUSTRIALIZATION

Models of Revitalizing Northeast China

OLD INDUSTRIAL CITIES SEEKING NEW ROAD OF INDUSTRIALIZATION
Models of Revitalizing Northeast China

editors

Mark Wang
The University of Melbourne, Australia

Zhiming Chen
University of Wollongong, Australia

Pingyu Zhang
The Chinese Academy of Sciences, China

Lianjun Tong
The Chinese Academy of Sciences, China

Yanji Ma
The Chinese Academy of Sciences, China

World Scientific

NEW JERSEY · LONDON · SINGAPORE · BEIJING · SHANGHAI · HONG KONG · TAIPEI · CHENNAI

Published by

World Scientific Publishing Co. Pte. Ltd.
5 Toh Tuck Link, Singapore 596224
USA office: 27 Warren Street, Suite 401-402, Hackensack, NJ 07601
UK office: 57 Shelton Street, Covent Garden, London WC2H 9HE

Library of Congress Cataloging-in-Publication Data
Old industrial cities seeking new road of industrialization : models of revitalizing Northeast China /
editors, Mark Wang, The University of Melbourne, Australia Zhiming Chen, University of
Wollongong, Australia Pingyu Zhang, The Chinese Academy of Sciences, China Lianjun Tong,
The Chinese Academy of Sciences, China Yanji Ma, The Chinese Academy of Sciences, China.
      pages cm
   Includes bibliographical references.
   ISBN 978-9814390538
   1. Industrialization--China--History--21st century. 2. Industries--China--History--21st century.
3. Cities and towns--China--History--21st century. 4. Regional planning--China--History--21st
century. I. Wang, Mark, 1960–   editor of compilation.
   HC427.95.O43 2014
   338.951'1--dc23

                                                                        2013033078

British Library Cataloguing-in-Publication Data
A catalogue record for this book is available from the British Library.

In-house Editors: Zheng Danjun/Dong Lixi

Typeset by Stallion Press
Email: enquiries@stallionpress.com

Printed in Singapore

Contents

Acknowledgements

This is a co-authored book. After Professor Mark Wang and Dr Zhiming Cheng completed the book's outline, each of the authors was charged with the drafting particular chapters: Chapter 1 by Professor Mark Wang and Dr Zhiming Cheng; Chapter 2 by Professor Pingyu Zhang; Chapter 3 by Professor Lianjun Tong and Dr Ruilinbg Han; Chapter 4 by Professor Pingyu Zhang and Dr Xin Li; Chapter 5 by Professor Yanji Ma, Ms Na Li, and Ms Jing Bai; Chapter 6 by Dr He Li and Professor Pingyu Zhang; Chapter 7 by Professor Yanji Ma and Ms Jing Bai, Chapter 8 by Professor Lianjun Tong, Ms Lihua Yang, and Ms Yanan Song; Chapter 9 by Dr Wenxin Liu and Professor Lianjun Tong; and Chapter 10 by Dr Zhiming Cheng and Professor Mark Wang. All chapters were then exchanged between all five authors and suggested changes were debated, accepted, and rejected. Final editing work of the book was mainly done by Professor Mark Wang. We would also like to thank Dr Xianzhe Xiong's for his assistance in reference checking and translation of Chinese references and Ms Charlotte Catmur for her editing support and language polishing. The authors also want to acknowledge the support from the editor and managerial.

We acknowledge the financial support of many agencies for research that is incorporated in this book: Professor Mark Wang for the support from two Australian Research Council grants (DPO0880244 and DP1094801) and from Northeast Institute of Geography and Agro-ecology, Chinese Academy of Sciences for the project of "Revitalization of old industrial base and coordination of resource management and environmental protection". The following competitive Chinese research grants made writing and data collection of the book chapters possible: National Natural Science Foundation of China grants 41071108 (Professor Pingyu Zhang); 41071086 (Professor Lianjun Tong); 41001076 (Dr Wenxin Liu); and 41001097 (Dr He Li); Knowledge Innovation Program of Chinese Academy of Sciences — No.kzcx2-yw-342 (Professor Pingyu Zhang and Professor Yanji Ma).

1

Introduction: Revitalization of China's Industrial Cradle

Since the mid-1970s, the notion of "restless landscape" has been used to describe the radical economic and socio-cultural changes that occurred in the metropolitan areas in Europe and North America (Knox, 1991, 1993). Since the opening-up reform, the notion has also been used to examine the dramatic changes in the post-Mao urban China (Lin and Wei, 2002). Prior research has particularly focused on more developed cities and regions such as Shanghai and the Lower Yangzi Delta along the Southern Coast (Marton, 2000; Shen and Wu, 2012). This is partially due to rapid economic growth along the coastal regions. In fact, the development of Chinese economy was typified by significant regional inequality and disparities between the coast and interior, and some regions were clearly left behind (Fan and Sun, 2008). Before the early-2000s, the notion of restless landscape was inapplicable to most cities in Northeast China (consisting of Liaoning, Heilongjiang, and Jilin provinces) that experienced economic stagnancy. In the mid-1990s, the region suffered from more negative shocks such as the massive state-owned enterprise (SOE) reforms which led to the retrenchment of millions of SOE workers in the region. Layoffs became an everyday topic and enraged many Northeastern Chinese workers to restlessly fight for their rights and benefits, and search for new employment (Won, 2004; Cai, 2005).

This negative first wave of restlessness was followed by a positive wave that resulted from the Chinese Government introducing the Northeast China Revitalization Program (NCRP) in 2003. Existing research has examined the impact of the SOE reforms on laid off workers in the region

(Won, 2005). However, research on the outcomes of the NCRP — the second wave of restlessness — in Northeast China is relatively scant. Aiming to fill the gap in knowledge, this book studies the second wave of restlessness that demonstrates different ways through which the once left-behind cities in Northeast China restructured their individual urban economies.

NCRP is an integral part of the program to amend the former leader Deng Xiaoping's coast-biased development strategy. When Deng introduced the open door policy, the coastal region was the center of attention (Lu and Wang, 2002). Over the course of the opening-up reform, the coastal region became the engine of China's economic growth, the major destination of foreign investment, and the manufacturing base of made-in-China products. The majority of the interior — including central, western, and northeastern regions — was, however, left behind. The focus on the coastal region was supported by an uneven regional development strategy and was further intensified after Deng's historical and influential tour of several cities in Southern China in 1992 (Tian, 2001). As a result, the socio-economic gaps between coastal and inland regions gradually became one of the major issues in China's development.

To correct the negative consequence of Deng's "letting the coastal region get rich first" in China's regional development, his successors have redirected China's regional development focus on a major scale. For example, the then president Jiang Zemin implemented the Great West Development Program (GWDP), or the "Go West" strategy, which aimed to deal with the regional inequality on the way to economic development by gradually eliminating the East–West disparities, consolidating the unity of ethnic groups, and promoting social development. In 2002, Hu Jintao, the then new president, introduced the policy on the revitalization of Northeast China; and later in 2005, he introduced the policy on the "rise of the central region", as an important element of his endeavor to build a "harmonious and balanced society". This book focuses on the former initiative.

To understand how individual cities, under the relatively new national priority policy, have transformed their urban economies, this book examines the various approaches adopted by six major cities in Northeast China which was once called the rust belt of China. This book carries some characteristics.

First, this book explains how a group of cities in China's industrial region avoided becoming ghost towns, and instead restructured and restored their flagging economies after the introduction of the Chinese Government's new regional development strategy. It outlines the Chinese version of how the rust belt revitalization model occurred in a region which was the cradle of China's industrialization since the 1930s but had been left behind after the economic reform in the late 1970s. The six different urban transformation models discussed in this book are less revealed in academic literature especially in English. In fact, they are products of the Chinese Government's new strategy of revitalizing Northeast China, and represent how cities dominated by the state sector (in terms of, for instance, local economy and employment) have found a new road to reindustrialization.

The transformation of resource-dependent and/or heavy industrial cities in Northeast China shares some characteristics with other countries' transformation experience. But, it is distinctive in terms of the key driving forces and mechanisms of transformation that are embedded within the various types of transformation models. One common feature of all the models implemented in Northeast China is that they are mainly incubated from inside rather than driven by external forces. This is different from the development models in the western region in which many cities are less industrialized before the implementation of GWDP and therefore, they have to rely on more external input. This also differs from the models that have shaped China's coastal region.

Second, this book analyzes specific places by focusing on how old industrial cities in Northeast China have sought new roads of reindustrialization. It suggests that these models of revitalization, though different in their own forms, should be examined in the context of the debatable China model of economic development and success (or the China model for short) which is typified by an (seemingly) effective mixture of authoritarian regime and market economy in achieving economic growth, or "authoritarian capitalism". The China model, in the name of "socialism with Chinese characteristics", is regarded as a potent alternative for economic governance rivaling those models from the West especially after the recent global financial crisis (Breslin, 2011).

Nonetheless, the conceptualization of the China model has largely drawn from the development experience of the coastal region. This book argues that the conceptualization and theorization of the China model, however, should not just be based on the experience of the coastal region which was more significantly influenced by external forces such as foreign investment and export-oriented manufacturing enterprises. The China model will be more distinctive if it is inclusive of the experience of local economies which were once heavily dominated by the state sector. In other words, the China model of development is sophisticated, not a black–white dichotomy of liberty against tyranny or democracy against authoritarianism. It exists in neither a liberal market economy, nor a social market economy. It is not a Stalinist command economy. It is an economy with an increasingly competitive labor market, free markets of commodities, and limited (but very soon freer) capital flow. What would have made the China model more distinctive after the inclusion of the Northeastern transitional model is the role played by the state. This book explains how governments interact with markets and enterprises, and more interestingly how governments work with other governments to transform their urban economy. To this end, we hope that this book will shed some lights on the strength and limits of the China model which has been under-researched to date (Peerenboom, 2008).

1. The "Northeast Phenomenon"

The transformation and development of resource-dependent cities is a key topic and a problem facing many countries (Yigitcanlar *et al.*, 2008; Yigitcanlar, 2010; Wong *et al.*, 2006; Inayatullah, 2011; Weisz and Steinberger, 2010; Engel, 2006; Cohen, 2006; Greg and Palmer, 2010; Qian and Li, 2009; Wang and Cheng, 2010; Zhang and Tong, 2011). In the West, cities in the rust belt areas have struggled to adapt to a variety of adverse economic conditions, such as the reallocation of capital and manufacturing facilities to overseas or other areas in their countries where lower labor cost was provided, the rise of automation in industrial processes, a decreased need for labor in the production of heavy industrial products, and the liberalization of existing foreign trade policies. Many resource-mining cities or cities from where economic activities shifted elsewhere have become ghost towns which were abandoned after mining activity failed to survive (e.g., Dallas, 1985). Classical examples include "boom-towns" where the single economic activity or resource (e.g., nearby mine, mill or resort) that created it has been depleted or the resource economy undergoes a "bust" (e.g., catastrophic resource price collapse). These boomtowns often shrank as quickly as they initially grew. In many cases the majority or even the entire population deserted the town, resulting in a ghost town. Increasing economic globalization also contributes to the dismantling of boomtowns due to the key economic sector in a boomtown shifting elsewhere for cheaper labor or access to a larger market, leaving behind economic collapse in the former town.

In industrialized countries, the notion of the rust belt has gained much research attention since the 1980s, especially in the U.S., where the rust belt refers to the area straddling the Midwestern and Northeastern U.S. in which the local economies traditionally specialized in large scale manufacturing of finished medium or heavy consumer and industrial products, including the transportation and processing of the raw materials required for heavy industry (High, 2003). After several periods of economic boom and prosperity between the late 19th and mid-20th century, cities in these areas struggled to adapt to a variety of adverse economic conditions thereafter in the late 20th century, such as the reallocation of manufacturing businesses to the Southeastern states due to their lower labor costs, the rise of automation in industrial processes, and the liberalization of foreign trade policies (Lopez, 2004; Meyer, 1989; Daniel and Stuart, 1987). Cities that struggled the most with these conditions soon encountered more difficulties including population loss, high unemployment, and a declining local economy (James, 1999).

Nonetheless, there are some examples of successful transformation of world-renowned resource-dependent cities. The examples include the Ruhr industrial area in Germany, the Wales region in Britain, the Los forest area in France, the Liege province in Belgium, and the Kitakyushu region in Japan. Some of the manufacturing sectors in the Northeast U.S. and Southern Ontario, Canada actually recovered faster from the late 2000s recession than other sectors of the economy. A number of public and private initiatives encouraged the development of alternative fuel technologies (Economist, 2011). The purpose of various reindustrialization programs is to generate new industry in the place of old industry, or in other words, to create new job opportunities for old.

In China, the economic miracle achieved since the economic reforms in the late 1970s has been mainly attributed to the rapid development of the coastal region. Most research into the country's development — and the China model — has focused onto this region. Development in the other regions of China, especially the rust belt, seems to be attracting relatively less research attention. In fact, the urban industrial restructuring is an ongoing process in inland China, notably in the recent decade, in terms of the scope and speed of restructuring. The old industrial cities in Northeast China were the cradle of China's industrialization, having significantly contributed to the industrialization of the nation during the

Mao era. After the reform, their competitive advantages were challenged by natural resource depletion, diminished demand of products, and a changing market structure which was no longer dominated by state orders. Meanwhile, China's international trade has grown in importance and drastically changed regional comparative advantages. Other regions, especially the coastal region, have shown a more dynamic and effective adjustment to these changing environment and opportunities. The initial specialization and lower susceptibility to investment inertia, as well as the flexible and business-friendly local government policies have contributed to the successful adjustments in the coastal region. In any case, the Northeast provinces, with an ageing population of skilled workers and less competitive industries in the emerging market economy, were on the path to becoming a rust belt region and became a burden to China's economic development. With a high concentration of state-owned heavy industries, cities in Northeast China suffered from heavy losses in revenue and a massive retrenchment of millions of state workers. Such phenomenon was labeled the "Northeast Phenomenon" or "Neo-Northeast Phenomenon". The once towering economic giant was dragged down. There was clearly a need for a major transformation in order to recapture the strong economic performance that once characterized the region's industrial history.

Since the implementation of the Chinese Government's Revitalization Strategy of Northeast China in 2003, cities in Northeast China have gone through various transformations. Based on their recent economic performance, some observers predict that Northeast China will become China's new growth engine and, in the longer term, catch up with other thriving regional economies such as the Pearl River Delta, Lower Yangzi Delta, and the Beijing–Tianjin region.

2. The Existing Transformation Models for Resource-Dependent and Heavy Industrial Cities

Three major types of industrial restructuring models are applied in the industrialized countries. The first type involves further diversification of the existing industrial sectors by transforming the urban economy from a single or a few dominant sectors to a combination of manufacturing, high-tech and modern service sectors. Examples of this restructuring model can be seen in the Ruhr industrial area of Northwestern Germany. The Ruhr area was famous for its coal and steel production. Both industries faced massive restructuring challenges due to the changes in global demand patterns and the loss of competitiveness to lower-cost international producers. After downsizing its large firms and establishing new economic activities, the Ruhr area has attracted many small and medium enterprises specializing in information technology, microsystems, solar energy technology, bio-medicines, and e-logistics (Hospers, 2004).

The second type of industrial restructuring model adopts an approach to replace existing urban industrial sectors by a new set of industrial chains which are not linked to the old ones. For example, high tech industries replace traditional industries and high valued-added industries replace low value-added ones. The capital, technology, and human resources needed for development of new industrial chains are either sourced by accumulation, by exploration of local natural resources, or through the attraction of outside investment. Industrial bases of Lorraine in France and Kyushu in Japan are good examples of this restructuring model (Case summary of old industrial bases in Ruhr of Germany and Lorraine of France, 2011). Both of them were heavily industrialized areas. Lorraine was one of the most heavily industrialized areas of France. But after industrial restructuring, certain traditional industrial activities lost their former importance. Iron ore, once being mined on a large scale, was no longer extracted. The steel industry that depended on this raw material has declined and steel-making is now limited to the area south of Thionville. The areas of Forbach and Vosges within this region have also experienced deterioration in coal mining and textiles industries, respectively. Other long-standing but smaller industries, however, have adapted better to a changed economic environment. For example, producers of glassware and crystal, food and beverage products, faience (earthenware), paper, and furniture have managed to stay afloat. Though many traditional industries are in decline, industrial conversion has nevertheless brought many new industries into Lorraine, including mechanical engineering, electronics, and electrical equipment manufacturing, and, above all, the vehicle assembly and components industry. Much of this investment has originated from economies outside of France — notably Germany. Funding from the French authorities and the European Union has also supported the development of new industries. Restructuring of the economy has also occurred with the development of science parks at Nancy and Metz, the establishment of a theme park in the Moselle Valley, and various other tourist attractions in this region (Case summary of old industrial bases in Ruhr of Germany and Lorraine of France, 2011; Xiao, 2010).

The third type of industrial restructuring model is the "rust belt revitaliza-tion" model. Besides the aforementioned rust belt cases in the U.S., the Pittsburgh redevelopment case is one of the classic and most well-known examples of shrinking industrialized cities in the U.S. As a consequence of the decline of its steel and manufacturing industries, Pittsburgh has lost a significant proportion of its population since the 1950s (Moe and Wilkie, 1997). But, in the 1980s, Pittsburgh started the so-called Renaissance II revitalization strategy to build a stronger and more diverse economy. A foundation built upon high-tech industries, education, health care, culture, and tourism. The implementation was managed through a "public–private–neighborhood partnership," representing the concerns of citizens and aim-ing at creating neighborhood involvement and participation. This was facilitated by the newly established Community Development Corporation (Lubove, 1996).

Pittsburgh's more recent revitalization efforts were based on a number of core projects known as the "Big Splash" (Pallagst, 2009). This endeavor focused on reviving high-end retail, new office buildings, housing units, and high-end hotels. Interestingly, the plan intended to create both additional parking spaces and pedestrian-friendly areas (Wang, 2003; Fasenfest and Jacobs, 2003). Pittsburgh's experience has generated interesting debate about appropriate responses to the problems of rusted-out industrial cities or shrinking cities. Florida (2010) argues that older industrial cities do not nec-essarily need growth to improve, but by making do with less, focusing on improvements in the quality of life for their residents, and bringing their level of infrastructure and housing into line with their smaller populations. The notion of "planned shrinkage" was originally proposed in the 1970s by the then New York housing commissioner Roger Starr. The most successful examples of planned shrinkage, such as Pittsburgh's, resulted not from top–down policies imposed by local governments, but from organic bottom–up, and community-based efforts. While Pittsburgh's government and business leaders pressed for big-government solutions (such as new stadiums and convention centers), the city's real turnaround was driven by community groups and citizen-led initiatives. Community groups, local foundations, and non-profit organizations (not city hall or business-led economic development groups) drove the transformation. Such groups played a key role in stabiliz-ing and strengthening neighborhoods, building greenery, and spurring the development of the waterfront and redevelopment around the universities.

Cities in Northeast China adopted some of these elements in revitalizing their own economies. However, these cities do not follow an existing model unconditionally. As mentioned above, they adopted distinctive approaches and found different ways to revitalize the local urban economy. Nonetheless what is common across all of the strategies to transform their urban economies is that industrial sector-oriented place-making and remaking was the focus. In fact, considering the increasing influence of globalization, market forces and competition pressure from China's coastal regions on cities and older communities in Northeast China, it is apparent that each city would be better served by proactively managing the process of economic transformation, thereby enabling those communities to improve their quality of life and realign with the new economic and fiscal realities. For many urban economists, the restructuring of the rust belt economies should put people first. At the end of the day, it is the people rather than the industries or even places that should be our biggest concern. As Clyde Prestowitz, president of the Economic Strategy Institute, aptly put it, "The plight of these people is also in a way our plight" (Florida, 2010). Those who are hardest hit by the SOE reforms and layoffs should be provided with a generous social safety net and the governments should invest in their (and their children's) education and skills. That does not mean we should give up on places. One major lesson learnt from the experience of the West over the past two decades is that large-scale top-down government projects to revitalize communities do not work properly as designed, and they frequently do more harm than good (Florida, 2010).

3. Northeast Revitalization as a Part of China's Modernization

The existing literature about Chinese urban industrial restructuring has been largely focused on the coastal region (Hu, 2011; Chen, 2004). There are reports on the Yangtze River Delta (Liu, 2006; Weng, 2010); research reports on the surrounding areas of coastal Bohai (Wang and Li, 2009; Zhou and Deng, 2009) or on Chinese cities becoming low carbon cities (Din and Zhou, 2008; Wan et al., 2011). Research on the transformation of resource-dependent cities or mining cities, in general, lacks a systematic analysis of transformation mechanisms: who are the key drivers and how do they interact to transform the urban economy? (Wei, 2010; Dong et al., 2007; Zhang and Tong, 2011; Sun and Liu, 2010; Li, et al., 2010; Zhang and Wu, 2001; Wu and Cheng, 2009; Wang, 2011).

This is also true for the research on the transformation of cities in Northeast China. Being more focused on the macro scale, they describe the general nature of the problem without delving into the root causes or mechanisms of how the problem came into being. (Xing and Gu, 2007; Cui, 2008; Pei and Yang, 2008; Zhang, 2008, 2009; Zhang and Tong, 2011; Chai and Choi, 2012; Hu and Liu, 2011; He *et al.,* 2009). Other researches include the transformation for the cities of oil resources (Li and Nan, 2011; Guo and Xu, 2011) and for cities of coal mines like Fuxin (Hou, 2007; Wei and Xing, 2007). All of our chapters are based on the individual case studies written by authors who have worked intensively in the above-said regions.

In fact, China's "rust belt" revitalization is just a part of China's overall macro regional development strategy. As Fig. 1.1 shows, when Deng came to power, he designed China's development strategy following the so-called "ladder-step doctrine". This doctrine treats different regions as steps on a ladder. The coastal region is akin to a higher step with better infrastructure, capital, technical level, management skill, and economic efficiency. Therefore, it was justified that the national development strategy should first concentrate on developing the better-situated coastal region with better provision of capital, energy, and foreign currency. This was deemed necessary if China was to modernize and catch up with its neighbors in economic development. Only after the coastal region was sufficiently developed, would development attention be extended to the inland region. In essence, the "ladder-step doctrine" is the Chinese version of the liberal argument that development will diffuse and spillover gradually from the center to the periphery ("trickle-down") (Chang, 2002; Yang, 1990). Therefore, after two decades of economic development in the coast, Deng's successor, Jiang, shifted China's development focus to Western China in 2000. His successor, Hu, formally started the revitalization of Northeast China program in 2003 when he came to power. The revitalization of Northeast China was aimed at building the region into the fourth economic pole, following lower Yangtze Delta (Shanghai, Jiangsu, and Zhejiang), Pearl River Delta (Guangdong) and Bohai Economic Rim (where Beijing and Tianjin are located) (see Fig. 1.1).

The central government's strategy for revitalizing Northeast China's old industrial bases is very broad, with no detail given about how to revitalize (State Council, Sept. 9, 2009 "Opinions of the State Council on Further Implementing the Strategy of Revitalizing the Old Industrial Bases Including Northeast China"). What the central government has offered to the locals is the autonomy to restructure the local economy and financial support for the local-initiated revitalization projects. The locals in the last few years have attempted various approaches and used different mechanisms to achieve their industrial transitions and realize an initial

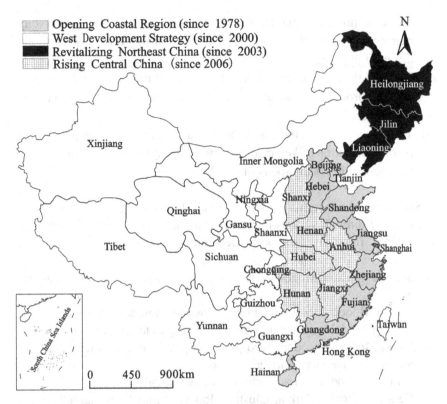

Figure 1.1. China's Macro Economic Regions and the Associated Regional Development Strategies.

sustainable development. The whole region has gradually solved its over-two-decade-long dilemma, and is now back onto the fast national development pathway. Overall, the recent urban economic transitions in Northeast China share the following characteristics:

i) The role of the local government is crucial for the city's transition. As discussed in Chaps. 4–9, district, municipal and provincial governments play different roles in different cases. In the West, national policies for "rust belt" revitalization are the introduction of trade barriers, creation of attractive investment climate, and ambitious job placement and retraining programs. The Chinese central government has done more than this, but it is the local government that has implemented such restructuring based on local conditions.

ii) There is no single model for the whole region; rather, every city requires a localized solution. The models in this book represent six different approaches.

iii) Because these models were developed based on local conditions and are the products of local initiatives, they are feasible and can be sustainable.

iv) The transition in all the case cities included in this book is ongoing; it is transformation of key mechanisms and players, rather than the final product, which is the focus of this book.

So, we can see that this book investigates how cities in Northeast China can take-off through various forms of industrial restructuring. It identifies six different reindustrialization models, namely:

— Shenyang Tiexi Model — repacking old industries in an industrial park;
— Dalian Model — beyond China's coast development model;
— Daqing Model — extension of the existing industrial chain;
— Fuxin Model — modern agro-processing industries replacing the coal mining to save city from "ghost town";
— Jilin City Model — low carbon reindustrialization;
— Central Liaoning Urban Cluster Model — negotiated/agreed industrial division.

This book consists of nine chapters in total. Chapters 2 and 3 provide a broad background of the history and revitalization of Northeast China. Chapter 2 explains the historical reasons for Northeast China's glory and contribution to China's industrialization during period of Mao. It then discusses what/why Northeast China has suffered and explains the "Northeast China phenomenon" during the post Mao period. Chapter 3 provides a comprehensive overview of Hu's revitalization strategies and performance.

Each of the remaining chapters portrays one particular model and answers the following questions: what is the model about? Under what conditions has the city transformed from old to new? How was the model city transferred and what were the processes? How does the new model work? Does it work? Who are the key players? Mechanism? What are the barriers, potential, and opportunities?

This book is a product of the collaboration between Chinese scholars working in Western universities and eminent Chinese scholars working in the Chinese Academy of Sciences. In the last two decades, they have been working on transitional issues in Northeast China. This book provides an inside interpretation and a local understanding of the "rust belt" transition experience, serving as an alternative to China's coast-dominated development model.

2

From Mao's Pet to Deng's Burden

1. Introduction

The Northeast region is an important geographical region in China. It includes three provinces: Liaoning, Jilin, and Heilongjiang as well as four prefectures in eastern Inner Mongolia, including Chifeng, Tongliao, Xing'an, and Hulunbeier. This region covers 1,251,800 km², which represents 13% of China's total land area. In 2010, the population of the Northeast region was 121 million, representing 9.04% of the national population. The Northeast region has a diverse ecological environment, and is rich in mineral resources, which was considered a good basis to develop modern industry. This region was the priority development area for the industries in "new" China. By the 1980s, the region had developed a relatively complete modern industrial system and was the industry leader in China. It has contributed significantly to China's industrialization and has provided solid support for the opening up of the Southeast coastal areas. In general, the region was late to embark on post-industrial reform, and was slow to deviate from its long-term economic system and focus on heavy industry. In 1990s, the Northeast old industry base experienced a recession labeled as the "Northeast phenomenon" which affected the entire region. This industry lacked competitiveness and failed to respond to changes in the economy. The Northeast phenomenon resulted in a range of impacts including a series of social problems. This chapter provides a background to and the reasoning why the "new" China chose this industrial model. It then analyzes the reasons why the Chinese central government chose the Northeast region as their number one priority for industrialization. This chapter also provides an analysis and evaluation of the historical contribution of the Northeast old industrial base, and the long-term effect of industrialization on the Northeast region. It then concludes with a discussion on the reasons for the deterioration of the Northeast old industrial base and gives theoretical explanations on the Northeast phenomenon.

2. Industrialization in "New" China and the Development of the Northeast Old Industrial Base

2.1. *Choice of industrialization model for the "new" China*

At the time of the foundation of the PRC government in 1949, the leaders had limited experience and theoretical knowledge to draw on, when developing the nation's economy. Learning from the Soviet Union was seen as the only best option for the country. The reasons were as follows: First, both the ideologies of the Chinese Communist Party and the Soviet Union Communist Party were based on Marxism. The socialist political and economic systems of the Soviet Union were a role model for all socialist countries. The Soviet Union believed that their experience with socialism was the universal law of socialism and of international significance. This belief was then forced on to other socialist countries, along with the Soviet model. Second, the Soviet Union and socialist countries in Eastern Europe provided financial aid to the "new" China. Finally, the United States and European countries were against the socialist model and tried to overturn the ruling of the Chinese communist party by implementing political sanctions; economic blockade and military siege; and leaving the new found government with no time to seek or advance to other development models (Tang and Jiang, 2001). In addition, Chairman Mao also thought that the development of socialism in Soviet Union set as a good example for rapid industrialization. After selecting the soviet socialism model, China's industrialization path focused on prioritizing the development of heavy industries. During the "first five-year" development period, under the guidance of Soviet Union, China identified and developed 156 projects. These projects have had a lasting influence on the Chinese modern industrial system. During the first five-year period, China invested 76.64 billion yuan on the construction of large industrial projects, which represented the start of Chinese modern industry.

What the Chinese learnt from the Soviet Union in the early 1950's was actually the "Stalin model", which included a high level of war preparation. The "Stalin model" focused on a centralized decision making system (Peng, 2006). Politically, the model was highly centralized and economically it focused on a single form of public ownership. It emphasized on giving priority to the quick development of heavy industries by adopting the military style of industrialization strategies. It also focused on collective agriculture, which ignored the light industry and agriculture that was central to people's livelihoods. The government also implemented a planned economic system, which limited the commodity correlation between money and value. During the period between the foundation of the "new" China and the economic reform, the "Stalin model" effectively rescued the Chinese economy, by quickly building modern industrial systems and enhancing national defense capabilities. However, the Stalin theory had some serious defects and practice abuse mainly because a mandatorily planned economic system cannot promote the healthy development of a nation's economy. An excessive concentration of political power and a high degree of personal ideals damaged the socialist legal systems' single and routine cultural management model (Peng, 2006).

In 1956, at the 20th congress Communist Party of the Soviet Union, the political, economic, cultural, scientific, and technological disadvantages of "Stalin model" were presented. The key issue was the negative effect that the extreme emphasis on the development of heavy industry was having on the development of light industry and agriculture. Chairman Mao had also begun to realize these defects. In 1956, Mao Zedong stated in his speech entitled the discussion of ten relationships, "Chinese economy is relying on heavy industry, which needs to be emphasized. However, agriculture and light industry also need to be focused upon" (Mao, 1976). Then in 1962, Mao Zedong proposed to develop and lead in the agriculture sector and in other levels of industries as well. Although Chairman Mao adjusted his theories, there was no change in the actual practice, with heavy industry still in the first place and low investments being allocated to agriculture and light industries. In June 1956, the ratio of investment between heavy and light industries only changed from $8:1$ to $7:1$. Investment in agriculture increased from 7% during the first five-year period to 10% during the second five-year period (Xia and Wang, 2010). There are three historical and political reasons for the unsuccessful attempt at implementing the "Stalin Model" during Mao's era. First, it is the impact of the international economic and political environment. After the World War II, the U.S. took their policies to the Soviet Union and other socialist countries. The differences in economic, political, military, diplo-matic, cultural, and ideological aspects resulted in the start of the "cold war" between the Eastern and Western world. This "cold war" coupled with the worsening of Sino–Soviet relations during the 1960s meant China was under intense national defense pressure. Under such condi-tions, priority was given to the development of heavy industries in line with the needs of combat readiness. Second, due to the dogmatic under-standing of Marxism, there was a misjudgment in the development of international socialism. The Soviet Union led to the implementation of a wrong political pathway, such as "anti-revisionism" as well as using "class revolution" as a key factor in strengthening the effects of the "Stalin Model" into China's political, economic, cultural, scientific, and technol-ogy fields. Third, the "Stalin Model" met the needs of Mao Zedong's desire to maintain a highly centralized communist party, government, and army. In addition, due to the acute shortage of funds and the lack of inter-national capital assistance after the founding of the "new" China, the government focused on reducing investment in agriculture and light industry and utilizing the products prices "disparity" approach in both sectors (Xia and Wang, 2010; Zhang, 2007). This was seen as the only way to accumulate the initial funding for industrialization. Therefore, looking just at the economic feasibility, the "Stalin Model" was seen as being suitable for China's economic conditions and the actual situation at this time.

2.2. Prioritizing the development of the Northeast old industrial base

After the Sino–Japanese War ended in August 1945, the Nationalist Party and the Communist Party entered into a civil war that lasted for four years. By the end of 1948, the Northeast region was the first region to be claimed by the Communist party. It then became the industrial base for the Communist party's army under Mao's leadership. By 1949, the time of foundation of the new government, the industry in the Northeast region had begun to recover. There are a number of reasons why the Northeast region became the industrial leader of "new" China.

First, in modern and contemporary China, industrial development was relatively weak. Over the first half of the 20th century, the Northeast region has been under colonial or semi-colonial rule. From 1931, the region was under Japanese imperialism occupation which resulted in the Manchuria puppet regime being established. During the 14 years of colonial rule, the Japanese plundered resources and wealth. They focused on the resource industry to supply the raw materials for the energy industry and machinery manufacturing for the military in order to support Japan's invasion of the Asia-Pacific region. During this period, more than 20 resource-based cities and manufacturing-based cities were formed. Although these cities did not have a complete industrial structure, they all had a dominant industry, which then formed the basis for the development of a modern industry. A regional railway network that linked the development of the cities and industries was built over this period. Although the Sino–Japanese war and then the civil war of the 1940s destroyed factories and equipment, the Northeast region was still the most industrially advanced region in the country. Second, in the "new" China, there was a general lack of industry expertise and skilled workers, which was seen as being more important than factories and machinery for the development of modern industry. Although many factories were devastated during the war, the more valuable industry technicians and industry teams were retained in the Northeast China, which was a clear advantage for the development of modern industry in the region. Third, the Northeast region has a wide variety of rich mineral resources which are well located around the region. For example, the industry has developed most extensively in the cities of Shenyang, Fushun, Anshan, Benxi, and Liaoyang in the Central Liaoning Province, because this region has over 10 billion tons of iron ore as well as the major coal producing areas of Fushun, Benxi, and Tieling. In addition, the Northeast region has rich supporting materials, for example, the magnesite reserve in Anshan city, which holds 80% of the total national reserve. The distances between the locations of the raw material and the producing sites are all within tens of kilometers, which makes production and transportation more convenient and inexpensive.

Finally, there were the benefits of being in close proximity to Russia. The Northeast region is in close proximity to not only Russia, but also Mongolia and North Korea. Its border line with Russia is over 3,000 km, and with North Korea it is 1,334 km. As a result of the Korean War in early 1950s, tensions rose to their highest levels in Northeast Asia. With the political history and the close relationship between the Northeast region and the Soviet Union, it was easier for the regions' industries to access skilled labor, equipment, and technical support from the Soviet Union. In a time of war, China could get prompt aid from the Soviet Union. In addition, with the centralization of the government, there was the benefit of accessing skills, technology, and material aids from anywhere within the country. With all the above factors considered at the initial stage of the "new" China, the Northeast region was the best pre-pared; it was well located and had the skills and experience within the industry sectors. Therefore, redeveloping the Northeast old industrial base was regarded as a high priority that resulted in the region gaining promi-nence during the both first five-year and second five-year periods.

3. Historical Implications and Contributions of the Northeast Old Industrial Base

3.1. *Mao's industrial base — beyond the "Stalin Model"*

After the foundation of the PRC and a period of economic recovery between 1949 and 1952, the nation implemented the first five-year plan. With support from the Soviet Union, China started to modernize its indus-tries. This was done through the implementation of 156 core projects and 900 medium to large supporting projects. Most of these projects were not completed until the second five-year period (Dong, 1999). In total, 150 of the 156 projects were actually implemented, which included 106 civil projects and 44 military projects. In the three Northeast provinces, 54 projects were completed during the first five-year plan (Dong, 2004), of which 24 were in Liaoning Province, eight were in Jilin Province and 22 were in Heilongjiang Province (see Table 2.1).

In the Northeast region, as well as there being a large number of pro-jects developed, it saw some of the first projects implemented. Of the total investment of 19.63 billion yuan, the three provinces received 44.3%; Liaoning received 5.075 billion yuan, representing 25.9%; Jilin received 1.455 billion yuan, representing 7.4% and Heilongjiang received 2.165 billion yuan, representing 11.0% (Dong, 2004). Apart from the 54 core projects, the three provinces in the Northeast region have also imple-mented almost 1,000 provincial and city level projects. The layout of these national and local projects provided the basic structure of industrialization for the Northeast region, and in turn made it the industrial base of China. The region had one of the highest rates of industrialization and urbaniza-tion in China prior to the national economic reform and opening up of the country.

For the reasons discussed above, prior to the reform and opening up, the economic growth rate of the three provinces in the Northeast region were higher than the national average. The progress in the industries' production

Table 2.1. Location of the 54 Key Projects Implemented in the Northeast Region During the First Five-year Period.

Liaoning Province (24)	Jilin Province (8)	Heilongjiang Province (22)
1. Fuxin Ping'an Vertical Shaft (Coal mine)	1. Liaoyuan Coal Mine Central Vertical Shaft	1. Hegang East Mountain No.1 Vertical Shaft
2. Fuxin Xinqiu No.1 Vertical Shaft	2. Tonghua Coal Mine Wangou Vertical Shaft	2. Hegang Xingantai No. 1 Vertical Shaft
3. Fuxin Haizhou Open Mine	3. Fengman Water Power Generation Plant	3. Hegang Xingantai Coal Washing Factory
4. Western Fushun Open Mine	4. Jilin Heat and Power Plant	4. Hegang Xingantai No. 2 Vertical Shaft
5. Fushun Longfeng Vertical Shaft	5. Jilin Ferro Alloy Factory	5. Shuangyashan Coal Washing Factory
6. Fushun Laohutai Inclined Shaft	6. Jilin Chemical Industry Corporation (Includes 4 Factories)	6. Jixicheng Zihe No. 9 Vertical Shaft
7. Fushun Shengli Inclined Shaft	7. Jilin Carbon Factory	7. Jixicheng Zihe Coal Washing Factory
8. Eastern Fushun Open Mine	8. Changchun First Automobile Works	8. Fulaerji Heat and Power Plant
9. Fushun No. 2 Oil Factory		9. Jiamusi Paper Manufacturing Factory
10. Fuxin Power Plant		10. Qiqihaer Steel Factory
11. Fushun Power Plant		11. Haerbin Northeast Light Alloy Processing Factory
12. Dalian Power Plant		12. Haerbin Boiler Factory
13. Anshan Iron and Steel Corporation		13. Haerbin Measuring Instruments and Cutting Tools Plant
14. Benxi Iron Enterprises		14. Haerbin Meters Factory
15. Fushun Aluminium Factory		15. Haerbin Steam Turbine Plant
16. Yangjiazhangzi Mineral Administrative Department		16. Haerbin Electric Motor Factory
17. Shenyang No. 1 Machine Tool Factory		17. Haerbin Electric Graphite Factory
18. Shenyang No. 2 Machine Tool Factory		18. Haerbin Bearing Factory
19. Shenyang Wind Motivated Tools Factory		19. Haerbin Dong'an Machinery Factory
20. Shenyang Electricity Wire Factory		20. Haerbin Weijian Machinery Factory
21. No. 1 Ship Manufacturing Factory (426 Factories)		21. Fulaerji Heavy Machinery Factory
22. Huludao Bohai Ship Manufacturing Factory		22. Acheng Electro-mechanical Equipment Factory
23. Shenyang Plane Manufacturing Company (112 Factories)		
24. Shenyang Liming Motor Manufacturing Factory (410 Factories)		

Source: Dong (1999).

Table 2.2.   1958–1978 Northeast Region Investment and Incremental Fixed Assets.

	Second five years (1958–1962)	Adjustment period (1963–1965)	Third five years (1966–1970)	Fourth five years (1971–1975)	Fifth five years (1976–1980)
Total investment (100 million yuan)	183.67	68.18	97.44	235.70	325.95
Incremental fixed assets (100 million yuan)	138.78	64.45	64.09	151.05	204.28
% of investment in national total	19.10	17.88	10.80	15.23	17.69

Source: Dong (2004).

represented a significant achievement in the development of the nation's socialist society (Chen, 2003). Overall, during the 20 years between the second five-year plan and the fifth five-year plan, the three provinces in the Northeast region established a relatively complete regional industry system by building on the initial 54 projects. By this time, the region became an important part of the nation's economy. Until the reform, the Northeast region was the key area for investment. Investments during the second, fourth, and fifth periods were over 15% of the national total (see Table 2.2) and only in the third period it dropped down to 10%.

3.2. The highly planned economic system and resource oriented heavy industry structure

The Northeast region was the first to implement the planned economic system; it also implemented the central government's commands for the longest period of time. The region was still following the orders to export thousands of products at production cost until the 1980s (Chen, 2003). The tax rates of the three provinces in the Northeast region, before reform and opening up, was the highest in China, and was even higher than the coastal regions after the reform and opening up. From 1950, the nation established a planned economic management system and produced yearly economic development plans. Subsequently, the scale and scope covered in the plans expanded each year (Wang and Li, 2004). During the first five-year period, the size of the state-owned economy grew rapidly because of the development of the national projects. At that time, the medium to large SOEs that were controlled by the central government implemented a centralized planned management system. From 1949 to 1952, these enterprises were managed by the Northeast region, and then from 1953 to 1957, they were managed by representative organizations that were selected by the central government departments. The local government managed the small and medium enterprises. The annual plans were distributed *in one go*, as the provincial Planned Economic Administration and the Material Administration had to apply for the required raw material supply from the central government. Any price changes firstly needed the approval of the governing administration and then the Northeast regional government. During this time, private-owned enterprises were managed by the government as a way of managing the processing, government purchasing, and selling and taxing. After the joint ventures were established between the private-owned enterprises and the government, financial plans were aligned with the state-owned enterprises. The fiscal system implemented a dividing range and classification of income and expenditure management processes in line with changes in the administrative and industrial management systems. The income from enterprises controlled by the province, the city or the town was distributed to the local government; whereas the income from the central government controlled enterprises was used by the central government. Provincial governments only controlled the mining of three types of materials while the important resources were managed by the central government. The construction of major infrastructure projects were also managed and funded by the central government. After more than 30 years of economic development, the Northeast region had the highest percentage and the most extensive allocation of SOEs; this is still the case today. The state-owned enterprises that are controlled by the central government still dominate the economy in the Northeast region. At the same time, the deep rooted ideas that come with a long time of planning are stifling the economic development, which will take a long time to implement changes.

Looking at the industry type of core projects that were developed during the first five-year and second five-year plans, the investments were mainly allocated to coal, electricity, smelting, machinery, and chemical engineering. The 54 national projects only had one project for the light industry, which was Jiamusi Paper Manufacturing Factory. These industrial sectors relied heavily on the local mineral resources, and with the long-term intensive mining the resources drained too quickly, thus creating a serious problem for the resource-based cities. The development since then has also relied on the heavy industry structure, which has made the possibility of transitioning to a light and heavy industrial mix slow.

3.3. Contribution of Northeast China cities to Mao's industrialization

During the 1960s and 1970s, there were many international and domestic factors that were compromising the development of the Chinese economy and affecting social development. This resulted in the Northeast region having the responsibility of ensuring the stability of the nation's economy and defense security as well as supporting the development of other regions. The Northeast region was not only trying to develop its own economy but also exporting a large amount of raw materials to support other industries. In addition, the region was exporting mechanical equipment and other industrial products that included over 1 million sets of mechanical equipment and over 500 million tons of steel. More importantly, the region was also the exporting base for skilled workers and technology. To cooperate with the need for tertiary development and national scientific and technological development, the Northeast region supported many enterprises and scientific research institutions across the nation. Many famous enterprises and public service organizations in China have some connections with the Northeast old industrial base. It can be said that the development of the Northeast old industrial base drove the development of the nation and contributed to the success of other regions' economies.

4. The Northeast Phenomenon and its Causes

In the early stages of reform and opening up, the Northeast region had moved into the "maturity stage" of development as a result of over 30 years of investment. Early stages of deterioration were becoming evident. At the start of the 1990s, China implemented a new wave of economic reform, which was different to any reform previously implemented. The tightened economic policy of the central government had differing impacts across the nation. In Southern and Eastern China there was a slight decrease in the rate of growth because of the higher cost of production material. Provinces in the Northwest and Southwest maintained a development rate higher than the national average because of their weak industrial foundation, whereas, the old industrial bases such as Liaoning, Jilin, and Heilongjiang Province experienced negative growth, as well as having high levels of debt to manage (Li, 2000). This situation of extreme contrast was named as Northeast phenomenon by Professor Shunhua Feng of University of Liaoning, this was the first time this definition was used by scholars and was recognized politically. The Northeast phenomenon refers to the economic slow-down and deterioration of the so-dominated Northeast old industrial base in the early 1990s, while other regions of China maintained high economic growth. The Northeast phenomenon is not only a regional phenomenon, but it can also be seen as an indicator for wider problems. It is a specific definition to describe the deterioration of China's old industrial base.

When analyzing the causes of the Northeast phenomenon on a macro level, it is evident that after the reform and opening up, China shifted its emphasis on economic development to the Southeastern coastal areas. China had the opportunity to learn from the western world about their experiences with the market economy and then started developing a socialist market economy suited to the Chinese market and moving away from the limitations of the Stalin Model. These macro strategy changes resulted in the Northeast old industrial base losing its traditional advantage. Ever since the reform and opening up was first implemented in the Southeastern coastal areas, the development emphasis shifted to that region. During the 1980s, China's industrial center shifted its location (Chen, 1993). Guangdong, Fujian, Zhejiang, Jiangsu, and Shandong Provinces became the new centers for the Chinese economy; they were the first provinces to receive development policies and soon became central to the nation's economic growth. Meanwhile, in the Northeast region, the provinces were unable to get support from any of the preferential policies since it was not a frontline area for the reform and opening up. Therefore, it fell into a position of competitive disadvantage in the opening up of the domestic market. As well as enjoying preferential policies in land, finance, taxing, and international trading, the coastal new industrial zones also chose a different industrial direction from the old industrial base; they invested mainly in light manufacturing industries and high technology industries. To boost the starting point of the industrial development, they imported a large amount of new technology and equipment. In addition, the enterprises in the new industrial bases adapted to the market economy and implemented modern management systems from the start, which utilized flexible human resources and income distribution systems.

Furthermore, the new enterprises did not have the burden of social responsibilities like the state-owned enterprises in the old industrial base; therefore, they could be more dynamic in their management systems. At this stage, the Northeast region was already facing difficulties, and was starting to be further disadvantaged by having to support the development of the new industrial zones. Whilst the new industrial zone was enjoying many tax discounting policies, the old industrial base was being taxed at increasingly higher rates. According to Chen (1993), the overall national income generated in this region was far greater than the amount being invested by the government, which meant that this region always contributed more than the investment it received from the government. On the other hand, the coastal new industrial zones contributed less than the government's investment they received. For example, during the period of 1980 to 1989, the gap between the GDP Liaoning Province had produced and the government investment received by Liaoning Province was 56.75 billion yuan whereas in the Guangdong Province, it received government investment of 1.04 billion yuan which was more than its GDP (Chen, 1993). Therefore, some scholars argue that the Northeast old industrial base had directly or indirectly subsidized the economic growth and covered the cost of the Southeastern coastal reform and opening up (Dong, 2004).

Why was the reform and opening up initiated by the Southeast coastal area and not by the Northeast region? At the start of the reform and opening up, the Northeast old industrial base was the most developed region of China; it had fully implemented the planned economic system, and, therefore, was related to the fundamental economic stability of China. Since the reform and opening up was undertaken to establish market economic systems, it brought with it some risks factors as well. The Southeast coastal areas have a low percentage of state-owned enterprises. The area also has a tradition of valuing commerce, therefore, choosing the Southeastern region to undertake a trial reform was a wise decision. In addition, the Southeastern coastal area has a good geographic location for trading with countries in the western world. Especially for the triangular area around the *Pearl River*, it is close to Hong Kong and Macao, which makes it the best place for trialing a market economy. At this time, the traditional resource advantage of the Northeast started to disappear and its location was no longer a benefit, it had become a draw-back for economic development. The historical political problems of the Northeast region proved that it was not an ideal place to attract foreign investments. For the

Northeast region, the most evident problems that resulted from the Northeast phenomenon was the bankruptcy of enterprises and a high level of unemployment. These two problems had the greatest impact on the regional economy and the wider society.

During the 1990s, most industrial products of state-owned enterprises in the Northeast region lost their market competitiveness, because of the types of products, quality, and price. Many enterprises had to be liquidated. For example, by the end of the 1990s in the Tiexi District of Shenyang city, many enterprises had an average leverage ratio of 90%, and had an accumulated debt of 26 billion yuan. In addition, 40% of enterprises had partially or entirely stopped their operations and the factory vacancy rate reached 50% (Bao et al., 2006). There are three main reasons identified for the downfall of the state-owned enterprises. First, the region fell back on their known systems. The state-owned enterprises lacked clarity in defining the division of responsibility and in the planning and of implementation of economic measures which led to the enterprises lacking in skills to operate in a market economy and were thus unable to boost employees' morale and creativity. Second, the region was slow in adjusting its rigid industrial structure. The Northeast old industrial base continued to focus on heavy industries like coal, metal smelting, petroleum, chemical engineering, and machinery manufacturing industries. The contribution of the light industry to the economy was low and new technology was underdeveloped. In 2001, the ratio between fixed assets in the light and heavy industries in the Northeast region was 17:83; the ratio between the added value of light and heavy industries was 15.6:84.4. The managers within the heavy industry sector were aware that the costs of technical upgrades were very high and that there were many barriers making it hard for private investors to enter the industry. This made it harder for the enterprises themselves to undertake structural adjustments and to implement technical upgrades. Third, since the enterprises lacked financial investments to fund technological upgrading, some industrial technical equipment being used was outdated, and there was a distinct lack of communication and technical upgrading within the region. In fact, most equipment was not being properly maintained. In September 1965, the Northeast Bureau of the Communist Party Central Commission working group undertook inspections of 874 sets of metal cutting machines in 21 Harbin city state-owned enterprises. They found that only 47% were in good condition and 53% required maintenance, of which 22% were desperately in need of maintenance. In addition, there were 10 enterprises whose complete machinery ratio was below 10% and there were three enterprises that had no complete equipment (Dong, 2004). During the 10 years of Cultural Revolution, the regulations of enterprises were abandoned, equipment management was in confusion, equipment wore out and the issues with lack of maintenance worsened. Entering the 1980s, China started technical reform of some key industrial enterprises, but this was only occurring on a small scale. In Shenyang city, only 1/10th of medium to large industrial enterprises were reformed. By the start of the 21th Century, Shenyang city only had 13.4% of total production equipment at the international advanced level, 19.2% at national advanced level and 70% of the old equipment from the 1960s were still being used (Qiao, 2004). In Changchun city, 60% of industrial equipment was in use for over 20 years. Without necessary technical upgrades, a cycle formed in the old enterprises, with the old equipment they produced old products, which could not be altered to meet the diversified market demand. Fourth, the heavy burden of social responsibilities of enterprises made the cost of reform very high. Meaning, that it was hard for the state-owned enterprises to support social development as well as to undertake reform within the market economy. For some mining enterprises that did not implement or complete transitional arrangements before the resources were drained — stopping production and liquidation was their only choice.

The shutting down of enterprises directly lead to large scale unemployment as workers were being laid off. Since late 1990s, the nation started systematic reform of state-owned enterprises with the aim of establishing modern enterprise system. It encouraged enterprises to merge and reorganize, with the aim to increase the presence of the share-based reform model and to effectively build new modern corporations. Since a large number of small to medium enterprises went bankrupt, and the newly established share-based enterprises cut employees to raise efficiency levels; there was a large number of workers being made redundant and unemployment was wide spread in the cities. According to the statistics from the Department of Labour and Social Security from 1997 to the end of 2002, the total number of workers made redundant of state-owned enterprises in the three provinces of the Northeast was 6.817 million, which represented 25.1% of China's 27.15 million laid-off workers. Of this total number of redundancies, there were 2.437 million in the Liaoning Province, 1.18 million in the Jilin Province, and 3.2 million in the Heilongjiang Province. However, the number of these workers who were reemployed during the same period was 1.524 million in the Liaoning Province, 0.825 million in the Jilin

Province, and 1.826 million in the Heilongjiang Province, with a regional total of 4.202 million, which represents 23.24% of China's 1.808 million reemployed laid-off workers (Chen, 2003). The Northeast region has always had a high unemployment rate; in 2002, the registered number of unemployed people in urban Liaoning, Jilin, and Heilongjiang was 756,000, 238,000, and 416,000 respectively, in total 1.41 million, representing 18.31% of the national unemployed population. The reason for the high level of unemployment and the difficulty of reemployment was because of the high percentage of state-owned enterprises in the region and the important role that state-owned enterprises played in the cities' social capital. In 1996, there were 828 state-owned industrial enterprises in Shengyang city, spread over to 30 industrial sectors. The actual capital of state-owned enterprises was over 59% of the total actual capital of all industrial enterprises. Among 12 industries, the capital of state-owned enterprises was over 70% of total capital of industrial enterprises, the highest was 99%. In 2002, the percentage of GDP of state-owned and state-controlled enterprises in total industrial GDP was 62.4%, 79.6%, and 77.9% for Liaoning, Jilin, and Heilongjiang, respectively, much higher than that of Guangdong Province (19.3%). Since this region had a too intensive percentage of state-owned enterprises and a high state-owned economy, there was no other social economic sector to absorb the shock when the state-owned enterprises were in difficulty. With a lack of reemployment opportunity, it became a serious problem for laid-off workers. Since the Northeast old industrial base did not have unemployment, medical and pension schemes in place, the laid-off workers were in very poor situations. Citizens had no choice but to go to the front door of the government and petition, or hold sit-ins and street protests, which however, in turn had a great impact on social security.

5. Theoretical Explanation of the Deterioration of Northeast Region

The Northeast phenomenon became a hot issue that drew attention from governments and scholars, all looking to solve the problem. Many have reached a common conclusion on the features and causes of the Northeast phenomenon, focusing on two areas; the structural factors and the systematic factors. The structural factors refer to the economic structure; including the three industry structures, light and heavy industry, industrial products, industrial equipment and technology, and regional economic ownership structure. The systematic factor refers to the interaction and the combined effect of the national economic policies, the state-owned economic ownership system, and the management system of state-owned enterprises. The unique system of the Northeast old industrial base had three outstanding features: the internal cycling of heavy chemical industry and the closed state-owned economy motivated one another, the vertical task delegation of heavy chemical industry combined well with the segmented management of the planned economy and the government purchase of the heavy chemical industry and the governments control of resource allocation helped with adapting (Wei, 2006). Chinese scholars generally state that the deterioration of the Northeast old industrial base was significantly due to systemic problems, which was different from the deterioration problem of old industrial bases in the western developed countries. Some scholars have stated that progressive reform processes and a shift in the focus of the national economy were important factors in the deterioration of the Northeast old industrial base. Systematic conflicts were the main reason for the deterioration of the Northeast old industrial base and systematic deterioration was the fundamental reason for the deterioration of the old industrial base (Bao *et al.*, 2006). Some scholars have also analyzed the causes of the phenomenon through the industrial (regional) development cycle theory, systematic structural effect theory, and regional cultural and ideology theory (Li and Li, 1996; Chen *et al.*, 2004; Ding, 2003; Lan, 2003; Liu and Chang, 2005). However, these theories do not provide a complete explanation. In addition, it is hard to understand that with such recognizable achievements from the Chinese reform and opening up policy, that the Northeast old industrial base still faced deterioration and transition problems.

North (1981; 1991) founded the path dependence theory of systematic transition. The theory states that path dependence is the key to the understanding of long-term economic changes, as is the same with technological changes, whereas system changes have self-enforcing and positive feedback mechanisms. This mechanism makes system changes self strengthen on the established direction once it is on a set pathway; ultimately it will depend on a systematic transition path (Zhao and Liu, 2007). North's path dependence theory provided a new theoretical scope for explaining the deterioration of the old industrial base. From this theory, Grabher made it clear when studying the Germany Ruhr old industrial region that there were three lock-in effects for the old industrial base: functional lock-in, cognitive lock-in, and political lock-in (Grabher, 1993). Xu Wei's analysis shows that in the Northeast old industrial base these three lock-in effects were also in effect. Functional lock-in was evident in the vertical relationship between local enterprises and the government; cognitive lock-in was evident in the insufficient supplying of a local efficient system; Political lock-in was evident in keeping its original organization and system (Wei, 2006). Enterprises in the Northeast region focused on vertical, traditional, and closed connections with the government for a long time and ignored connecting with other enterprises, inter-industrial relationship and interaction, focusing instead on isolated enterprises' development without forming effective specialized task delegations and supporting systems, therefore, unable to enjoy the clustering effect of social connections. These formed the unique functional lock-in. Since the enterprises were unable to conduct specialized task delegation and innovative cooperation through a cooperative network, they failed to innovate through interaction and learning from each other. Enterprises had weak technical innovation skills and the isolated enterprises technical development was severely *stifling* the overall technical innovation level. Also, enterprises had insufficient cooperation, connection, and knowledge and communication between enterprises and colleges; agencies and organizations; and scientific and technical research institutions. This limited the development of regional innovative capability. Cognitive lock-in mainly refers to the inability to breakthrough traditional processes due to some habitual thinking and hence they were unable to reform and innovate. People were mainly focused on solving technical upgrading issues and the problems of industrial development itself, and did not realize the effect that a weak innovative environment had on technical innovation and in addition, the necessity of developing a local industrial system and industry clusters for maintaining and raising industrial competitiveness. In the Northeast region, arrangements were made to ensure the property rights of state-owned enterprises and to secure their allocation of resources, leaving almost no room for economic activities of other types within the economy. This ensured that the central and local government remained the most important and in some areas the only economic activity. Since most large enterprises were controlled by the central government, they implemented more profound and complete planned economic policies and locked-in increasing income rates through the system; at the same time, in consideration of local interests, this type of political lock-in was shown in the resource allocation between administrative divisions. Although scholars have tried to explain the reason for deterioration of the Northeast region with North's path dependence theory, without profound and detailed case studies, this theory has not become a dominant theoretical explanation. Since the development environment and the reasons for deterioration were different across various regions, cities, and enterprises, and there are different features and characters, further work is required to examine the different factors, and some common problems and features that are different to cases of the western world. This book seeks to go some way to discuss these differences through a series of more detailed case studies.

3

Revitalization Strategies of Old Industrial Cities under Hu: Overview

1. Introduction

This chapter is mainly about how the Northeast region of China shifted from a pathway of decline to one of revitalization, since the implementation of the revitalization strategies. The two main areas discussed in this chapter are the revitalization policies for the Northeast region and the progresses of revitalization.

1.1. *The proposal of revitalization strategies for the Northeast old industrial base*

Since the economic reform and opening up in the late 1980s, the economic development of the Northeast region has progressed well. However, compared to the coastal area in Eastern Chinese, the pace of economic development in the Northeast region is clearly slow and the difference has increased over time. In 1978, the GDP per person in the Northeast region was 560.34 yuan, higher than that of Eastern China by 94.99 yuan. However, since the 1990s, the GDP per person in the Eastern region has surpassed that of the Northeast region. In 1991, the difference was 66.48 yuan, and then by 2010 it had increased by more than 170 times, the amount to a difference of 11,451 yuan (Fig. 3.1). In 2002, the industry GDP of the three provinces of the Northeast region was only 60% as that of Guangdong Province of the Southeast region. This statistics attracted the central government's attention, and proved to be a driving force for giving higher priority to the revitalization of Northeast China on the agenda. The Northeast region has rich natural resources, solid industrial foundations, and a highly-skilled workforce. Therefore, it was seen as being most efficient of the Northeast region to make a transition based on its existing strengths by implementing systematic and mechanical innovations, and to change the thinking habit and management structures away from the traditional planned economy to the new market economy. Thus, the central government proposed the strategy of revitalization with guidelines around utilizing competitive advantages and providing equalized public services for all residents. A new regional cooperative development structure was formed with clearly defined main functions and channels for the cooperation of the Eastern, Central, and Western regions. On 5 October 2003, the "Suggestions for revitalization of the Northeast old industrial base" was published by the State Council and Central Government, representing the start of the implementation of the revitalization strategies.

It was important and necessary to quickly implement old industrial based revitalization strategies. The Northeast old industrial base was the mother of new China's industry (Lu and Liu, 2003) and had made tremendous contribution to the formation of Chinese independent and complete industrial system and national economic system. However, these old

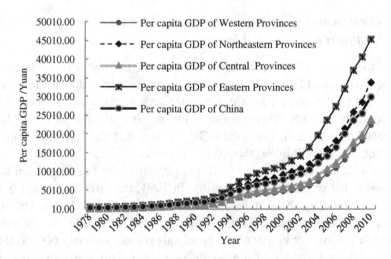

Figure 3.1.   Per capita GDP of China.

Source: China Statistical Yearbook.

industry methods were not adapting to the new market mechanisms that came with the reform of the 1990s. The issues included:

i) low market engagement and lack of dynamic economic development
ii) single ownership structure with a high percentage of state-owned enterprises
iii) slow pace in the industrial structure adjustment
iv) old equipment and technology
v) heavy social burdens for enterprises to perform social responsibilities
vi) high pressure on social security and employment
vii) deterioration of dominant industries in resource based cities.

The region had a competitive advantage and with low input it had the potential for quick results. The Chinese government highly regarded the economic reform and development of the old industrial base of the Northeast region and took a series of measures to promote reform of state-owned enterprises, establish a social security system, and adjust the industrial structure. The Northeast old industrial base gained valuable experience during the reform process.

1.2. Unique policies and motivation mechanisms used in the revitalization process of the Northeast region

During the implementation of the revitalization strategies, all the departments and all levels of government actively participated and provided policy support for the Northeast region. The focus of these policies included resources, tax, electricity, and opening up and cooperation, food subsidies, and resource based cities transformation (Table 3.1).

2. Revitalization Policies

2.1. Policy package

In 2003, the document "Suggestions for the implementation of revitalization of the Northeast old industrial base" by the State Council

Table 3.1.   Preferential Policies of the Northeast China Revitalization Strategy.

Year	Document	Main content
Taxing		
2004	"Regulations in enlarging the scope of added value tax deduction in Northeast region" and "company tax discount for enterprises in Northeast region"	Raised the depreciation ratio of fixed assets, shortened amortization years of intangible assets, raised pretax tax free threshold for taxable income, added value tax deduction changed from production type to a consumption type, that is a deduction on all expenditures; enlarging the scope of added value tax deduction means to include production-used fixed assets as deduction item. It is aimed at reducing costs for domestic enterprises, reducing tax liability for VAT, and attract investment and motivate enterprises technical improvement.
2004	National ministry of taxation and national ministry and Finance issued clarification on preferential policies for Northeast old industrial bases company tax, effective 1 July, 2004	Enlarged deduction scope of VAT, adjusted taxation standard for resource tax and company tax discount, etc.
2004	Statement of adjusting resource tax of some mining and oil drilling enterprises in the Northeast region	According to the actual conditions of oil fields and mines and their financial ability, resource tax standard was reduced within 30% for low-abundance oil wells and mines in the resource draining stage. The policy reduced resource tax of resource based cities.

(Continued)

Table 3.1. (*Continued*)

Year	Document	Main content
2004–2005	The "2004 measurements of enlarging VAT deduction scope for Northeast region" "regulations of enlarging VAT deduction scope for Northeast region" "Statement for implementing company tax discount for Northeast old industrial base"; and "2005 statement of enlarging VAT deduction scope of Northeast region".	Clarified with the detailed practices of Northeast China's VAT reform and deduction measurements of fixed assets' VAT. These measurements reduced tax burden for enterprises of the Northeast region and increased the basic salary of workers.
2006	"Statement of waiving historical tax liability of Northeast old industrial base"	The policy has supported old industrial enterprises in the Northeast region on all aspects. The tax liabilities incurred prior to 31 December 1997 were waived (except for tax incurred outside the Northeast region).
2002–2004	Policies on increasing improved variety subsidy and expand the area of rice planting	In 2002, central finance department invested 100 million yuan as improved variety soya bean subsidy, and the area of improved variety demonstration land was 10 million acres. In 2003, the government continued to increase the land for high oil content soya beans subsidy project by 20 million acres, at the same time 10 million acres of improved wheat variety subsidy land, with subsidy of 200 million yuan and 100 million yuan, respectively. In 2004, to implement the guideline of No.1 Document of the central government, the government extended subsidy area to four wheat products including soya bean, wheat, corn, and rice.

(*Continued*)

Table 3.1. (*Continued*)

Year	Document	Main content
New high technology		
2004	National Development and Reform Commission's Statement of commercializing first group of new high technology of the Northeast region	This policy supported the new high technology industry on all aspects. By developing new industries to promote industrial structure adjustment in the Northeast region.
Social		
2000	Pivot plan for completing urban social security system	Liaoning Province, Jilin Province, and Heilongjiang Province issued their pivot plan for completing urban social security system
2004	Central government's preferential policies to support revitalization of the Northeast old industrial base	Waived agricultural tax first in Heilongjiang and Jilin Province; in those two provinces started pivot projects of completing social security system; paid bankrupt enterprises subsidy to over 60 enterprises in the three provinces of the Northeast region of 16.3 billion yuan; in some state-owned enterprise implemented the pivot project of separating social functions from enterprises.
Reform of state-owned enterprises		
2005	The State Council passed the proposal of trial reform of collectively owned enterprises	Related to asset and liability treatment, employees' placement and labor relationship treatment; social security policies and their implementation measurements. This work would solve reform problems of large SOEs of Northeast region.

(*Continued*)

Table 3.1. (*Continued*)

Year	Document	Main content
Opening up and cooperation		
2006	List of foreign invested advantageous industries of Liaoning city	Foreign invested projects in the lists enjoy preferential policies for encouraging foreign investment. Foreign invested projects under construction that comply with the list's rules can also enjoy the policies in the list.
Mining resource		
2005	Policy and measurement of Northeast region land and mining resources	Implement land using preferential policies (increase efficiency of granting permission for construction land to provide outstanding land using service for economic development; enhance policy support for land using to accelerate reform of state-owned enterprises; promote land adjustment and reclamation to create better production and living conditions; implement stable land policies and promote ecological restoration; implement mining resource preferential policies; enhance resource discovery and promote sustainable development; enforce market realization, and deepen the reform of mines ownership; increase policy support for mining companies to develop; accelerate socializing services for geologic documents, information and technology).
Transformation of resource based cities		
2007 and 2009	"Suggestions of promoting sustainable development of resource based cities by the State Council" the central government distributed annual fiscal transfer payment	Develop continuous industry and solve unemployment. Enhance environmental restoration and ecological protection. Enhance management of resource discovery and mine ownership. Raise policies support

Source: Revitalizing Northeast China Website: http://chinaneast.xinhuanet.com.

mentioned the following 10 aspects of detailed strategies of revitalization:

i) System and mechanical innovation: Promote innovation to eliminate system barriers that hinder economic development and integrated reform; strategic adjustment of the national economy; deepen the reform of state-owned enterprises; create a friendly environment for economic development of non-public owned enterprises; shift the government responsibilities to separate non-governmental enterprises.

ii) Promote industry structure upgrades: Upgrade and optimize secondary industry; discover and take full advantage of the current industrial foundations; enhance enterprises' independent innovation capability and technical equipment level; take advantage of competitive advantages and accelerate development of regional industries and dominant industries.

iii) Develop modern agriculture: An important aspect of revitalization is to enhance the agriculture sector whilst acknowledging the ecological environmental protection of the relatively good environment of the Northeast region.

iv) Actively develop tertiary industry: Take the opportunity to reduce enterprises social responsibilities by promoting the socialization, commercialization, and industrialization of the service industry; develop traditional service industries; develop and complete the distribution of primary agricultural products; and also develop the tourism industry.

v) Promote the economic transformation of resource-based cities: For those cities that still possess rich resources should enhance the usage of the resources and extend the industrial chain; for cities with resource draining should find an alternative way to develop continuous industry; for cities with already or close to drained resource should also develop continuous industry.

vi) Enhance infrastructure construction: Transportation, water, and power infrastructure are important factors for supporting the revitalization of the old industrial base; promote industrialization of waste and water treatment, implement environmental protection projects that focus on residential living or treatment of pollution; invest in public health infrastructure and improve the medical response infrastructure.

vii) Further expand the opening up of the economy, both domestically and internationally: Optimize the investment environment; extend opening up of finance, insurance, commerce, and tourism industries in the old industrial base; put efforts into the improvisation of the utilization of foreign investments and actively seek to attract foreign investments into the Northeast region; accept international industrial transfer and asset transfer. Take advantage of the regions location and enhance its trading cooperation with the surrounding countries. Promote internal markets and breakthrough regional barriers and market segmentation.

viii) Accelerate the development of scientific and technology educational sector: Take full advantage of the cluster of tertiary institutions and scientific background to enhance the cooperation along the process from "production to studying and researching"; create key technologies and famous brands with proprietary intellectual property rights; import advanced foreign technology and enhance the technological content and market competitiveness of products. Build a system and environment that will motivate skilled workers to stand out; develop various methods of skillful training to train compound talents and practical skills as well as pay attention to train highly skillful technical workers and technicians' team. In addition, develop cultural sector and a cultural industry to develop a spiritual civilization.

ix) Set out complete policy measurements: All the functional departments of the government should create suitable conditions for the reform of state-owned enterprises; to release enterprises from performing social functions; the cost incurred should be subsidized by the central government ministry of finance. Provide support to the old industrial base through fiscal tax policies; simplify the granting process of old industrial base transformation projects.

x) Enforce organizational leadership: Coordination among all levels of government should be enhanced so policies are aligned and implemented related to the necessary enterprises; establish the idea of old industrial base revitalization through opening up of markets and broader reform and self-motivated development.

Revitalizing Northeast old industrial region is important not only for the regions' viability but also as a measurement of success for the whole countries' social and economic development. The "suggestions" by the State Council were based on the realistic situation of the Northeast region, and focused on a number of key problems. These included, adjustment and upgrading the pace of the industry, the structure of reform and opening up policies, regional cooperation, and economic transformation of resource based cities, re-using building resources and building an environmentally aware society, development of important social services including education, health service, culture and sports, expansion of employment, and completion of a social security system. The goal was to promote total revitalization of the economy and society. In detail, the tasks included:

i) To maintain rapid and healthy economic growth. As a result of optimizing profitability and reducing consumption, the regional GDP per person was doubled.

ii) To achieve relatively large improvements in economic structural adjustment. The weight of the service industry and the value add of the non-public economy relative to regional GDP both experience a significant increase. The innovation capability of independent enterprises was enhanced; with a series of well-known enterprises that possess intellectual property rights to new technology.

iii) To enhance the ability of sustainable development. The usage of resources led to the rise in the efficiency level and deterioration of the environment slowed. Significant progress was made in treating water pollution in the Liao River and the Songhua River, as well as the local marine environment. Work was also done on air pollution.

iv) To increase the social development level. The basic public services were enhanced, the education, health service, and social security system were advanced, and the level of poverty was reduced. The ability to preventing and reducing the impact of disasters was improved. The strategy of building new villages under the socialist system was a success. The increase in the rate of disposable income per person of urban residents and the gross income of rural residents was higher than the national average. The registered unemployment rate in the urban area was reduced to less than 5%.

v) To make significant progress in implementing the reform and opening up strategy. The market economic system was successfully implemented and the reform of state-owned enterprises was nearly completed. The opening up was focused mainly on coastal areas, country borders, and in major cities. External economic cooperation was further developed as international trading has rapidly increased and the quality and the utilization of foreign investment were enhanced.

In March 2012, the Chinese government passed the 12th "five-year plan for revitalizing the Northeast region". The "12th five-year period" is seen as an important period for stabilizing and improving the revitalization achievements, and a critical period for laying solid foundations for further development. The planned development directions in the latest five-year plan include:

i) To develop a stable modern agricultural system with the aim of ensuring the nation's food security. At the same time achieve improved living conditions in rural areas and build wealthy new villages.

ii) To continue modernizing the industrial system. The plan requires enterprises to optimize traditional industry and accelerate the development of strategic new industries and develop the service industry.

iii) To optimize the spatial allocation of city development and promote the development of industrial areas. At the same time, the region should utilize the technical advantage and skilled labor to enhance regional innovation capability.

iv) To promote the sustainable development of resource based cities. These cities should seek to develop industries that have a future, solve historical problems and develop a long-term mechanism for sustainable development.

v) To improve infrastructure to build a comprehensive transportation system and a diversified clean energy system.

vi) To strengthen the protection and treatment of important environmental zones such as forest, grassland, wetland, and rivers. At the same time, focusing on reducing the resource use, saving energy, and emission reductions.

vii) The plan requires the region to take various measurements to increase employment opportunities as well as accelerate the reform of the shantytowns and provide guaranteed house construction projects.

viii) To continue deepen reform of state-owned enterprises and develop non-public economy. At the same time, the region should seek to promote reform of managed forestry and the farming system. The region should also increase the level of opening up and re-label itself as the important hub for trade with Northeast Asia.

2.2. The advantages of policies in Northeast region compared to the policies in other key areas

The four main regional development strategies implemented by the Chinese government were aimed at balancing the regional development difference. They included:

i) Leading the development of the East,
ii) The grand development of the West,
iii) The revitalization of the Northeast and
iv) The rise of the Central area.

The development policies were all based on the overall regional development strategy.

The focus of development along the East coast area was important to develop and advance overall wealth by driving the development in the undeveloped areas. The policies sought to create an environment conducive to innovation by promoting industrial structural optimization, developing new technology, changing economic development mode, expanding external communication and promoting regional balanced development (Chen, 2006). The preferential policies for revitalizing the Northeast region were mainly showing support and adjustment function to address the "Northeast Phenomenon". These policies more specifically included:

i)   Tax and finance policies which provided an important opportunity for revitalization and were used the most in the development policies
ii) Industrial development and enterprises reform policies
iii) Social security policies were key and had a positive social impact as well as stabilizing reform.

Others supportive policies included general and regional opening up policies, spatial policies, and skilled workers training policies.

The grand development of the West was aimed at lessening its difference with the East and balancing regional differences. The Chinese government outlined five key aspects of the strategy for the Western region (Xiang et al., 2006):

i) Accelerating infrastructure development
ii) Enhancing environmental protection and development

iii) Successfully implement industry structural adjustment
iv) Develop scientific and technical education and accelerate skilled worker training
v) Deepen reform policies and expand the opening up of the region.

The policies identified for the West were linked closely to the other regions' development policies, as well as focusing on environmental protection. The policies in general included, policies to increase funding, policies to improve investment in the environment, policies to attract skilled workers and policies to develop science and technology.

The rising Central China strategy was aimed at making full use of the regions' advantages, optimize the regional development structure and accelerate the formation of new regional coordinated enterprises. The set out of preferential policies of Central China highlighted the regions role in supporting and coordinating with other regions. The policies put emphasis on tax reform and to take advantage of existing industries such as energy, grain, and mechanical manufacturing industry. At the same time creating opportunity for industry integration and forming industry clusters.

3. Achievements of Northeast Revitalization Strategy

3.1. *The transformation of resource based cities*

The resource based cities of the Northeast refer to a special type of city that raised development of local forestry and mining resources, and relied on resource oriented industries to support the city's economy. Since resource based cities strongly depend on their resources, these cities normally face two pathways when their resources drain — deterioration or transformation (Liu, 2002).

During the first thirty years after the foundation of the People's Republic of China, the construction of energy resource mining enterprises were based on the priority strategy of developing heavy industry that utilizes domestic resources. A large number of resource based cities were formed across the country with the Northeast being the main region for development. After the foundation of the PRC, the central government invested heavily in the Northeast region, mainly on resource mining and processing. Surrounding the location of some important projects, a series of resource based cities were formed with energy and resource development as the main function. These cities are now an important part of the Northeast region. Among 36 cities in the region, 14 are resource-based cities, 6 of which are large cities with populations of over 500,000. Currently, most of these cities have entered the mid or end period of resource mining and their economic and social structures are in a state of transition. Because they lack a competitive industry system and investment environment, these cities are experiencing slow economic development and deterioration. In detail, the problems that existed were:

i) Structural conflicts were evident in cities during transformation. Economic development was highly dependent on the natural resources and the existing industrial strucutre. The heavy industry was a burden on the Northeast region. The imbalance in the industry portfolio seriously stifled the development of urban economy (Meng, 2006).

ii) There were a large number and different types of cities in transformation, resulting in a heavy financial pressure. The central government implemented measures to enhance support to the Northeast old industrial base, however, with limited funding from the central and local government, the financial needs could not be met by the government alone. This situation put financial pressure on both the central and local governments, especially when the transformation process becomes more difficult.

iii) The development pathways for industries were hard to define. Resource cities in decline needed to take different development pathways by focusing on continuing industries.

iv) A positive relationship was not formed between resource mining and urban development. The service industries of the cities were outdated and were developing slowly. The development of infrastructure and public projects were slow. Centralized management and integrated planning were difficult due to the mines remote spatial location, which stifled the clustering effect and the formation of a positive development mechanism.

The main features of resource based cities in transition are:

i) To redefine the cities' development and function. Based on the regional economic development, the future development direction and the redefined functions of the city and changing the simple "industry and mining city" into new cities with complete functions called as the service industry.

ii) To diversify industry development strategy. Choosing sustainable industry building on existing industry infrastructure and moving away from the single industry structure. For example, building connected industries in a coal mining city could be metal smelting, building materials industry, light industry, textiles, medicines, mechanical manufacturing and construction; forestry cities can develop connected industries for example wood processing, furniture manufacturing, planting, farming, building material, transportation, forestry chemicals and ecological tourism industry.

iii) Enterprise management reform by accelerating the transition in enterprise management, the systematic reform was deepened; the enterprises focused on the main body of their production, separated the supporting product lines, eased the enterprises from social responsibility and sought share-based ownership reform and public listing of enterprises.

iv) Layout of resource based cities was adjusted and population and production factors were spatially collated. For example, small mines with drained resources were closed.

v) Restoration measurements of resource based cities are to enhance environmental restoration of the mine areas with advancements in land reclamation technology; discover the true resource potential, at the same time enhance waste usage within the industry cycle.

3.2. The "Northeast Phenomenon" and state-owned enterprises reform

The Northeast Phenomenon describes the slowing down and in some cases there is a decline in the economic development of the Northeast industrial base, whilst other regions continued to see rapid development. As a result, the Northeast region was facing a series of social problems. The Northeast Phenomenon was amongst other factors, a result of the unique development process of the old industrial base and changes in the domestic and international development environment. The Northeast region existed because of the development of state owned enterprises and also failed because of the rigid structure of the SOEs. The reform of regional SOEs was progressing in the revitalization of the Northeast region.

3.2.1. *Major problems of the state-owned enterprises*
      in the Northeast region and their causes

First, the state-owned enterprises had a large influence on the region's economy and due to their rigid structures and their history it was difficult to implement reform and adjustments (Zhang, 2004). In 2001, the importance of the state-owned enterprises on the economy of Liaoning, Jilin, and Heilongjiang province represented 72.8%, 86.2%, and 87.2%, respectively, all much higher than that of the national average of 64.9%. Table 3.2 shows the scale and weight of state-owned enterprises in 2001.

The state-owned economy of the Northeast region was comprised mainly of traditional mining and processing industries. Within the heavy industry sector, the percentage of mining and raw material industries was 64.2%, higher than the national average by 14.5%. Of the 913 central government controlled enterprises, 149 were monopolies. Of all enterprises the asset amount, sales revenue, and employee amount was 58.2%, 52.8%, and 53.0%, respectively. Further 281 enterprises were in basic industry, with their asset amount, sales revenue, and employee figures being 64.1%, 50.0%, and 58.2% respectively. In 2001, the state-owned enterprises GDP for the three provinces all exceeded 50% (Table 3.2). The sheer volume of state-owned enterprises meant that the cost of reform in the Jilin Province was on average three times higher than that of the coastal areas, and it was the same, if not more, for Liaoning and Heilongjiang Provinces. Therefore, the reform of the state-owned economy of the Northeast region into a market economy was very difficult, partly as it was hard for state-owned enterprises to exit the market.

Second, the Northeast region had outdated ideas and a prominent single ownership structure, which resulted in a distinct lack of preparation for market competition. The Northeast region was the original area where the planned economy was implemented and where it had most success. The contribution of the industrial sector in the Northeast region to GDP fell from 17% of the national industrial contribution at the start of the reform, to around 9% in 2012. There were a large number of enterprises filing for bankruptcy and an increase in the number of unemployed. Analyzing the predominant industry structure, it is evident that the simple ownership structure was the cause of a lack of self-motivation structural adjustments. SOEs were dominant in all the Northeastern industries, but the structural transformation of Northeast region was mostly led by the central government. Since SOEs lacked the self-motivation for structural transformation, they fell

Table 3.2. Number and Proportion of State-Owned Industrial Enterprises in China and Northeast China in 2001.

Project	No. of state-owned enterprises and non-state-owned enterprise over delegated scale	No. of state-owned and in controlling interest enterprises	Percentage of/No. of industry enterprises (%)	Industry GDP of state-owned enterprises and non-state-owned enterprise over delegated scale (100 million yuan)	GDP of state-owned and in controlling interest enterprise (100 million yuan)	Percentage in industrial enterprise GDP of state-owned enterprises and non-state-owned enterprise over delegated scale (%)
National	171256	46767	27.3	95448.98	42408.49	44.4
Liaoning	5847	2188	37.4	4480.32	2928.95	65.4
Jilin	2608	1392	53.4	1876.65	1505.03	80.2
Heilongjiang	2500	1328	53.1	2365.44	1957.20	82.7

Source of Information: China Statistics Yearbook-2002.

behind in the movement of working toward a market economy. This situation was a barrier in the transformation of the Northeast old industrial base.

Third, the reform of SOEs in the Northeast region fell behind, the adop-
tion of the market economy was low and the implementation of reform
policies was slow. In 2000, the comprehensive indices for the development
of the market economy ranked Liaoning's city 18th out of the 31 inland
provinces, Jilin Province ranked 19th and Heilongjiang city ranked 21st.
Although the products made in the Northeast region were mostly commercialized, the supporting markets were still in an early development stage,
especially the development of the labor market. The production factors had
a low degree of commercialization and it was hard to optimize the allocation of resources and reorganize assets according to the requirements of a
scaled economy. The degree of market success in the Northeast was considerably lower than the eastern coastal areas. Although the products and the
pricing in the Northeast region were market-based, the production factors
such as ownership, capital, technology, and labor still had strong features of
the planned economy. This resulted in most products produced by the
Northeast region's SOEs being uncompetitive in the market economy. This
led to an increase in unemployment. These results occurred partly because
the reform was not properly integrated into all aspects of the economy.

Fourth, the SOEs crowd-out effect on the private-owned enterprises
stifled the market development. Although the three provinces of the
Northeast region had already realized the importance of POEs, their presence was still far less than in the Southeast coastal areas, and surprisingly
was even worse than in some inland areas. Most industries were dominated by SOEs, which meant it was easier for them to get opportunities to
develop. At the same time, SOEs had responsibility for various social
services that should have been carried out by the government. Hence, the
government had to exercise administrative authority by giving preferential
treatment to the SOEs. This imbalance in the resource allocation stifled
the development of the market economy.

Fifth, there were three pre-existing situations that made reform difficult
in the Northeast region and resulted in the enterprises being uncompetitive. In detail, they were:

i) Enterprises funding and carrying out social functions. There were
   3,476 organizations carrying out social functions that were established by enterprises controlled by the central government. These

organizations employed 310,000 employees and received a 12.99 billion yuan subsidy from the enterprises. There were a large number of collectively-owned enterprises, most of which had negative profit and were experiencing difficulty.

ii) Excess number of employees, too many retirees and laid-off workers, resulted in low morale and working efficiency. Most enterprises had an excess number of employees by over 20%. With this heavy historical burden of high employment numbers, the cost of social security system and the need for social stability had increased; there was an increasing risk of a regional financial crisis and security problems.

iii) High leverage, poor asset quality, and low economic benefit. The enterprise financial reports by the Chinese Ministry of Finance stated that the three provinces in the Northeast region were all ranked at the bottom of the list when compared with other provinces, in the indexes like total profit, leverage ratio, net asset profit margin, and non-performing asset by interest ratio. Furthermore, the assets of the enterprises were mostly fixed assets, which resulted in poor asset quality. In addition, these enterprises were unable to increase their profitability because of the old equipment being used, single product variety and high expense on excess employees.

These difficulties made it very difficult for the enterprises in the Northeast region to grow.

Sixth, the degree of opening up in the Northeast region was not high enough and the investment environment was poor. The level of difficulty in asset reorganization is closely related to the level of development of the market economy and the level of opening up. Compared with the development of the coastal provinces, the Northeast region was weak in opening up, and the gap between the regions expanded. In detail:

i) In terms of opening up to the global market, the international trading dependency level was only 20.37% for the three provinces of the Northeast region, far lower than the national average of 43.57%. The amount of foreign investment attracted to this region was only 6.89% of the national total.

ii) In terms of domestic opening up, the effective implementation of the opening up policy by the Southeast coastal areas made itself the best choice for foreign investment and industry transfer. Thus, the coastal areas became the window for opening up to domestic market, which led to the Northeast region seeing a loss in funding and human skills.

3.2.2. *How were SOEs reformed during the revitalization process*

There were four main processes used in the reform of SOEs. They are described below:

i) Mergers and acquisition: This has always been a dominant process in the reform of SOEs (Liu, 2003). Internationally, the success rate for merging was only 25%, however, it was lower for merging SOEs in China. Factors influencing the low success rate included system inefficiencies, market changes, and changes in national industry policy. Subjective reasons included: First, there was an excessive focus on expansion and inaccurate calculation on the benefits of merging of both the parties involved. Second, after merging, enterprises' lacked concern and attention to the integration of assets, liabilities, human resources, management, and culture. Third, there was excessive government intervention and finally, the laws and regulation on merging were incomplete. Therefore, merging and acquisition was mainly undertaken to attract foreign investment and private capital. The involvement of large international corporations not only provided a boost in funding, but also brought in pre-existing management styles, technology, and international marketing network. This effectively improved the management skills and enterprise competitiveness of the SOEs.

ii) Liquidation and reorganization: The government strategically implemented policies to promote the liquidation and reorganization of assets based on the government funding and the state-owned commercial bank's ability to write off bad debts. The liquidation process eliminated unprofitable enterprises and industries. It also accelerated the pace of regional and industrial economic structural reform. In the process of liquidation employees of these enterprises were looked after through the promotion of the social security system. Gradually, a mechanism was established for the disadvantaged SOEs to exit the market, this ensured the economy remained stable through the economic transition period.

iii) Asset reorganization: The reform of medium to large SOEs can be seen as the reorganization of some monopoly industries. This was done to optimize resource allocation and create competition, as well as to develop a number of large enterprises with international competitiveness. The SOEs were still the key factor for industries involving national security, for those that formed natural monopolies, industries supplying important public products and services, important resource industries and some new high technology industries.

iv) Debt reorganization: In general, the heavy liability of SOEs was evident from the large debt figures, the unreasonable debt structure, high leverage, high historical debts, and high insolvency risk. During the economic transformation period, the large number of bad debts became a key factor in the success or failure of the transformation process whilst resolving the debts led to fundamental conflicts in the economic system which were difficult to solve. Through debt cancellation, enterprise trustee mechanisms, debt conversion, market negotiation, and debt to equity conversion was implemented.

3.2.3. State-owned enterprises found new development path after reform

In the Northeast region, the enterprise reform, merging and reorganization was accelerated and SOEs were seen as reforming. By the end of 2003, there were 13,000 SOEs in the Northeast region, of which 900 were controlled by the central government. Since the implementation of the revitalization strategies of the Northeast old industrial base strategy, the SOEs had made great progress in reforming. Since 2003, finance departments of all banks have packed and treated bad debts. At the same time, the government implemented preferential policies for combining social securities (50% contribution by central government, 30% by provincial government, and 20% by enterprises), which culminated at the end of 2005.

The management system of SOEs was separated from the government (Liu and Li, 2003). Previously, it was the government who directly led the enterprises, with state-owned capital belonging to the governments and the government appointed managers for the enterprises. After the reform, a double management system was established; it changed the state-own assets agent relationship from political agency to economic agency.

A commercialized agency relationship was implemented, which maintained and increased the value of most state-owned assets.

Combined with the adjustment of the state-owned economic structure, the majority of SOEs completed a share-based ownership reform. During 2004–2005, the Northeast region started the hard battle of reforming SOEs. The general guidelines provided included using the ownership structure reform as core, gaining strategic investors, and achieving diversified enterprise ownership. For resource-oriented enterprises that had competitive advantage, the government promoted reorganization which included the integration of other favorable enterprises. Except for the large coal enterprises, it was recommended to remove the limitation on the percentage of shares available in the state-owned enterprises, regardless of their sizes. A small number of large enterprises still remained under the control of the central government. By the end of 2005, 90% of the reform process of state-owned industrial enterprises in the Northeast region had been completed (the reform of the large–medium enterprises was 86% completed), and the reform of regional SOEs was 70% completed. By 2009, the reform of state-owned enterprises in the Northeast region had achieved its basic progress goals (see Table 3.3 a, b, c).

There was support for the strategy which released enterprises from performing social responsibilities and reduced employee figures. The government took over social public servicing organizations and administrative organizations, such as primary and secondary colleges, the police force, People's Procuratorate and People's Court, health organizations, and community management organizations. Then, the government gradually separated the public welfare organizations such as hospitals, public transport, and waste management organizations. Combined with reforming the social security system, the government supported the opportunity to eliminate excess labor to ease the burden of enterprises. In 2009, the percentage of staff of SOEs in Liaoning, Jilin, and Heilongjiang was 13.78%, 12.3%, and 17.81% of the total employees, respectively. Compared to 1990 levels it had dropped by 52.35%, 18.635%, and 54.22%, respectively for three provinces.

The alterations to the ownership policies included changes in the ownership and management of state-owned assets by different levels of governments. It was set out in the management system of different types of state-owned assets and was managed accordingly. The establishment of independent management organizations specifically for the state-owned assets and the promotion of layered management practices of state-owned assets.

Table 3.3.   (a) Basic Situation of State-Owned Enterprises in Northeast China, 2009.

Province	No. of state-owned enterprises	Total No. of enterprises	Total No. of industrial enterprises	No. of industrial state-owned enterprises	Total industrial GDP (10,000 yuan)	Industrial GDP of state-owned enterprises (100 million yuan)	Social investment in fixed assets by state-owned economy (100 million yuan)	Total social investment in fixed assets (100 million yuan)	Employees of state-owned enterprises/ total No. of employees in industry (%)	Average salary (yuan)
Liaoning	48682	345754	23364	424	28152.73	2705	2845.6	12292.6	13.78	31878
Jilin	28063	131982	5936	186	10026.55	1342.89	1927.10	7259.50	12.3	27070
Heilongjiang	37285	164241	4408	505	7301.6	4362.38	2068.9	5028.8	17.81	25635

Table 3.3.   (b) Basic Situation of State-Owned Enterprises in Northeast China, 2000.

Province	No. of state-owned enterprises	Total No. of enterprises	Total No. of industrial enterprises	No. of industrial state-owned enterprises	Total industrial GDP (10,000 yuan)	Industrial GDP of state-owned enterprises (100 million yuan)	Social investment in fixed assets by state-owned economy (100 million yuan)	Total social investment in fixed assets (100 million yuan)	Employees of state-owned enterprises/total No. of employees in industry (%)	Average salary (yuan)
Liaoning	—	—	6017	2045	4249.46	1326.14	649.4244	1267.6873	26.17	9221
Jilin	—	—	2728	1667	1377.42	710.43	491.20	586.86	21.22	8145
Heilongjiang	2337	5346	2666	826	3540.9	2071.1	449.8	859.2	73.41	7792

Table 3.3. (c) Basic Situation of State-Owned Enterprises in Northeast China, 1990.

Province	No. of state-owned enterprises	Total No. of enterprises	Total No. of industrial enterprises	No. of industrial state-owned enterprises	Total industrial GDP (10,000 yuan)	Industrial GDP of state-owned enterprises (100 million yuan)	Social investment in fixed assets by state-owned economy (100 million yuan)	Total social investment in fixed assets (100 million yuan)	Employees of state-owned enterprises/ total No. of employees in industry (%)	Average salary (yuan)
Liaoning	—	—	—	21211	3424	1606.93	983.92	262.88	66.13	2388
Jilin	—	—	—	178600	2380	552.39	380.39	66.94	30.95	2068
Heilongjiang	—	—	—	14884	3455	863.51	695.3	162.9	72.03	2014

Source of document: China Statistics Yearbook.

The production efficiency increased significantly with a rise in the profitability of state-owned assets (Qi, 2003), but it was still lower than the national average. In 2009, the GDP of state-owned or state-controlled enterprises in Liaoning, Jilin, and Heilongjiang provinces were: 270.5 billion yuan, 134.289 billion yuan, and 436.238 billion yuan, respectively, representing an increase of 18.95% in Jilin, decrease of 19.78%, and 15.19% in Liaoning and Heilongjiang when compared to the previous year.

3.3. *Industry upgrade and structural reform mode*

3.3.1. *Northeast region industrial upgrade*

The key to revitalizing Northeast old industrial base was to take advantage of the comparative advantage of special industries and develop other industries with competitive advantage. The traditional advantageous industries were still the main direction of development (Xu, 2006). For the dominant industries, their reform practices were:

Equipment manufacturing industry:

i) The Northeast region should undertake strategic adjustment in the state-owned equipment manufacturing industry, they should support key enterprises, achieve diversified investment bodies, and develop intermediate industries.

ii) To develop a performance evaluation system and a motivation system and connect the GDP with other green indicator systems.

iii) To set up organizations as intermediaries, combine the government, production, education and research into an integrated chain and build a regional brand image; establish information gathering and product distribution organization.

iv) To combine domestic production and international marketing and benefit from the development of the Northeast Asia economic circle and to build up a local production system and adapt it to the global system.

Automobile industry:

i) To support the profitable enterprises and eliminate the unsuccessful enterprises and accelerate organizational adjustment. The regional government should support the development of products in the automobile parts industry; stimulate small to medium enterprises that manufactures automobile parts that have potential to raise the level of skills.

ii) To build a core network and enhance competitiveness within the industry cluster.

iii) To encourage enterprises to form an alliance to enhance the market share of the industry cluster. For example, the region should promote technical cooperation and innovation between domestic automobile industries with enterprises in developed regions such as Shanghai.

iv) To encourage the development of intermediaries within the car industry. For example, establish the automobile industry development fund to support the flow of domestic and international funding to the automobile enterprises of the Northeast region.

v) To establish the Northeast region automobile research and development center to improve product development. Also, develop a national center for automobile parts, to improve the development of some critical parts that matches the developments of car technology.

Medicine production:

i) Integrate resources to motivate the development of industry cluster. As the industry relies on new technology and technological innovation, the regional could enhance its independent innovation capability of medicine production.

ii) To develop large manufacturing and distribution corporations. The industry should build up the regional comparative advantage and the core competitiveness of the pharmaceutical industry and also develop pharmaceutical distribution systems for both the domestic and international market. Build up medicine retailing chain enterprises with a good international reputation.

iii) To develop all kinds of medicine-related markets. The region should develop all kinds of medicine-related market with specialized division of labor, especially the upstream and downstream industries in the pharmaceutical industry and sub-industries.

iv) To implement a production and research system. The region should establish a joint research and development mechanism surrounding the pharmaceutical companies, and make use of research institutions in and out of the Northeast region.

v) To upgrade the entire pharmaceutics manufacturing industry with advanced technology.

Food processing:

i) To accelerate the upgrading pace of the food processing industry. The region should further improve the quality of the agricultural products and build up the largest green food industrial base.

ii) The emphasis of this strategy is dietary products, soybean products, grain processing, potato related products, meat products, beer and beverages, and mountain delicacies. More investment should be put into green products.

iii) To accelerate the development of food processing production and distribution enterprises. The region should support influential enterprises; build distribution enterprises and establish agricultural wholesale market.

iv) To utilize the regional advantage to cooperatively integrate into the international market. Liaoning Province should focus on developing trade with Japan; Jilin Province should take advantage of its location to develop economic cooperation with South and North Korea; and Heilongjiang Province should enhance trade with Russia.

Petrochemical industry:

i) To increase the production capacity of ethylene and the market share of its downstream products. The current technology of ethylene production devices should be upgraded; the region should take full advantage of its integrated petroleum and petrochemical industry; focus on developing cracking furnace and separating technique with high capacity, high quality, high heat efficiency, and high durability.

ii) To use new production methods and change the traditional raw material production method.

iii) To improve the technical innovation system and enhance the development ability. The region should accelerate the incorporation of petrochemical research institutes; import competition to promote the commercialization of new technologies and products.

iv) To develop a national petrochemical industry cluster to improve profitability. Take full advantage of both the domestic and foreign market and achieve optimized resource allocation. For example, the Northeast industrial base should develop the Ha-Da-Qi national petrochemical industrial cluster with Daqing Oil Field as core.

3.3.2. *Upgrading the industrial structure drove a change in the regional ownership structure*

3.3.2.1. Establish an exit mechanism for state-owned capital and optimize the layout of state-owned economy

First, the old industrial base should establish an exit mechanism for state-owned enterprises. The exit mechanism can be established through the following methods:

i) Use the security market, through whole assets trade-in, part ownership selling, holding interest in other enterprises, restructure and list enterprise to attract private capital and achieve diversified investment.

ii) Rely on the ownership market, accelerate liquidation policy and legally enforce liquidation to motivate state-owned interests away from small and medium enterprises.

iii) Use methods such as merging.

Second, optimize the location of the state-owned enterprises. The state-owned economy should exit from industries with outdated technology, poor product quality, and a narrow market space. At the same time, the state-owned fund should concentrate on supporting large enterprises and enterprises in important industries that are related to the nation's economy.

Third, concentrate on supporting the competitive enterprises. The strategic reform of SOEs is the micro foundation of optimizing the state-owned economic layout. The three breakthroughs that the old industrial needs achieve are: First, accelerate the pace of cooperation and joint investment of large state-owned enterprises. Only a few large enterprises that have the potential to impact on the national economy or are part of the military industry should be solely owned or controlled by the national government, other large state-owned enterprises should establish a modern enterprise system. The second breakthrough is to accelerate the pace of privatization of SOEs. The final breakthrough that needs to be achieved is to liquidate and shut down enterprises that have a long history of making a loss and are impossible to make profitable, as well as enterprises that are high polluters, resource wasting and not complying with safe production regulations.

3.3.2.2. Develop diversified investment bodies and complete the mixed ownership economy

First, develop a share-based economy as the major form of public ownership. Through the reform, the development of the public ownership economy can be connected to the non-public ownership economy, which can enhance the liquidity of funds and promote asset-optimizing reorganization.

Second, enhance the opening up of the domestic and the international market. In detail, the opening up strategy should include:

i) To accelerate the regional economic reorganization and integration and establish a united market.
ii) To expand the opening up to other regions of China. The Northeast region can take full advantage of its transportation, industry foundation, labor resources and rich agricultural products to develop light manufacturing industries.
iii) To enhance the external opening up with economic cooperation in the Northeastern Asia. The Northeast region should carry out economic structural adjustment with the aim of global economic integration and to participate in the global market.

3.4. *Change in macro layout of the old industrial base*

The Northeast old industrial base achieved a balance in the development of the region by adjusting the region's macro layout (Lu, 2009). Some measurements that were beneficial for building regional structure and space included the establishment of the Liaoning Province coastal economic belt, the Chang-Ji-Tu national pivot for reform and opening up and the, Shenyang city economic zone. These measurements helped in the building up of new regional economic development zone by utilizing the competitive advantages of the provinces through regional cooperation and a clear task division system. Ultimately, it helps in achieving a balance in the development between humans, natural environment, and the society.

3.4.1. *Coastal Liaoning Economic Belt*

3.4.1.1. Shift in development strategy of coastal Liaoning Province and regional introduction

During the 1990s and in the beginning of the 21st Century, the Liaoning Province implemented the economic strategy of using coastal cities as "*tap*" cities to drive regional economic development.

In 2005, the strategic development idea of "five points and one line" was proposed. In February, 2006, five key development zones in coastal Liaoning Province were identified (Fig. 3.2):

i) Dalian city Changxing Island Port Industrial Zone,
ii) Liaoning Province (Yingkou) Coastal Industrial Base (Including the Panjin Ship Manufacturing Industrial Base),
iii) Western Liaoning Jinzhouwan Coastal Economic Zone (Including the Jinzhou Xihai Industrial Zone and Hulu Island North Port Industrial Zone),
iv) Liaoning Dandong Industrial Zone and
v) Dalian Huayuankou Industrial Zone.

The total area covered by the strategy was 582.9 km². The "one line" refers to the coastal road between Dandong and Huludao Suizhong, with a length of 1,443 km. The main principle was to drive economic development to an area within 100 km to the coastal line.

In June 2006, the "five points and one line" strategy was expanded to all coastal cities of Liaoning Province including Dangdong, Dalian, Panjin, Yingkou, Jinzhou, and Hulu Island (Fig. 3.3). On 1 July 2009, the "development plan of Liaoning coastal economic belt" was approved by the State Council to be upgraded to a national strategy.

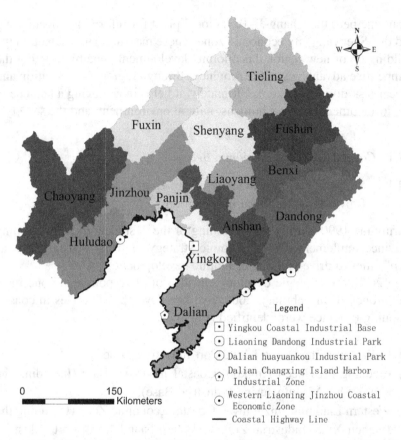

Figure 3.2. "Five Points and One Line" in the Coastal Economic Belt of Liaoning Province.

3.4.1.2. Emphasis of regional development

The Liaoning coastal economic belt is an important zone for China's border development and opening up. It is an important door and platform for economic and technological development of Northeastern Asia and an important new development point of Northeast region.

The strategic positioning of the coastal economic belt in Liaoning Province means it is backed up by the whole Northeast region, whilst serving the whole nation. It is the face of Northeast Asia, as well as developing the coastal economic belt into a featured and competitive portal for industry clustering. It is ranked as top in China, and the Northeast Asia as

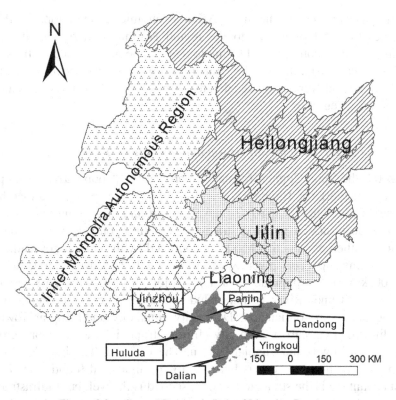

Figure 3.3. Coastal Economic Belt of Liaoning Province.

an international shipping center and international logistics center. In addition, the coastal Liaoning economic belt is also intended to become the pivot zone for reform, innovation, and opening up. This is the first choice of investment while being a new city that's suitable for living, and the core engine for revitalizing the Northeast region.

3.4.1.3. The implications of the strategy

Accelerating the development of Liaoning's coastal economic belt is beneficial for completing China's coastal economy and for forming new economic growth zones. It makes use of the driving effect of revitalizing the Northeast old industrial zones, it raises the development level of northern coastal areas and promotes the integration between the Northeast region and the Bohai circle area. It is also beneficial to participate in the Northeastern Asian economic cooperation, as this reduces the cost of export to the inland Northeastern region. It will strengthen the economic and technological cooperation with countries in the Northeast Asia, deepen the strategic cooperative partner relationship with Japan and Korea, and accelerate the process of Northeastern Asia's economic integration.

3.4.2. *Chang-Ji-Tu national reform and opening up pivot*

In 2009, the State Council formally approved the "cooperative development framework for Tumen River region, China", which signaled that the construction of the Chang-Ji-Tu development and the opening up of the pivot zone is now a national strategy. Until this point, it was the only region on the boarders that had been approved by the central government for opening up. The pivot zone of Chang-Ji-Tu covers an area of 30,000 km^2 and a population of 7.7 million. It covers the core region around the Tumen River, which includes Changchun city (encompassing Changchun metropolitian area, Dehui city, Jiutai city, and Nong'an Town) in Jilin Province, part of Jilin city (Jilin metropocitian area, Jiaohe city, and Yongji Town) and Yanbian Burgh. The Chang-Ji-Tu pivot development and opening up zone is built on a good industrial foundation. The first advantage is the strategic location, second is the well built infrastructure, third is the extensive economic and trading cooperation and fourth is the strong industrial and scientific support available.

3.4.2.1. Development key points

The Tumen River region is an important platform to enable China to participate in the Northeastern economic market. The four strategic positions of the Chang-Ji-Tu region are:

i) It is an important zone for China's opening up and development along the border,
ii) It is an important door into the Northeast Asia,
iii) It is a key platform for economic and technological cooperation,
iv) It is a new important growth polar of the Northeast region that can promote revitalization of the old industrial base together with Liaoning and Heilongjiang Province.

3.4.2.2. Implications of the strategy

First, the strategy has effectively resolved the development problems faced by the Tumen River region. Yanbian Burgh, Changchun city, and Jilin city were all included in the Tumen River international cooperative development projects to enhance the overall development prospects of this area. Second, the strategy promoted the revitalization of the Northeast old industrial base, it motivated China's cooperation with other Northeastern countries in balancing the regional development. Third, the strategy provided experience for China in expanding the opening up policy. As the Chang-Ji-Tu region is on the border and is close to the sea, this pilot region sets an example for the opening up of other border areas in China. Fourth, the strategy promotes the stable development of ethnic minority areas close to the border. The Yanbian Burgh is close to the border and is the only Korean minority autonomous prefecture. With the implementation of the strategy, it will see significant economic and social development, which can have a positive impact on the stability along the border regions and support unity between all the ethnic groups.

3.4.3. *Shenyang economic zone*

The Shenyang economic zone was poised to be developed as an important growth zone for the new national industrial base (See Fig. 3.4). More specifically, the aim was to build into an advanced equipment manufacturing industrial base with international competitiveness and as a processed raw material industrial base, while building it as the demonstration area for other resource based cities who are transforming and developing continuous industries and shifting to more diversified industrial development. In addition to it, it develops a pilot for driving modern agricultural development through modern industrialization and achieving integration of the urban–rural economy and social development.

3.4.3.1. Implications of the strategy

The approval of the Shenyang economic zone to be the National industrial synthetically reform testing district was in line with the national industrial development direction and the general requirements of revitalizing the Northeast old industrial base. In general, the establishment of the Shenyang economic zone is beneficial for promoting economic

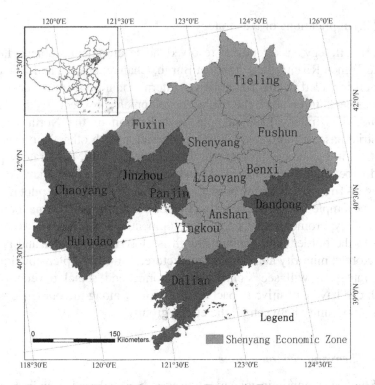

Figure 3.4. Shenyang Economic Zone.

cooperation of China with the wider Northeast region. It is beneficial for accelerating the economic transformation of resource based cities and enhancing sustainable development, as well as being beneficial to the implementation of the national strategy of regional development.

4. Conclusion

In 2003, the revitalization strategy was implemented in China's Northeast region. The strategy covered a broad range of aspects including the regional system, industrial structure, industrial development, city transformation, infrastructure constructions, external opening up, scientific education, culture, and health and hygiene. Comparing the strategies used in other regions, the preferential policies of the Chinese government for the Northeast region were providing a supportive and adjusting function. Under the implementation of the revitalization strategy and preferential policies, the Northeast region has seen an overall revitalization. The major signs of revitalization are:

i) The structural conflicts of the resource based cities in the region were eased by adjusting the city's structure through overall development of continuous industries.

ii) State-owned enterprises achieved reform by merging, liquidating, and asset and debt reorganizing, which separated the government from the control of enterprises and completed the share based reform. It also reduced enterprises' social responsibilities which resulted in a significant increase in the asset usage efficiency.

iii) The dominant industries in the Northeast region were reformed, which included equipment manufacturing, automobile, pharmaceutical, green food processing, and petrochemical industries; the regional ownership structure was changed with the exit of state-owned funds and the introduction of a mixed ownership economy.

The coastal Liaoning economic belt, Chang-Li-Tu national reform and the opening up of the pivot zone, and the Shenyang economic zone have been recognized as national key development zones. The prioritized development of these regions can promote the regional task divisions and the overall balance in the regional development.

4

Tiexi's Reborn: The Revitalization of the City's Old Industrial Zone

The old industrial zone in Northeast China consists of many old industrial cities. The rise and fall of the old industrial zone is essentially the rise and fall of the old industrial cities. The old industrial cities vary in size and function. The deterioration of Shenyang City, the largest old industrial city in Northeast China, is representative of what other cities may experience and its leading role in the revitalization of the state-dominant urban economy is an example for the rest of the regions' old industrial cities.

In the Mao era, urban planning and the economy were largely copied from the former Soviet Union (Tang and Jiang, 2001). Therefore, before the implementation of the economic reform in the late 1970s, many Chinese cities had industrial districts with a vast number of state-owned enterprises' (SOEs) clusters. These districts were self-sufficient and predominantly had just one function i.e. manufacturing. Many large state-owned *'Danwei'* (work units) were concentrated in these districts where each unit provided all social and economic services to their workers. However, when the market economy was gradually introduced, they became problem areas with slow growth rates and high unemployment (Jin *et al.*, 2006). Tiexi, Shenyang's most important industrial district, had a similar experience. Since the foundation of the People's Republic of China, 100 national-level industrial projects were set up in Tiexi. The district became the leader in China's machinery manufacturing industry until the start of the economic reform and opening-up. Another aspect that brought glory to Tiexi district is that it has been in the first place in China for 500 items (Dong, 2007a). However, the deterioration affected the

Tiexi district severely, by the end of the 1990s, 90% of the enterprises in the district had entirely or partially stopped production, and 43% workers had been laid off (Dong, 2007b). In 2002, the Shenyang municipal government started to implement the reform strategy for the old industrial district. This chapter provides an insight to how Tiexi district revitalized itself.

This chapter first describes the development process and the historical contribution of the Tiexi district, Shenyang city. Then, it presents the model used in the revitalization of Tiexi and how it works. Finally, it discusses the implications of the "Tiexi Model".

1. The Development Process and Historical Contribution of Tiexi District, Shenyang City

Shenyang city is the capital city of Liaoning Province. It is the largest economic, cultural, and transportation center of the Northeast region of China, and is one of the most important modern equipment manufacturing industrial cities in China. Shenyang city is ranked as the top 10 largest cities of China, with an urban population of 6.248 million. Tiexi is one of the five urban districts in Shenyang city. Tiexi was the largest modern equipment manufacturing center in China and one of the largest in Asia, and it gained a reputation as *the eldest son of Chinese industry* and as an important industrial town of Northeast region. Tiexi district was the growth engine of Shenyang city's economy, therefore, the rise and fall of the district had a direct impact on the rise and fall of Shenyang city.

Tiexi district was a product of the colonial economy. In July 1889, the Qing government was forced to sign a contract with the Russian government called the "Agreement of the Northeastern Railway Company" (the area during that time was known as South Manchuria), in which about 6 km² area of land was classified as land for railway development and was controlled by Russia. The 6 km² area of land was to enable the Russians to control the Northeast region of China and to conveniently transport energy (Tiexi District Shenyang City Government Local History Office, 1998). This was the early development of the Tiexi district.

In 1904, the Russia–Japanese war began in China. Japan, as the victorious country, took over some of the 6 km² railway land and renamed it "The Manchuria Railway Affiliated Land". Until 1932, under the puppet Manchuria Regime, the Japanese government moved a large number of Japanese migrants into the areas that they controlled in Shenyang. They invested in factories and started urban planning and development in the city. In 1938, the Japanese puppet government pushed forward with the establishment of the Tiexi district. The district followed a colonial city lay-out with residents in the South and factories in the North, with a construction road dividing line between two areas (Tiexi District Shenyang City Government Local History Office, 1998). To keep the Japanese immigrants separated from the Chinese, spatially segregated residential areas were purposely developed. Japanese citizens lived on the east of Guihe Street with quality infrastructure, while a shanty town with limited infrastructure was built on the west for the Chinese residents. Tiexi was a poorly selected location for the development of the manufacturing industry, as it is located upwind from the Shenyang CBD which resulted in an increase in pollution in the city center.

Tiexi district experienced a rapid expansion in the 1930s and the early 1940s. Tiexi became an important heavy industrial site (See Fig. 4.1. and Fig. 4.2). Japanese-owned enterprises gradually took over Tiexi's economy. For

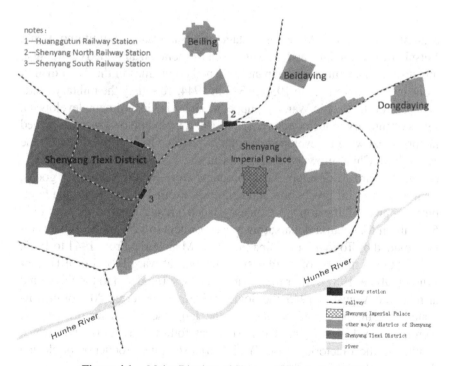

Figure 4.1. Major Districts of Shenyang City in the 1930s.

Figure 4.2.   Urban Landscape of Shenyang Tiexi District in the 1930s.

example, during the Manchuria stage, Kansai Osaka, Sumitomo Bank, Mitsui Trust & Banking, and the Mitsubishi Corporation all started operating in this district. The number of Japanese-owned companies in the Tiexi district alone increased from 28 in 1930 to 323 in 1944. To satisfy the military needs of Japan for the Pacific War, the puppet Manchuria Government developed a series of military industry enterprises in 1942, including 63 Japanese-owned factories that were redeveloped in order to produce military products. At the same time, Chinese-owned enterprises in the Tiexi district were finding it extremely hard to develop. Their products were mainly consumer goods, such as grains, oil processing and ceramics. From 1917 to 1944, the combined capital of the top 57 Chinese-owned private enterprises was only 5.2 million Manchuria dollars; this was equivalent to 52% of the initial capital provided by Toyota for the first factory in Manchuria. From 1941 to 1945, Tiexi, as with the rest of Northeast China, was at war (Tiexi Local History Editing Office, 1987). After the Japanese army surrendered to the Soviet red army in the August of 1945, the Soviet red army transferred 80% of the raw material, equipment, and products in the Japanese-owned factories to the former Soviet Union (Qin, 2010). This was followed by a civil war which resulted in most factories in the Tiexi district stopping production or closing doors until 1948 (Chen, 2009).

Tiexi district is also a product of Maoist industrialization. Its colonial legacy made it an attractive option for investment by communist China after the foundation of the PRC. The new central government, under the support of the former Soviet Union, started systematic, large-scale industrialization of heavy industry during the first five years (1952–1957). In the first 10 years of the People's Republic, the central government allocated a sixth of its total budget to the equipment manufacturing industry in the Tiexi district of Shenyang city (Dong, 2007a), with the aim of building an equipment manufacturing industry base and an exemplary model of socialist industry. For example, during the first five-year period, based on the strong technical expertise, with a readily available work force and existing equipment, the Chinese central government allocated three out of a total of 156 Soviet aided projects to the Tiexi district. The government also built 12 new medium to large enterprises and upgraded 40 industry enterprises, which alone cost over one million yuan. During this period, the total number of industrial enterprises reached a record of 650, of which 20 were highly ranked in China in terms of the scale of production and technical level (He, 2007). During the second five-year period (1958–1962), Tiexi expanded its manufacturing capacity further and some of its industrial products were in a dominant position in the Chinese market, such as the blower and metal cutting machine tool (Table 4.1). By 1963, 30 out of the 31 types of manufacturing industries in China had been established in Tiexi (Wang, 2005). An industrial system with a complete range of outputs and relatively strong supporting services had been formed with a focus on equipment manufacturing including, metallurgy mining, chemical industry, building materials, and textiles. Therefore, after the first two five-year plans (1952–1957, 1958–1962), Tiexi district was able to manufacture heavy machinery for pump-valves; power transmission and transformation; and metallurgic mining. Its products

Table 4.1. Main Industrial Products, Production Amount and Market Share of the Tiexi District in 1960.

	Blower	Metal cutting machine tool	Electricity transformer	Electricity wires
Production	27,000	17,000	1.054×10^{10} volts	60,000 tons
Market share	25.3%	14.9%	40.6%	25.1%

manufacturing capacity and technical level represented the highest achievement in China at that time (Dong, 2007a).

From the start of the third five-year period to the beginning of the opening up and economic reform (1965–1978), Tiexi district still played an important role in the nation's industry because of its solid industrial base and the advantage of scale. In 1982, the assets of state-owned enterprises (above municipality level) accounted for 46.7% of Shenyang's total assets value, equal to the total of Changchun city and Qingdao city. The gross profit accounted for 65.3% of Shenyang's total profit, which was equal to the total of Chongqing city, Haerbin city, and Xi'an city. Tiexi district provided support for the development of new industrial bases across China through their technical expertise. For example, the Shenyang High Voltage Switch Gear Factory produced the first 800 kilowatts hydraulic generator in China for the Sichuan Power Station; the Shenyang High and Middle Pressure Valve Factory produced military gear that China urgently required; the Shenyang Bridge Construction Factory built seven railway bridges overseas building the reputation of the Chinese railway bridge construction team (Wang, 2005). During the cold-war period and the "third front" construction period (1964–1980), China established military–industrial bases in "safe haven" regions including, the inland provinces of Sichuan, Chongqing, Guizhou, Shaanxi, and Shanxi. In addition, 16 factories from the Tiexi district sent 14,000 technicians and skilled workers to assist in the newly established manufacturing industries in the "third front" areas. At the same time, these factories were providing training for the workers heading to the third front factories (Tiexi Local History Editing Office, 1987).

Before Deng introduced the open door policy, Tiexi was China's most important industrial district. A famous phrase in China at that time was *Liaoning Province leads China's industry, Shenyang City leads Liaoning's industry and Tiexi district leads Shenyang's industry.* By the end of the 1980s, Tiexi district had been noted for 500 specific achievements in the development of the Chinese industry since the foundation of PRC, of which over 300 were related to the equipment manufacturing industry. In 1978, at the beginning of the opening-up and economic reform, China had three key industrial bases: the Beijing–Tianjin area, Shanghai, and Liaoning Province. During Mao's era, the position and technical level of the equipment manufacturing industry of the Tiexi district was irreplaceable and its contribution to China's industrialization was significant (Dong, 2007a). However, the other two industrial bases listed were coastal development zones and their rapid growth continued beyond 1978, whereas the Tiexi district experienced a decline in the industry sector and its economic position shifted from contributing half of Shenyang city's industrial output to becoming one of the most problematic areas of China. Like many other parts of Northeast China, the economic reform and opening-up made many enterprises in Tiexi bankrupt and workers were laid off. By the end of the 1990s, 90% of enterprises in Tiexi district either had totally or partially stopped their operations with assets valued at more than 50 billion yuan staying idle (Liu, 2009). At the same time, 232 medium to large state-owned enterprises did not have the money to pay salaries to their workers and the average leverage ratio of enterprises in Tiexi district was as high as 90% (Qin, 2010). Besides poor economic development outlook, the unemployment problem became more noticeable. Social conflicts worsened because of the poor social security system. In total, over 40% of workers were laid off, with the majority not having a secure pension fund, unemployment support or medical insurance. As a result, local residents had low morale and social stability became an issue. For example, workers who had been laid off demonstrated by blocking the roads 127 times in 2000 to seek help from the higher authorities (Liu, 2009).

2. The Causes of the Deterioration in Shenyang's Tiexi District

Like China's other traditional industrial zones, Tiexi district developed rapidly with the investment in heavy industry from the central government. The domination of the state sector made it difficult to break through the path-dependence and meant that it was hard for Tiexi to compete with the latecomers, such as the Pearl River region and the Lower Yangzi delta. The institutional problems can be seen at all levels, including, government, organizational, community, and individuals. The conflict between the old and new systems caused by the human resource system was one of the difficulties faced by the SOEs. Until 2000, China's SOEs had no clear direction; there was a question as to who was in control, the government or the enterprise managers? All SOE managers continued to be appointed by the government authority (Feng and Long, 2000). At the same time, SOEs were using a discriminating performance appraisal system, which reduced employees' production motivation and led to low production efficiency and heavy social burdens. The communities in Tiexi were over-dependent on the government and enterprises; this was mainly because the employment, medical treatment and education of employees and their family members were all provided by the enterprises. The situation of *enterprises performing social functions* resulted in enterprises lacking resources and capacity to undertake reforms and to develop. From an individual's perspective, people were too dependent on the enterprises and previous employees were not actively seeking new jobs because they were happy being dependent on the government for support. By 2000, Tiexi district had become run-down: there was high unemployment rate and a significant reduction in skilled workers and technicians. For example, the number of engineering and technical staff in the equipment manufacturing industry of Tiexi district decreased by 25.7% from 1990 to 2000, and staff turnover in 2000 was 1.3 times more than what it was in 1990. In addition, enterprises in Tiexi with a production value of over 100 million yuan lost 36 of their highest qualified professional staff. From 1990 to 2000, the equipment manufacturing enterprises reduced the number of frontline technical workers by 21.53% and workers with highly relevant qualifications by 16.9% (Wang, 2005).

Structural problems were also one of the important factors that led to the economic recession in the Tiexi district. Since the foundation of the PRC government, the Tiexi district focused on the development of heavy industry. The light industry developed rather slowly in comparison. In 1985, the light industry was only contributing 29% of the total industry value (Li, 1993). After the implementation of the economic reform and opening-up policies, the demand in the domestic market shifted to light industry goods and the central government started to support the development of light industry. At this stage, the Tiexi district was unable to produce new light industrial goods that satisfied the market demand. Therefore, the district's products were not competitive in the market. Further, equipment being used in the Tiexi district was outdated. Enterprises had previously been required to produce goods that met China's industrialization needs without much need for technological innovation. In Tiexi, for example, more than half of the equipment used in the mechanical and electrical, chemical engineering, and automobiles industries were made in the 1950s and 1960s, with 27% made in the 1970s and 21% in the 1980s (Li, 1993). A lack of technological innovation and upgrading of equipment was also reflected in the top 500 industrial awards received by the enterprises in Tiexi: 55% were achieved in the 1950s and the 1960s, 40% were achieved in 1970s and 1980s and less than 5% were achieved toward the end of the 20th century (Su, 2004). This suggests that the technical knowledge of Tiexi district was seriously outdated by the end of the century and subsequently it had lost a lot of its market competitiveness. The new industries were developing slowly, by the 1980s the GDP of new industries was only around 1% of total industries' GDP (Li, 1993).

The change in both the international and domestic economic environments was another important factor in the deterioration of Tiexi district. After the economic reform and opening up began, the Chinese government gradually shifted its industrialization strategy from according top priority to heavy industry to focusing on consumer goods (Han, 2004). It also searched for and developed new institutions and mechanisms for enterprises, in order to shift toward a market economy. Concurrently, capital, technology, human resources, innovation, and information became key factors in motivating the global economic development. Foreign capital investment was attracted by the favorable policies offered by China's costal region, which has emerged as a global manufacturing center. On the contrary, the Tiexi district in Shenyang city missed the opportunity to attract international industrial transfer due to its deteriorating resource advantage and isolated development environment. To compound the districts difficulties, under the dual-track price system, the district was forced to sell raw materials and primary industry goods at heavily reduced price or for no profit at all. This meant that the old industrial zone has played only a minor role in supporting the newly developed economic regions. In addition to the dramatic drop in demand for manufacturing equipment from the surrounding resource based cities, including Anshan, Benxi, Fushun, and Fuxin, the Tiexi district has also lost the income from its traditional domestic market.

3. The Formation of the Tiexi Model

The spatial structures of most Chinese cities normally consist of variously sized old industrial zones or districts. Two critical issues for restructuring old industrial districts that are commonly discussed by Chinese urban municipal government officials and academics are: "where does the money come from? and where do the people go?" Essentially, they are questioning, where is the capital going to come from to support the old industrial districts' restructuring? And where is the unemployed going to find a job? The first question addresses the financial viability of the district and the second question is about the social cost of change in the economic situation. So far, several important stages of restructuring can be identified: in 1986, the central government listed Tiexi district as the first urban district to restructure its old industrial base in China. Even after 10 years of effort (1986–1996), the restructuring attempts largely failed, as will be demonstrated below. The "Tiexi Syndrome", as described above, became more obvious in the late 1990s. From 2002, the Shenyang Municipal government decided to introduce a new way of restructuring the old industrial district, the approach taken to "reform enterprises by reforming industrial zones by reforming enterprises" reflected the new thinking. The next section first explains why the first ten years (1986–1996) of restructuring failed and then explains how the municipal government has adopted various measures in their attempts to save Tiexi (Zhang, 2006).

3.1. Technology upgrade program, 1986–1998

In February 1986, the State Council of China passed the "plan for total reform of Tiexi Industrial zone", which listed Tiexi's restructuring as the only pilot project in the national "seventh five-year plan". The plan for Tiexi was also present in the eighth and ninth five-year plans. The main aim was to upgrade the level of technology of enterprises. In 1988, the Liaoning provincial government listed Tiexi district as one of the three pilot zones that formed the opening of Liaodong Peninsula. Since announcing the pilot zones, Tiexi district not only had financial support from the central government but also received foreign investment. For example, by the end of 1999, Tiexi had been allocated 2,300 fixed asset investment projects with a total funding of 18.2 billion yuan (1,712 projects were for technology upgrades with associated costs of 13 billion yuan) (Northeast Revitalisation Committee, 2006). After a decade, the Tiexi district had two key achievements: a number of enterprises had managed to improve their technology levels and there had been improvement in the urban infrastructure, mainly in the shanty town areas. Through the upgrading of enterprise technology, the scale of production and the technical abilities of the key enterprises were improved, including machine tool manufacturing and electricity transformation and transmission. Through upgrading technology, some enterprises were reclassified as national manufacturing bases for important technical equipment (making China less dependent on foreign imports). These enterprises include the Electrical Transformer Factory, High Voltage Switch Gear, Water Pump Factory and the Air-blower Plant. Also, some new large corporations were formed like the Northeast Electricity Transmission and Transformation Corporation, Northeast Pharmaceutical Company, and Shenyang Hongmei Company. In addition, 20 key enterprises took advantage of China's *special loan for technology reform* to expand their operations in the Shenyang Economic Development Zone and the Yuhong Industrial zone. These upgrades to the urban infrastructure included improvements in the living environment. First, Tiexi district used the special loan to relocate and separate 60 high polluting enterprises from 2,000 residential houses. Second, the district cleaned up the Weigong Open Trench and improved the urban landscape alongside Jianshe Road. Third, the basic urban services for residents were upgraded so that two-thirds of the district's residents had improved access to services. Meanwhile, two new furniture markets were developed: China Furniture city and Xiang River Furniture Market. These two markets contributed to the development of the tertiary sector in Tiexi. Finally, the shanty town projects in the Huaxiang residential area included the construction of Huaxiang Park and Huanxiang Square both of which improved the environment of local residents as well as promoting the development of entertainment, trading, and service industries (Shenyang City Plan Committee, 2001). The central government's investment in the upgrade of Tiexi's technology level was successful to some extent; however, the SOEs' management problems and institutional barriers remained unsolved.

3.2. Systematic reform of state-owned enterprises from 1998 to 2001

Starting from 1998, all SOEs in the Tiexi district were required to participate in China's SOE reform program. The central government estimated that by introducing new institutional changes, the losses would cease within three years. To reach these targets, the central government allowed SOEs to merge; debt could be converted to shares and interest could be discounted for technical renovation. Medium to large enterprises in the Tiexi district benefited from this policy. Through the debt to share conversion, the leverage ratio was reduced so that the interest cost and credit risk were reduced (Northeast Revitalisation Committee, 2006). In 2000, the Shenyang Machine Tool Limited Company signed an agreement with its creditors: the asset management companies Huarong, Dongfang, Xinda, and Changcheng. This agreement reduced the company's debt by 449.45 million yuan, which brought the leverage ratio down to 55% from 65%. The involvement of asset management companies not only promoted transition, but also made the management of enterprises more diverse and efficient, which was seen preferable for floating production and management (Wang and Tan, 2000). For some SOEs with a long history of negative profit, the national policy was to file for bankruptcy and to encourage acquisition, in order to free unused assets and to compensate employees. These measurements helped to solve some of the issues associated with workers who had been laid-off, by cutting employer numbers to improve efficiency and reforming the social security system. With the policy and monetary support from the government, the Shenyang Smelter, as a major pollution source, declared itself bankrupt and repositioned laid-off workers. This action eliminated one of the biggest environmental pollution sources, and removed the strategic environment barrier for the implementation of "the reduction of secondary sector and increasing share of tertiary sector" policy.

The above two phases of reform were motivated by both the central government and the Liaoning Provincial government, both of which provided macro policies and financial support to the Tiexi district. The Shenyang Municipal government was the major player and the Tiexi district government provided a supportive role. This is very different from the restructuring experience of old industrial zones in western countries. The Tiexi experience did not see much involvement from enterprises, social groups, and individuals before 2001. Through these two stages of restructuring, the most important achievement was the institutional changes. The SOEs and other enterprises in Tiexi were able to make decisions according to market needs and not just having to follow the state authority's instructions. However, Tiexi district still did not take off. Looking back at the reform practices, two lessons can be drawn: first, the plans need to realize that revitalization of Tiexi as a whole is a comprehensive, complex and long-term task; second, the measurements taken were mainly focused upon technical reform, therefore, failing to account for the integrated reform (Jin *et al.*, 2006).

3.3. *The Tiexi Model: the path to revitalization of the old industrial zone*

The previous reform policies obtained limited achievements, therefore the Shenyang municipal government decided to change its approach from the old practice of reforming the enterprise to reforming the whole industrial zone.

To do this, two major actions were taken: it first expanded the Tiexi district's jurisdictional area through merging the Tiexi district and the recently established Shenyang Economic Development Zone; and it then relocated enterprises in the east (near the CBD) to the west near the Shenyang Economic Development Zone.

On 18 June 2002, the Shenyang Municipal government combined the two districts. The two administrative authorities, Tiexi district and Shenyang Economic and Technological Development Area (SEDA), became the New Tiexi district (Fig. 4.3). The new district was delegated to city-level authority for the approval of land use planning, land sales, and the collection of various land-use fees (Dong, 2007b). This merger expanded the Tiexi jurisdictional area from 40 km² to 128 km². Not only did Tiexi expand physically, the new Tiexi district was able to benefit from the central government's policies, same as the coastal cities. This was because SEDA was listed as one of the national economic and technology development zones in 1993 by the State Council. This recognition gave the zone the same policy advantage as 14 coastal cities (Dong, 2007a). These changes made it possible for Tiexi to undertake industrial restructuring: including the intra-district enterprise relocation from the east to the west area and the conversion of the former industrial land functions into commercial housing and office buildings. This meant that the profit from these conversions could be used to support the upgradation of the technology of relocated enterprises.

The relocation of enterprises was not simply a physical movement. The municipal government classified its enterprises into potentially

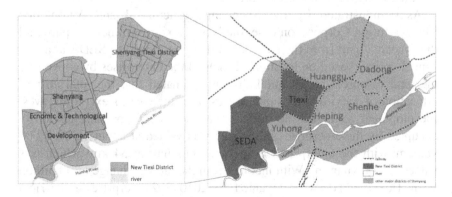

Figure 4.3. New Tiexi District Function Zones in 2004, Heiping and Shenhe are the Two Major Commercial Centers or CBD.

profitable and those with no future which were either closed down or merged. The potentially profitable enterprises were provided funding from the land conversion which covered unpaid financial bills, including salaries and bank interests. This meant that enterprises could start to compete with others in the new district without excessive financial burden. For example, the Shenyang Agricultural Machinery and Automobile Corporation was the first to move into SEDA through the relocation program. The corporation was previously an SOE named Shenyang Tractor Manufacturing Factory, which was the birthplace of tractor manufacturing in China and had produced volumes of agricultural machinery. After the 1990s, the enterprise was trapped because of its inability to adapt to the market competition. The organization had to file for bankruptcy and with the assets recomposed to form the Shenyang Agricultural Machinery and Automobile Corporation. However, the fact that its products had no market, resulted in the company getting into difficulty again. In 2002, the company started to move from the east to the west according to the government's strategy. During the moving process, the enterprise sold its 240,000 m^2 land to the New Tiexi district government at 1,000 yuan/m^2, it then used the 240 million yuan to pay the wages, medical and heating costs that it owed. At the same time, it started to provide 3,000 employees with standard pay packages. The company then used the remaining funds to build a 45,000 m^2 new factory and update equipment. After resettlement, these enterprises increased their industrial output value from 400 million yuan in 2001 (before resettlement) to 1.6 billion yuan in 2005 (after resettlement) (Revitalising Northeast Region Committee, 2006).

As demonstrated by the Shenyang Agricultural and Automobile Manufacturing Corporation case, the New Tiexi government acquired all the "vacant" land from the enterprises that had moved to SEDA at a reasonable price (based on location). It helped the enterprises by converting the land resources into capital. It was estimated that the total cost of relocation of Tiexi district's enterprises from the east (Tiexi) to the west (development zone) was 30 billion yuan. About 20 km^2 land previously occupied by the enterprises in the east was valued at about 1,500–2,000 yuan/m^2 with the enterprises in the west purchasing 34 km^2 which was valued at 200 yuan/m^2. With income from the land exchange of 30 billion yuan, Tiexi could do what it wanted. By 2010, 302 enterprises in the Tiexi district had relocated to the development area and they had released 9 km^2 area of land and gained 14.2 billion yuan from the land price difference (Tiexi District Government, 2010). Of the 14.2 billion yuan income, 5 billion yuan was retained for enterprise's development, 3.5 billion was used for building infrastructure, and 5.5 billion was used to repay debts (Qin, 2010). The income from the land exchange not only enabled the enterprises to pay off their debts, build factories in the new zone and upgrade technology, but it also helped solve social problems, including reducing staff and supporting laid off workers. The New Tiexi district government used the funds from the land exchange to ensure 100% support for all workers in all state-owned and collectively owned enterprises, such as pensions, unemployment insurance, and medical insurance. To solve the high unemployment rate, the Tiexi district invested heavily in the labor intensive sectors in order to provide jobs for the 130,000 laid-off workers. At the same time, the district government managed to gradually introduce a pension system in rural areas: the government, individuals, and the public, respectively pay the premium at $4:5:9$ proportionally and individuals have access to monthly repayments of over 3,000 yuan (Wang, 2005).

The relocation of enterprises in Tiexi did not face the *not in my backyard* (NIMBY) problem. Tiexi urban planners say that NIMBY is a western problem, and that as China is a strong state and also more importantly, all urban land belongs to the government, the government can solve the acquisition of land without any barriers.

Another important move was the restructuring of Tiexi's economic structure. The government's idea was to "strengthen the secondary industry and activate the tertiary industry". Strengthening the secondary industry meant extending the advantage of the secondary industry by building on the existing industry's foundation and by promoting the development of secondary industry group in SEDA. Activating the tertiary industry meant that when the manufacturing enterprises moved out of the Tiexi district, the land they previously occupied was used for developing modern service industries such as logistics, finance, and IT. In the Tiexi district, the district government redeveloped the newly vacant land on the north side of the Jianshe Road for modern service industries and residential housing.

In SEDA, enterprises were sectioned into different sub-zones, such as equipment manufacturing, automobile parts manufacturing, and electrical appliances. Some of the key equipment manufacturing enterprises were located in the southwest of the development area, including the Shenyang Machine Tool Company, Shenyang Blower Company, and the

Shenyang Mining Equipment Company. An industry cluster of equipment manufacturing companies was formed. In 2010, there were 428 equipment-manufacturing enterprises in the designated area of the New Tiexi district, which reached a size of 52 km² and added value to the Shenyang city (33.6%) and to Liaoning Province (12.7%) (Shenyang Tiexi District Plan Museum, 2011). Of the seven broad types of equipment manufacturing, the industries that the New Tiexi district had competitive advantage for, were general equipment manufacturing; professional equipment manufacturing; transport equipment manufacturing; and electrical, mechanical, and equipment manufacturing industries. Of these industries, six types of equipment manufacturing industries became the pillar industries of the New Tiexi district, including the numerical control machines; general petrochemical and energy equipment; electricity transformation and transmission equipment; construction machineries; heavy mining machinery; and automobile parts manufacturing industries.

4. Impact of the Tiexi Model

China's implementation of the revitalization strategy for the Northeast old industrial base has seen the Tiexi district gradually shift from a traditional old manufacturing zone to a modern service industry with a strong manufacturing industry zone (Fig. 4.4). The development of the New Tiexi district is seen as a great achievement and its development progress has been recognized through many international and national awards. The major awards include: "display zone for reforming the Tiexi old industrial base and developing equipment manufacturing industry", "the UN sustainability demonstration city", "Chinese new industrializing demonstration base" and one of the first "pioneer zone for comprehensive reform of service industry". The awards and titles were not only the recognition for the progress of the reform in the old district and development of the new district, but they also recognized the future regional positioning of the New Tiexi district.

4.1. *Urban economic structural change and changing land use*

Through continuous reform, both the industry structure and land use structure have changed dramatically. The old spatial layout — of residents in the south and factories in the north — has become history. The Tiexi district became the third biggest commercial service zone in Shenyang

Figure 4.4. Old Factory Zone Becomes Residential/Business Zone in Tiexi District (2007).
Source: Hudong Document of Tiexi District (2011).

and tried to differentiate its service types from the other two traditional commercial service zones (Shenhe district and Heping district). The economic structure of Tiexi has also changed. The secondary sector, mainly the equipment manufacturing industry has recovered quickly. The share of the secondary industries output value increased quickly, surpassing the tertiary industries share from 2004 to 2007. However, from 2008, along with the completion of the enterprise relocation strategy, the commercial service industry in Tiexi district grew at a high speed. By 2009, the weight of the secondary industry dropped to 25.83% and the tertiary industry became the dominant force driving the economic development of Tiexi district. By then, the GDP generated by the major manufacturing enterprises in the Tiexi district dropped from 13.66% in 2005 to 1.07% in 2009 (Fig. 4.5). This implies that the Tiexi district had put an end to its 100-year-long industry history and had successfully converted into a new district with a new major industry function of commercial services. The change of land use also reflected the ongoing trend in China. As shown in Table 4.2, in 1997, manufacturing land use accounted for nearly 55% of total land use in the Tiexi district but by 2008 this had dropped to

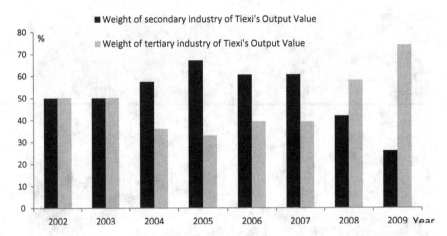

Figure 4.5. Share of Industrial Output Value by Secondary and Tertiary Industries in Tiexi (2002–2009).

Source of data: Shenyang Statistical Bureau (2002–2010).

Table 4.2. Land Use Structural Change of Shenyang Tiexi District.

	Percentage of land area (%)			
Land type	**1997**	**2002**	**2005**	**2008**
Residential	39.45	36.92	43.06	51.97
Industrial	54.7	55.19	46.64	33.3
Commercial	1.92	3.24	5.64	8.16
Education and medication	3.04	3.27	3.36	3.29
Other	0.88	1.37	1.3	3.28

Source: Zhang *et al.* (2011).

33.3%. The residential land use increased from 39% to 51% and commercial use and others increased from 5.8% in 1997 to 14.7% in 2008. By 2011, there were only three large industrial enterprises in the Tiexi district. They form the remaining legacy or the "live museums" of old Tiexi.

The new area now hosts several specialized industrial parks, such as the Modern Architecture Industrial Park, Casting and Forging Industrial Park, American Industrial Village, and Taiwan Industrial Park. Six of the enterprise groups produce an output value over 100 billion yuan/each. All resettled enterprises in the west (development zone) are now performing better. In 2010, the industry added value of enterprises reached 57.53 billion yuan, 18 times of that in 2002.

The recovery of the manufacturing industry and the rapid development of the tertiary industry have produced a large number of employment opportunities. From 2005 to 2009, the total population that had moved into the Shenyang Tiexi district was 47,131, on average about 10,000 persons per year. Tiexi district has become the number one choice for real estate investment and residential house investment in Shenyang.

5. Implications of the Tiexi Model

The formation, development, deterioration, and reform process of the Tiexi district is a representation of the Chinese way of reforming the old industrial zones. The district shares many features with other Chinese cities and industrial districts. The Tiexi Model is one of the few reform models for the development of Chinese old industrial zones, with unique Chinese features. Its theoretical implications and practical revelations still need further monitoring and evaluation.

One of the findings of the implementation of the reform is the importance of merging. The Shenyang Municipal government creatively merged the Tiexi district and the Shenyang Economic and Technology Development Area and integrated the administrative authority. The relocation of enterprises from the east to the west enabled Tiexi to promote development of the tertiary sector and regrouping and upgrading of relocated enterprises at the new manufacturing site. All of this was possible because of the differences in land value and rental value in the two districts. The district converted the land resource into a regional reforming fund to pay off the debt problems and for the reemployment of the unemployed workers and their social security. These measurements solved most of the problems of "where to get money from and what laid off workers do for employment". These two problems were not unique to the Tiexi district, they are also common issues for the restructuring of all Chinese cities. The Tiexi Model broke the old reform practice of focusing solely on enterprises. The new model is a profound, systematic, and open city transition strategy, since it encompasses the whole city through spatial reorganization and the merging of the old district with the development of a new district.

The Tiexi experience shares some common features with the reform of other old industrial zones in China, but it also has its own unique factors. First, in 2003, two key strategies were implemented: the strategy for revitalization of the Northeast region by the central government and the Shenyang strategy for merging the Tiexi district with the Economic and Technology Development Zone and the relocation of enterprises from the east to the west. These strategies provided an historical opportunity for the promotion of reform in the Tiexi district. Second, the Tiexi district is next to the CBD area of Shenyang city, which represented a significant location advantage. The area had a high land value for commercial development and real estate while the enterprises who decided to relocate to the west created an additional financial resource through the difference in land value. Third, the merging of the Tiexi district and the Shenyang Development Area enabled the development of the New Tiexi district. It was possible because the enterprises were a party to the national government's favorable policy; they also had a solid industrial foundation and location advantage, which secured the smooth implementation of the reform process.

The history and factors of decline in the Tiexi district are different from those seen in the western world. Many of the approaches and practices would not be appropriate outside of China. The ability to change the administrative border is a practice that is commonly done in China but this is not the case in other western countries. The Tiexi deterioration syndrome is not uncommon in China but the Tiexi Model cannot be copied directly for other Chinese cities. This timing is crucial as well as the cities' industrial districts being part of the central government's strategy. In addition, it is important that the reform of an old industrial zone has a solid strategy to follow that has built on the governments planning. Reforming an old industrial zone is a more complicated task than the development of a new district, since it not only involves resolving any historical problems, but also includes rebuilding a new spatial order, which is essentially a profound adjustment of interest groups and stakeholders relationship. If not done properly, it can easily lead to conflicts and tension.

Restructuring old industrial districts and the modernization of the traditional manufacturing sectors does not need to lead to the destruction of everything. The government needs to realize the importance of protecting the culture and heritage of an old industrial zone. The Tiexi district was called "the Eastern Ruhr" in China as it held a rich industrial heritage and culture. However, during the recent relocation, the old factory buildings and employee residences were almost entirely removed. These buildings held a lot of the culture and memory of the Tiexi district, when this urban context was destroyed, the community culture disappeared and the industry specialty of the Tiexi district was lost and can no longer be passed on from generation to generation. For example, the Shenyang Smelting Factory, built in 1936 had access to a complete set of smelting industry processes and equipment. When it was demolished, all that was left to be reminded of the industry were historical documents which can be read to experience the charm of an old state-owned industrial giant (Chinese Communist Party Shenyang City Tiexi District Party School, 2008). It was lucky that Tiexi's land exchange experience did not lead to much social conflict unlike the present times where the NIMBY movement is prevalent in China. People and enterprises are no longer just doing as they are told. They request proper compensation before they agree to relocate, any relocation projects, like in the Tiexi case, could now trigger social conflicts. This is because the incomplete market and the management systems often result in the forced demolishment of homes and poor arrangements to families being relocated (Zhang, 2006).

5

Dalian Coastal New Industrial Base Development Model

1. Introduction

Dalian is located at the south end of the Liaodong Peninsula in China's Northeast region. It is an important industrial city and the most important transportation hub in Northeast China. It has always been defined as the water gateway to the outside world for the three provinces in Northeast China and the eastern part of Inner Mongolia. Historically, Dalian's development was influenced by both Russia and Japan. But the most significant event was in 1981 when Dalian was listed as one of China's fourteen coastal cities (Wang, 1995). The GDP increased from 4.2 billion yuan in 1978 to 100 billion in 2000 and to 2,000 billion in 2005. Since then, Dalian has been listed within China's top six cities for comprehensive development (Liaoning province bureau of statistics, 2009). Dalian's urban economic transformation model differs from all other cities in Northeast China. The "Dalian Model" that will be presented in this chapter has two distinctive components: first, similar to China's coastal cities model, Dalian has set up various zones (industrial parks and high technology zones) as nests for development of designated industries; second, different to the coastal city development model, Dalian has successfully strengthened its heavy industry sector whilst still achieving fast growth in the service sector and other new economic areas. The Dalian Model contains many of the successful elements used by other coastal cities such as export-oriented industrialization, utilization of both FDI and industrial zones, rapid growth of the service sector and new economic sectors (such as the software industry) but different to other cities; it also includes an element of reindustrialization of its heavy industrial sectors.

This chapter first explains the inevitability of and the conditions for Dalian's industrial transformation. Then, it describes the formation process of the Dalian Model. This includes the rules of different practices carried out in different development stages and how each key sector has been upgraded or introduced. Finally, this chapter highlights the potential challenges Dalian faces and recommends the countermeasures.

2. Development Conditions for the Dalian Model

In the early stage of the People's Republic of China (PRC), Dalian's heavy industry was rapidly expanded as a result of the large-scale investment by the central government. The development strategy of Dalian was solely focused on heavy industries, and although this strategy led to a rapid growth in the GDP, the light industrial sectors and agriculture sectors suffered. In 1978, the ratio of output value by primary, secondary, and tertiary sectors was 16:66:18 and the ratio between light and heavy industry was 31.5:68.5. As is the nature with heavy industry, there was a high demand and consumption of energy, pollution was high and there was a low value addition in the industry's performance.

Since the open door policy was introduced in 1978, the industrial structure has been characterized by two trends: First, up to 1992, the tertiary sector registered a steady increase while the secondary sector registered a steady decline. But from 1992 onwards, these two sectors have produced a similar output value (see Fig. 5.1). Second, the shares of the heavy industry sectors slightly dropped from 1978 to 1990 but increased after 1990. Figure 5.2 shows the structural change that indicates that the reindustrialization process in Dalian has been dominated by heavy industry.

From 1978 to 1990, the major problems for sustainable industrial development in Dalian were institutional barriers and low productivity, which was similar to the problems faced in the other cities of Northeast China. In Dalian, over 65% of the industries were state owned enterprises (SOEs) therefore, Dalian suffered similar problems in the Northeast Phenomenon, as was discussed in Chap. 3. However, the SOEs' reform in Dalian which was implemented in the late 1990s was viewed as the most successful reform case. Dalian successfully transformed the ownership of SOEs with little social cost due to the fact that redundant workers were

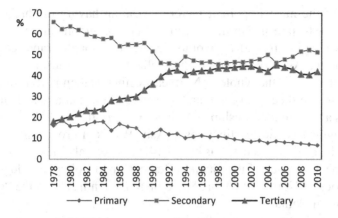

Figure 5.1.   Changes of Industry Structure in Dalian from 1978–2010.

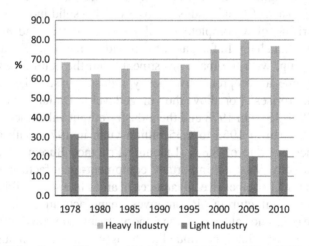

Figure 5.2.   Share of Heavy and Light Industrial Output Value (1978–2010).

promised new jobs that were being created through the development of the new sectors (Zhang and Lin, 2006). In Northeast China, only Dalian had strong competitive advantages in the service sector which was due to its tourist resources and open coastal city status. The municipal government was able to develop its tourist sector to provide jobs for the workers who were made redundant so that the unemployment rate in Dalian remained the lowest in Northeast China (Shan and Zhao, 2011).

Two of the most important factors in Dalian having the highest economic growth rate in Northeast China were geographical and political.
Dalian's location provided favorable conditions for the rapid economic
development. As a coastal city with excellent port facilities, Dalian served
as the gateway for the whole of Northeast China. Dalian port handles over
70% of the Northeast sea cargo and over 90% of the containers. Dalian not
only has a trading relationship with major ports of the world but it also has
direct flights to major destinations of Asia, Pacific, Europe, and America.
Politically, Dalian was listed as one of 14 open coastal cities by the central
government in 1984. Such status offered Dalian policy privileges over
other cities of Northeast China. Since then, Dalian has been the "get rich
first" city in China.

Heavy industry has been the key economic sector in Dalian, unlike
other coastal cities where economic growth has been predominantly
driven by the light industry, processing for foreign products or service
sectors. It is one of China's industrial bases with a solid industrial foundation comprising of a complete set of industry sectors and a relatively
strong industrial chain. In fact, after the foundation of the PRC and before
the opening-up, with the mass investment from the central government,
Dalian became a comprehensive heavy industry base. The number of
industry enterprises at or above the village level in Dalian increased from
183 in 1949 to 1390 in 1978 and the industry output value increased from
1.16 billion yuan in 1953 to 6.35 billion yuan in 1978, with an annual
average increase rate of 8.8% (Liaoning Province Bureau of Statistics,
1999). The city was an important equipment-manufacturing base in
China, and it had competitive advantages in areas like ship building, heavy
machinery manufacturing, locomotives manufacturing, machine tool
manufacturing, and electrical machinery manufacturing. What made
Dalian special was that it continued to strengthen its heavy industrial sector, unlike most other cities in the region. In 2003, the industry output
value of enterprises above the designated scale reached 154.24 billion
yuan, which put Dalian first among 14 cities of Liaoning Province.
Shipbuilding enterprises, like the Dalian Shipbuilding Heavy Industry Co.,
had a high level of competitiveness. Other enterprises had a competitive
advantage at the national level, including the Dalian Heavy Industry Co.
and the Dalian Bingshan Co., the machine tool manufacturing firm —
Dalian Machine Tool Co. and the precision bearing producer such as
Dalian Tile and Bearing Co. The information technology (IT) industry in

Dalian also maintained a good momentum. In 2010, Dalian produced 22.5% of Liaoning's total industrial value.

After 1978, along with the gradual opening-up, Dalian's advantages in developing an export-oriented economy become obvious. As one of the open coastal cities, Dalian set up its Economic and Technology Development Zone, Tourism and Resort Zone, Free Trade Zone, Export Processing Zone, New and High-technology Industry Park, and National Software Industry Base. These parks and zones attracted large amounts of foreign investment. By 2003, Dalian accounted for over 40% of utilized FDI in Northeast China. The establishment of these areas enabled the city to make use of foreign investment, import technology, develop the economy, promote reform of the economic system, and upgrade industrial structure. At the same time, the opening-up measurements created opportunities for Dalian city to compete in the global market.

Dalian had the advantage of being able to access high level human resource capacity, including scientists and technicians who then secured the development of new economic sectors in Dalian. There are a large number of universities and research institutions located in Dalian, such as Dalian Science and Engineering University, Dalian Maritime University, Dalian Jiaotong University, Dalian Industry University, Northeastern University of Finance and Economics, University of Dalian, and Dalian Institution of Chemistry and Physics of Chinese Academy of Science. In 2010, there were 419.07 university students per 10,000 people in Dalian, higher than that of national average 187.53. Dalian city had access to highly skilled and educated workers who could provide support for the reform and upgrading of industries and to the development of a new industrial base.

Dalian is one of the most livable cities of China, though its economy is dominated by the heavy industries. Located between the mountains and the sea, Dalian has a pleasant climate and environment. It has long been one of the China's famous tourism spots. Dalian city was granted the "most suitable for human living city award" and was acknowledged as one of the "top 500 cities of the world" by the United Nations (UN). It has also been awarded for a number of other positions; National green city, National top ten cities for Comprehensive Environmental Restoration, National Clean city, Nationally Designated Garden city, National Model city for Environmental Protection, China, suitable-for-living city award from the Chinese Ministry of Construction and was selected as a Pilot city for Environmental Restoration in the Asia Pacific region by the UN.

3. Formation of the Dalian Model

3.1. *Industrialization during Mao*

During the period of the first five-year plan (1953–1957), the central government identified 156 projects to be implemented around China, two of these were industrial projects in Dalian: the Dalian Second Power Plant and expansion of the Dalian Shipbuilding Factory. During the first five-year period, Dalian received an annual investment of 86.3 million yuan for its heavy industry sector which supported the restoration of petroleum and gas factory and the Jinzhou Heavy Machinery Factory, it also supported the expansion of 745 enterprises and building new factories like the potassium chlorate producing factory and the plastic factory (Wang, 1995). The heavy industry-oriented investment during this period helped develop a solid foundation for Dalian's economic development. The national competitive advantages of the heavy industry sector meant that all post-Mao industrial restructuring had to find a way to support the revitalization of the sector. The light industry and service sectors which had been ignored during the Mao era grew rapidly in the post-Mao period.

3.2. *Opening-up stage*

As mentioned above, in 1984, Dalian was listed as one of the 14 open coastal cities by the central government. Associated with this was the upgrading of Dalian's political power. Dalian is one of the few cities of China whose urban and economic plans are directly administered by the central government. This system is called the *jihua danlie shi*, (individually planned city) which means that the city's overall development is aligned to achieve the central government's plan. Meaning Dalian became one of the central government's "pet city".

All these special statuses made Dalian an attractive place for foreign investment. For example, the gradual opening up of Dalian, including the establishment of the Dalian Economic and Technology Development Zone, attracted foreign investment and developed foreign trade and cooperation. Also starting from 1985, Dalian was allowed to directly conduct international trade. During this stage, industry growth increased with annual growth rates of industry output value from village level and above increasing by 24%.

Dalian's industrial structure was also altered over this period. It accelerated the development of the food and textile industry and also supported the development of the electrical industry, producing mainly color televisions, video players, recorders, and radios. During the period of 1984–1991, light industry in Dalian grew at an annual rate of 19.8%. Meanwhile, the private and foreign-owned economy also grew rapidly. However, during this period, SOEs in Dalian suffered similar problems to those affected by the Northeast Phenomenon.

3.3. *1992–2003*

The year 1992 was an important turning point with Deng's "private visit" to southern China pushing the top Chinese leaders to focus even more on the opening up. Following this, Dalian introduced the "managing Dalian" idea, which resulted in an increase in "management" strategies being used to upgrade the tertiary sector and producer services. The strategy was to push for rapid development of the tertiary industry. In 1993, Dalian clearly stated that it wanted "not to be the biggest, but the best city". The desire differed from all other Chinese cities, many of who aimed at becoming a world city or global city based on the expansion of their population (Wang and Li, 2002). The first step was to create a business friendly environment and a green or garden city. From 1993 to 2000, Dalian built a number of parks and forests, which included over 230 gardens and 20 km^2 lawns and public open spaces. These "greening" programs have made Dalian famous throughout China (Yang and Rong, 2001). At the same time, almost all of the high-energy consuming and high polluting factories were relocated from the city center into the designated industrial park or zone. When they were relocated to these newly established zones, these factories had to meet minimum environmental standards, which included emission standards. Similar to Tiexi's approach, the Dalian government also converted the vacant land previously occupied by the factories in the city center into properties to be used for commerce and residential purposes (Li, 2001). The profit from the land conversion was used partially to support job creation programs and other social welfare programs to support those who had been made redundant and also for low-income families. It was reported that Dalian was the only municipal government in China that promised every redundant worker from the SOEs would be offered a new job. This was possible partially as a result of the success of the land conversion.

Along with the improvements made to the urban environment and the establishment of various types of industrial parks and zones, foreign investment poured into Dalian. The Dalian Tax Protected Zone and the

Jinshitan Nationbal Holiday Resort were established in 1992 and the Dalian Software Park was established in 1998. In 2000, Dalian's New and High Tech Park was listed as one of the China's Industrial Export Bases and the Dalian Export Processing Zone was also established. By 2003, there were 9,112 enterprises that had received foreign investments with a total of US$2.11 billion; this was an increase of 4.7 and 3.1 times from 1992, respectively. In 2003, enterprises with foreign investment achieved a production value of 79.06 billion yuan and a gross profit of 3.8 billion yuan, this was an increase of 11.9 and 15.5 times from 1992, respectively (Dalian City Bureau of Statistics and National Bureau of Statistics Dalian Investigation Team, 2005). At this stage, the industrial structure had changed slightly and there was a small increase in the tertiary sector development. The ratio of primary, secondary, and tertiary industries changed from 13.1:50.8:36.1 in 1992 to 8.9:47.9:43.2 in 2003. During this stage, the new and high tech industry developed rapidly and became a new economic development sector for Dalian.

Over this period, the Dalian municipal government adopted the "urban management" concept and managed its urban development along the line of "improving the urban environment and function and changing the priority order for the three sectors with tertiary first, secondary second and primary last" (Luo, 2004; Huang, 2002). Dalian's urban development slogan was famous throughout China, "strive not to be the largest, but to be the best". Associated with this urban development slogan was the policy that all residential areas included over 25% of green space. Together with the establishment of many new public spaces and green areas in urban Dalian, per capita green space in Dalian reached 8.5 m² and urban green coverage reached 40.5% in 2001. Dalian worked towards being a neat and clean city by demolishing several thousands of illegal buildings and improving urban waste water treatment facilities.

Meanwhile, many manufacturing factories in the inner city were relocated to the newly established industrial parks, leaving 3 million m² of inner city land available for commercial use. The resettlement of these factories generated 3.1 billion yuan for the factories and 1.7 billion profit for the municipal government (Diao, 2001).

Many of these newly established industrial parks registered rapid growth. For example, in 2003, the Dalian Software Park generated 2.4 billion yuan income with a total of US$85 million coming from overseas markets as this was the highest income for an industrial park in China (Peng and Yang, 2004).

3.4. *Revitalization stage: post-2003*

The pre-2003 economic development in Dalian was still path-dependent: industrial growth was largely based on the expansion of the scale of production and was less dependent on innovation and research and development (R&D). In 2003, when the central government shifted its development focus to the Northeast China, Dalian proposed the "one center, four bases" strategy. One center refers to Dalian becoming the international transport hub for the entire Northeast China and the four bases refer to 1) petrochemical 2) shipbuilding; 3) modern equipment manufacturing; and 4) electrical and software industry. The first three are the existing sectors in which Dalian has a competitive advantage. However, they were upgraded to reduce energy and material consumption; and to cut down pollution and increase technology level.

Dalian spent 64 billion yuan from 2004 to 2010 to upgrade its port facilities and shipment capacity to become the center of international shipping in Northeast China. This investment was 12 times more than the total investment of this port for the period of 1949 to 2003 (Dong, 2012). Since the starting of the revitalization of Northeast China program in 2003, Dalian has handled over 1.9 billion tons of cargo and 32 million containers, with an annual average growth rate of 13.18% and 18.7%, respectively. In 2012, the Dalian Port was ranked as the 19th largest container port in the World.

The four base industries that Dalian targeted registered rapid growth (see Fig. 5.3). They contributed to over 58% of Dalian's total value added industrial output in 2011. Dalian's new economy, software and information service was targeted as one of the city's key growth engines. Dalian has established the largest software industrial zone in China which has attracted some of the world's software giants to set up operations in Dalian (Chen, 2011). Since 2004, Dalian's new and high tech industry has grown at an annual rate of over 30%.

The other three base industries are traditional sectors. Their rapid growth was driven by two approaches: On the one hand, companies in three different sectors were merged and industrial clusters were formed. For example, in 2004 the Northeast Special Steel Group was formed after Dalian Steel took over Fushun Special Steel and Beiman Special Steel. Then in 2005, the Dalian Shipbuilding Industry Corporation was established after the Dalian Shipyard merged with the Dalian New Shipbuilding Heavy Industry Co. Ltd. (Li and Wang, 2011). On the other hand, Dalian

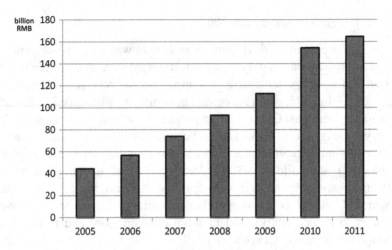

Figure 5.3. The Value-added Industrial Output of the Four Base Industries in Dalian (2005 to 2011).

set up large industrial parks. For example, 11 new industrial parks occupying over 400 km² were set up to accommodate Dalian's industries (Xu *et al.*, 2011). These parks offer the best facilities for industry production in Dalian, but for a firm to be allowed to set up in an industrial park, it is required to reach the minimum environmental standards.

Dalian's story highlights the importance of the special policies granted by the central government which affected the transformation of its economy. When compared to the other cities of Northeast China, Dalian was the only city that received two different sets of central government special policies: the first set was in 1984 which were all related to Dalian's open coast city status and the second set were the special policies on the revitalization of the Northeast China that was introduced in the year 2003. Along with the open coast city status, Dalian became the center of Liaoning's coastal economic zone which was a part of the central government's national development strategy. Dalian used all of the benefits of these policies to support the transfer of its traditional heavy industry sector into a high value add modern manufacturing center. After tens of years of development, in 2010 Dalian's GDP reached 500 billion yuan and per capita income reached US$11,000. Dalian is the hybrid city of Northeast China. By 2010, the industrial output value, added value, and profit had increased by 4.29, 4.81, and 4.60 times from 2003 levels, respectively. The four key industry sectors were consolidated and upgraded. Not only its traditional sectors — equipment manufacturing, shipbuilding, and petro-chemical have been upgraded but also IT industry — a new economy — has become one of the major industrial sectors. In 2010, these four sectors produced output value of over 154 billion yuan, representing 70% of Dalian's total. Meanwhile, other service industries such as logistics, commerce, and tourism also saw rapid development. Since the implementation of the revitalization strategy the tertiary industry grew at an annual rate of 13.7% and the tertiary industry added value in 2010 reached 216.75 billion yuan, which was 3.1 times of that in 2003.

Foreign investment in Dalian reached its highest point yet. From 2003 to 2010, foreign companies invested US$ 29.7 billion in 5,006 enterprises in Dalian; it was increasing annually by 80.14%. In 2010 alone, FDI amounted to over US$ 10 billion, 4.5 times of that in 2003. In addition, international trading increased, since the implementation of revitalization strategy, the accumulated self-managed exportation and importation amount was US$233.028 billion (Dalian City Bureau of Statistics and National Bureau of Statistics Dalian Investigation Team, 2011). This represented a total increase of 18.9% per annum, of which the accumulated self-managed exportation amount was US$ 12.86 billion, representing an increase of 18.6% p.a. In 2010, the self-managed importation and exportation amount was US$ 26.046 billion, 3.1 times of that in 2003. During 2004–2010, the accumulated cargo handling amount was 1,536.9 billion tons, containers handled was 26.2862 million, representing an annual increase of 13.0% and 18.1%, respectively. During the seven years, the city completed a number of infrastructure projects including the second stage extension of Dalian Airport, the reconstruction of the old terminal and the extension of the apron. Over the seven years of revitalization the total number of customers was 52.108 million representing an annual increase of 17.9%. In 2010, the handling capacity of Dalian Port reached 250 million tons, and the handling capacity of containers reached 11 million standard containers. The development plan for the Dalian Northeast Asia Shipping Center started and is scheduled to be completed by 2020 and then Dalian's position in Northeast Asia shipment will be consolidated (Yun, 2007).

4. Discussion: Problems and Potentials

Dalian's urban economic transformation model contains legacies from both Mao and Deng. In Northeast China, Dalian was the city most privileged by Deng's open door policy. Dalian's various open zones and associated special policies supported the success of the development of a new economic sector and attracted a large amount of foreign investment. However, we can also see Mao's legacy in Dalian's transformation model. Dissimilar to most of China's other coastal cities, where the service industry and labor intensive sectors are the growth industries, Dalian has managed to boost its traditional sector which was developed under Mao.

The major problem of urban economic growth in Dalian is its high dependence on imported energy and other natural resources — per GDP consumption level of energy is still high. Heavy industry is Dalian's key economic sector, which means Dalian needs to enforce energy savings and emission reductions, eliminate outdated products to reduce energy consumption per production unit. Circuit economy projects have been promoted by the municipal government but more efforts need to be put in to the development of a green economy, renewable energy economy, and a low-carbon economy; and to the promotion of energy-saving technology and products.

A general problem in Dalian is that enterprises lack self-innovation capabilities and research and development input is still relatively low. Current industries in Dalian are mainly in the downstream sector, they are characterized by low technological input and there are limited products that have independent intellectual property rights. To improve this situation, Dalian needs to enhance its self innovation capabilities, upgrade its industries to be upstream of the global production chain, and increase the contribution of science and technology to the increasing economic growth.

In order to improve innovation and technology, spread the industries with national and global competitiveness, which will expand the industrial clusters/chains. This will also increase the competitive advantage of the regional industries and will be beneficial for increasing the usage efficiency of regional resources. Dalian's key traditional enterprises need to continue upgrading their technology. In addition to it, Dalian's dominant position in the equipment manufacturing industry and the shipbuilding industry in China should be further consolidated. This can be done, in part, by increasing the production capacity and expanding the product chain of the key equipment manufacturing enterprises. The Dalian Heavy Industry Weight Lifting Corporation and the Dalian Bingshan Corporation can be expanded further to form a heavy machinery manufacturing base. Further, the city would benefit from increasing the competitiveness of the machine tools produced by Dalian Machine Tool Corporation, locomotives produced by China Northern Automotive Corporation, precision bearings produced by Bearing Corporation. By increasing the core competitiveness of the equipment manufacturing industry, the city would be able to create giant enterprises that have absolute competitive advantages nationally and build up industry clusters (Peng, 2008). For example, by promoting task sharing and cooperation between the big enterprises like Wafangdian Bearing Corporation and all the related small to medium enterprises in Wafangdian city, a bearing industry cluster could be created. In the process of developing clusters, the city needs to make use of the market system, emphasize brand effects and encourage technical cooperation between enterprises, universities, and research institutions. In addition, the government can support the development of industry clusters by providing fine development conditions.

Dalian's petrochemical base hosts both of China's major oil processing companies: Petro-China Dalian Petrochemical Company and Western Pacific Petrochemical Corporation. The strong R&D resources in Dalian mean that there is a new opportunity for Dalian to become a leading city in the petrochemical industry. The Petro-China Dalian Company could be the home for another petrochemical industrial park for the processing of oil products and for Western Petrochemical to develop downstream industries of the petrochemical industry and deeply-processed petrochemical products. All of these factors together have the potential to make Dalian a world class petrochemical base.

The new sectors that Dalian has developed, including the modern service industry and the IT and software industry will remain important to the economy if Dalian consolidates them and continues promoting the development of the software, IT, biomedicine, modern manufacturing, animation, digital audiovisual, and car multimedia industries. This may assist in upgrading Dalian from being China's national software industry base to one of international significance.

If Dalian achieves all of these goals it will make it one of the most livable cities in China. The city also attracts tourists by hosting many international festivals such as the summer Davos Forum, International Fashion Festival, International Beer Festival, and software and IT service trade fair. The traditional industries (equipment manufacturing and petrochemical industries) and the software industry make Dalian a meeting place of the old and the new.

6

Daqing Model of Industrial Chain Extension

1. Introduction

The existing literature has identified four stages of resource-based city transition: beginning, growing, maturing, and declining or revitalizing (Bradbury and St.-Martin, 1983; Tapela, 2002; Fan *et al.*, 2005). The final stage is critical to achieve sustainable development because first, city may become a ghost town after the resources it is dependent on are depleted or are not demanded, second, revitalization requires more wisdom. How successful the transition is would depend on factors such as not only resource type, mining stage, and location, but also social and political as well as choice of urban industrial restructuring models. China has a failure case of an oil-based city transition. China's first oil-based city — Yumen city in Gansu Province has become a ghost town. The oil resource drained and substituted industries were not developed, the population was resettled entirely since 2003.

On the contrary, Daqing city has started to explore a new way to achieve industrial transition before its oil and gas drains, mainly through extended oil industrial chain by exploring, drilling to further processing, and petrochemical related sectors. It has proactively reduced its annual oil production to gain time for extending industrial chain. Meanwhile, it has also put more effort into exploring new oil fields and processing oil from Russia and Mongolia so that it has enough raw materials for its newly established petrochemical processing industry. In addition, Daqing has been further developing its petrochemical industry by upgrading its technology and reducing the production of refined oil without changing the processing amount of crude oil. Productivity of basic organic chemical materials and deep processed petrochemical products such as synthetic fiber, Polyolefin and synthetic rubber were increased. Daqing has also worked cooperatively with academic staff from the Chinese Academy of Sciences and other universities to develop its natural gas chemical industry. This extension of industrial chain has greatly increased the industrial added value and overall economic performance. It has also promoted the development of horizontally related industrial sectors, such as petroleum and petrochemical equipment manufacturing industry and petrochemical products logistic industry. These changes strengthen the competitiveness and sustainability of Daqing, without becoming another "ghost town".

The extension of industrial chain model adopted in Daqing is a commonly seen transition model in resource-based cities whose resource is not yet exhausted (Fig. 6.1). This transition model is implemented when the city still has rich oil resource supply but substituted industries are not fully developed. This model provides an example of industrial transition in other resource-based cities. It is an important part of urban transformation model in Northeast China. This chapter first introduces the background and pathway of the Daqing industrial extension model. Then it analyzes how the extension is possible and what are the outcomes. Finally, this chapter recommends suggestions to optimize this outcome and discusses how it can be useful for the economic transformation of other resource-based cities in China.

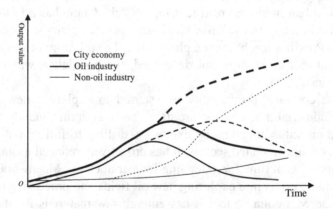

Figure 6.1. Two Possible Senarios for Daqing's Industrial Chain Extension.

Notes: The solid line is the boom-and-bust economic cycles of mining city, dotted lines represent alternative growth path of Daqing City.

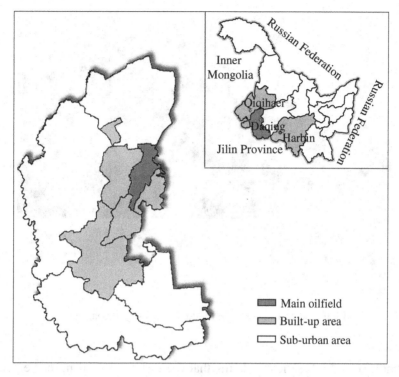

Figure 6.2. The Location of Daqing City.

2. Background

2.1. *Mao's pet city*

Located between the two large cities, Harbin and Qiqihar of Heilongjiang Province (Fig. 6.2), Daqing city was Mao's "pet" city. Daqing did not exist until an oilfield was set up and named Daqing (meaning in Chinese: Big Celebration — celebrating oil drilling. This is especially important during the cold war period when China's oil importation was restricted) in 1959. It became a big city almost overnight when thousands of petroleum drilling/ processing workers and technicians were moved there. In 1964, Mao issued the call — "In industry, learn from Daqing" — made Daqing national model for industrialization because Daqing was the first major oilfield opened up since the foundation of China (Fig. 6.3). To prove that China could do without the support of Soviet technicians and assistance, and to

Struggle to create some ten 'Daqing' oilfields, 1978

Figure 6.3.   Daqing is the Model for Industry' Propaganda.

counter (mostly American) claims that the country would never be self-sufficient in oil though major exploration activities were started in early 1960. To maximize working efficiency, the state-owned petroleum and petrochemical company directors had been appointed as local administration officials until the year 1984. The characteristics of planned economy still exist in Daqing after more than 30 years of abolishment since the economic reform in late 1970s. State-owned petroleum and petrochemical companies still play a dominant part in Daqing city's economy.

According to statistics, Daqing has provided China 2 billion tons of oil since its establishment and maintained an annual production level of 50 million tons over 27 years. On the one hand, this high level of production drives the city's economic growth substantially. On the other hand, this resource-based growth model creates lots of structural and institutional conflicts. Hence, the local government started to actively seek a pathway for industrial transition since 1990s. Significant achievements were seen in economic structural optimization and upgrading over the past 20 years. In 2005, it was selected as the pilot city by the State Counsel for transition of oil mining cities. The following statistics shows that Daqing remains as China's biggest oil production base and an important petrochemical industrial base: Its GDP reached 290 billion RMB in 2010, among which 52% was petro-related and 48% from non-petro sector. The urban economic ownership is dominated by the state sector and private sector accounted less than 20% of total GDP. Per capital GDP was over 100,000 yuan, the highest in the Northeast region and oil production of over 40 million tons per year, representing 1/5 of national oil production amount.

2.2. The reasons for transition

2.2.1. Depleted resource: proved oil reserve increase rate slows down, and drilling gets harder

From 1959 to 1976, the annual oil production of Daqing city increased from Nil to 50 million tons and this highest production maintained until year 2002 (Table 6.1). However, due to a long period of extensive exploiting, proven oil reserves increased rate began to slowdown and newly-found proven reserves remained far less than the oil production amount for most years since 1970s (Table 6.2). This induces high stress for maintaining high production. At the same time, after more than 30 years of drilling, the oil field enters high water cut (meaning water contained in the oil field) stage: water cut rate raised from 1.38% at the beginning of drilling to 78.12% in 1989. The reduction in the degree of oil abundance makes drilling more difficult. This has led to the change of production method and technology: 94.4% of oil wells adopted mechanical drilling, changed from previously flowing well by 1990 (Heilongjiang economic development, Editorial Board for 50 years, 1999). By statistics from 1978 to 1989 (Zhang, 1993), Daqing oil field's electricity consumption per ton

Table 6.1.   Annual Oil Production in Daqing (10^4 tons), Selected Years from 1960 to 2008.

Year	Production	Year	Production	Year	Production	Year	Production
1960	97.1	1982	5194.2	1992	5565.8	2002	5013.1
1962	355.5	1983	5235.5	1993	5590.2	2003	4840.0
1965	834.2	1984	5356.4	1994	5600.5	2004	4640.0
1970	2118.4	1985	5528.9	1995	5600.6	2005	4495.1
1975	4626.0	1986	5555.2	1996	5600.9	2006	4340.5
1976	5030.0	1987	5555.3	1997	5600.9	2007	4169.8
1978	5037.5	1988	5570.3	1998	5570.4	2008	4020.0

Table 6.2. Newly-found Proved Reserve Change in Daqing from 1960–1989.

Period	Yearly newly-found reserve (10^8 tons)	Per well proved reserve (10^4 tons)
1960–1970	2.44	945.6
1971–1980	0.4	158
1981–1985	0.33	36.86
1986–1989	0.67	26.65

Source: Summarized from Zhang (1993).

of oil increased by 1.6 times; the cost per ton of oil increased from 18.94 yuan to 108.5 yuan, representing 4.7 times and the profit per ton dropped from 79.03 yuan to 10.04 yuan. This increase in the cost of production is a driving force for Daqing city to start economic transition.

2.2.2. *High risk with a single-sector dominated industrial structure, low sustainability to develop*

To satisfy national demand for oil, Daqing's economy becomes over-dependent on oil resource. For example, the increase in oil-based profit counted as much as 64.7% of the total economic profit in 1990. Petro-industry plays the dominant role in the city's economy for a long time and the economic structure of Daqing has been dominated by single sector. Although the rich oil resource has substantially contributed to the quick rise of the city, the increasing cost of oil production in Daqing and fluctuated international oil price have slowed down Daqing's economic growth. Its GDP growth rate became lower than the average of the province (Fig. 6.4). Disadvantages of the oil-dependent industrial structure are fully exposed, such as low stability, high risk, and low sustainability. This is another driving force for the city to seek new economic growth point by diversifying its industrial structure, in order to achieve sustainable development.

2.2.3. *SOE related institutional barriers*

Daqing city was a product of Mao's typical planned economy and its oil fields and economy have been dominantly owned by the state. In the mid 1990s, 90% of Daqing's GDP was produced by the state sector. Such high degree of state ownership has led to three institutional problems after market economy was gradually introduced since 1980. First, in Daqing,

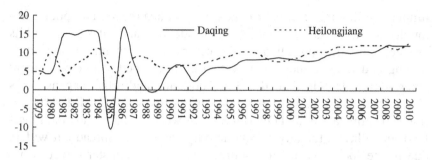

Figure 6.4. Annual GDP Growth Rate (%) of Daqing City and Heilongjiang Province.

Notes: Rate calculated as comparable rate. Data are from Daqing City Annual Statistics and Heilongjiang Province Annual Statistics.

two governing bodies use compartmentalized administrative management: state-owned resource-based enterprises (central government owned) and local government are administratively separated, each with its own public facilities, such as water and gas supply, school, and medical services. Such duplication has wasted lots of resources, which not only puts heavy burden on enterprises, but also makes local governments difficult to control economic performance. Second, two sets of economies (state-owned enterprises and local economy) are separated, without much integration. Hence, these central-government-owned enterprises care more about their own interests, hardly aiming to promote local economic development. In addition, local government almost lost control: without full cooperation from state-owned enterprises, any local government's plan to develop urban economy cannot be implemented. Third, these enterprises pass on most of the oil-mining profit to the central government, thus the local government was not benefiting. As a result, the local government has conflict interest with state-owned enterprises in oil resource, projects, human resource and funds, which is a huge draw-back for the city to grow as an integrated whole.

2.2.4. *Uncompleted urban function*

As it was built for the central-government-owned enterprises to explore oil resources, Daqing's urban development has always been stifled by its primary function — oil drilling and production. Until 1990s, the urban infrastructure and facilities were still incomplete: inferior infrastructure, limited public facilities, poor education and healthcare, and poor community services. As for economy, the production and sales of oil and its products are still controlled by the central government, so the city's trading and finance industry is yet to be developed. The environment deterioration, largely related to oil production and urban expansion, is also evident, such as over-extraction of groundwater; land desertification and salinization; and deterioration of wetland, farmland, and grassland. In addition, the city's main activity centers are spread out widely due to the locations of oil resources. Hence, the cluster effect is not present in the city. All of the above factors make the city an undesirable place for investors and unattractive to human resource. Therefore, Daqing has to promote industrial transition and change its positioning as a raw-material source, in order to enhance the comprehensive functionality of the city.

3. Conditions for Industrial Chain Extension in Daqing

Due to its important oil industry status and historically-celebrity-city reason, Daqing's industrial transition issue has attracted the central government's attention for a long time. This is one of the reasons why Daqing will not become a ghost town. The other favorable factors for Daqing to adopt oil-production chain are below:

i) The rich oil resource can provide long-time support for oil gas industrial chain extension

Daqing Oilfield is the China's biggest oil field on the continent. Its quality and quantity provides good material ground for Daqing industrial chain extension. Daqing oilfield has a known reserve of 6 billion tons, with nearly 4 billion tons remaining. At the same time, oil in this oilfield is light sweet crude, which is an ideal material for petrochemical industry. The oil field maintains an annual production of 40 million tons. In 2004, the enterprises' goal was to keep oil production and oil drilling sustainable for another century. Meanwhile, Daqing has rich natural gas resource: an estimated total of 1,170 billion cubic meters of gas, known reserve of 100 billion m^3. The natural gas production reached 3 billion m^3 in 2010 and natural gas can also provide resource for the development of petrochemical industry.

ii) Solid petrochemical background is an advantage for oil/gas industrial chain extension

The petrochemical industrial has been continuously growing since the 1960s. With several medium to large size petrochemical companies, Daqing's annual processing capacity reaches over 7.5 million tons of oil in 1990s, with the ability to refine oil, produce petrochemical products, fertilizer and chemical fiber. The professional storage and transferring facilities for petrochemical products, oil pipes, railway, and waste treatment facilities have been fully built up. These improvements together mean a solid foundation for oil gas industrial chain extension.

iii) Excellent technical support for industrial chain extension

Since Daqing has long been relied on oil resource, various high-skilled petrochemical experts and workers have been employed in oil exploration, production, and processing. During the central planning period under Mao, the state allocated large skilled workers and technicians to Daqing. In the post-Mao period, Daqing still is attractive to many petrochemical technicians even though it is an inland city. According to the statistics (Zhang, 1993), Daqing now has over 64,000 technicians, among which 2,472 people have senior qualifications (equivalent to associate professor and professor). Oil Exploration and Production Research Institute and Oil Field Designing Institute are the leading major research institutions in their fields in China. The exploitation technique of high water cut oil well reaches an advanced level in the world.

iv) The industrial extension attempts to attract high attention from central government and the head office of PetroChina

As China's largest oil production base and the most important profit source for PetroChina (the state-owned oil giant in China), the sustainability of Daqing's oil production could impact the energy security of the nation and the development of the enterprise as a whole. Therefore, it has attracted high attention from the central government and PetroChina. The city was appointed the pioneer city for petro-resource-based city transition project and the provincial government has also listed Harbin–Daqing–Qiqihaer as the urban and industrial corridors. The oil giant, PetroChina has also given full support to Daqing Oil Field in resource allocation so that it can extend its industrial chain. With the support from all the above bodies, Daqing city has gained primary advantage in its industrial chain extension.

v) Industrial chain extension is a common practice for an oil-based city Comparing with other types of mineral resources, crude oil has a long transportation radiation and high added value for its processed products. This indicates a high potential for oil-based cities to further develop the processed oil products. Therefore, it is possible to vertically extend its industrial chain, then horizontally expand its operations. For example, the famous oil-based city in the U. S., Houston, went through this process to achieve a diversified industry structure in a oil dominant economy. When Daqing started extension of its industrial chain in 1990s, the urban economy was highly dependent on oil resource, and substituted industries were still at the beginning stage. It is wise to continue with its oil resource as the backbone of urban economy to support growth of infant industries and the extended set of industrial chains. When these infant sectors are well established, the city can benefit from such value added sectors.

4. Pathway of Industrial Chain Extension

The transition attempts started relatively early in Daqing city, back dating to the 1990s when Daqing Oil Field had a stable annual production of 50 million tons. At that time, the transformation of resource-based cities in China was not yet widely noticed. Daqing started action after the former top leader Jiang Zemin addressed the importance of sustainable development of the cities', when he visited Daqing in 1990. Since then, Daqing industrial restructuring plans have been supported by both provincial government and the State Council after Jiang's speech. The most important support from the State Council has been its approval for Daqing to set up a national level high-tech industrial zone to motivate the technology innovation of petroleum and petrochemical enterprises in 1992. This is the marking stone of Daqing's economic transition and since then the city has emphasized on the following areas to promote industrial chain extension over the past 20 years:

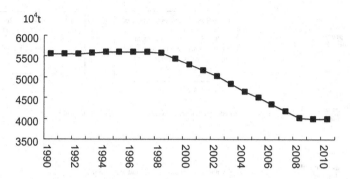

Figure 6.5.   Annual Oil Production in Daqing (1990–2010).
Notes: Data from Daqing City Annual Statistics.

i) Purposefully decrease oil production, making use of overseas oil
   resource
   Since 1976, Daqing oil field has been maintaining an annual production level of more than 50 million tons for 27 years, by improving its
   exploitation technology. In 1997, the annual production level reached
   a record of 56 million tons. After that, PetroChina decided to reduce
   its production level by 1.5–2 million per year and by 2008, its annual
   target dropped to 40 million tons (Fig. 6.5). The central government
   wants Daqing to keep a production level of 40 million to meet the
   increasing demand for oil in China. Such quota is based on the con-
   siderations of both, the demand for oil in China and sustainability of
   the Daqing oil field. Meanwhile Daqing is allowed to build up
   imported Russian oil storage and transporting base, and acquired
   three oil fields in Tamtsag Basin in Mongolia. By reducing production
   purposefully and importing oil from overseas, a longer servicing time
   of Daqing oil field can be achieved to ease the stress of domestic
   demand. It gains more time for fostering substituted industries and
   provides raw material supply source for petroleum industry chain
   extension.
ii) Extending oil/gas industrial chain
   Industrial chain extension can be in two forms: vertical extension and
   horizontal extension. The former means to add new production process through technical innovation to the existing industries. The latter

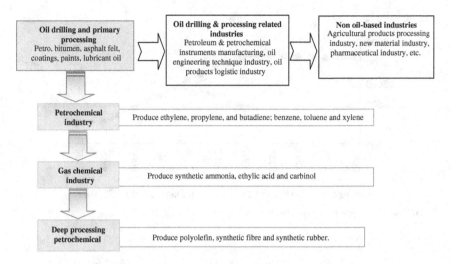

Figure 6.6.   The Industrial Restructuring of Daqing City.

means to import industries that are closely related to the existing
industries or whole new industries to achieve a horizontal industrial
chain extension (Wang and He, 2003). As Daqing has not entered its
resource exhausting stage, industrial chain extension is the main pathway for regional industrial upgrading and discovering new economic
growth engines, which would significantly drive the economy of the
city. Daqing has significantly deepened the degree of processing oil
and gas and diversified urban industrial structure by industrial chain
extension (Fig. 6.6).

Firstly, for vertical extension since 1990s, Daqing has promoted
its petrochemical industry to increase the added value of its products.
This way, the city was able to gain same levels of profits even when
annual production level was decreased from 50 million tons to
40 million tons. Except for producing primary petrochemical products, such as petro, bitumen, asphalt felt, coatings, paints, and lubri-
cant oil, the city has adjusted its production process by reducing petro
production, increasing the production of basic organic petrochemical
products such as three alkene and three benzene products (ethylene,
propylene, and butadiene; benzene, toluene and xylene) to extend
industrial chain for ethylene, propylene, and arene. Daqing now is

able to produce 600,000 tons of ethylene, 300,000 tons of polypropylene and 760,000 tons of urea. In the year 2010, the added value of Daqing petrochemical industry has reached 36 billion yuan, representing a 27.8% increase from last year (Xia, 2011). At the same time, Daqing has been promoting gas-chemical industry as a dominant part of the high technology industry zone since its foundation in 1992. The PetroChina and Chinese Academic of Sciences Gas-chemical Test Center was found in Daqing on 22 August 2001. Founded in 2003, Daqing Oil Field Petrochemical Company has been treating gas-chemical business as a major business area. Located in the Daqing–Hongwei industrial zone, this company is a leader in driving the gas-chemical industry, major products including synthetic ammonia, ethylic acid, and carbinol. Daqing is actively promoting deep processing of polyolefin and organic chemical material, with the view to become China's deep processing base for six petrochemical products, like polyolefin, synthetic fiber, synthetic rubber etc.

Secondly, for horizontal extension, Daqing promotes the development of related industries derived for oil exploring and processing, such as petroleum and petrochemical instruments manufacturing industry, oil engineering technique industry, and oil logistics industry. Relying on other competitive advantages, Daqing has also developed agricultural products processing industry, represented by dairy products processing industry; pharmaceutical industry, represented by Chinese medicine producing, chemical medicine and biomedicine; new material industry, represented by chemical, building, and agricultural material industry. These non-oil related industries as substituted industries could reduce the loss brought by the oil production cut, and hence, promoted the diversification of city's economy.

iii) Institutional reform

Daqing is also implementing reforms in enterprise organizational structure, ownership structure, and management structure to overcome systematic problems that stifles industrial extension. First, to support the industrial extension of Daqing, PetroChina Enterprise has restructured its business in Daqing to significantly raise its competitive advantage: Daqing Oilfield Petrochemical factory merged with Linyuan Petrochemical Company into PetroChina Ltd Company Daqing

Processing Division in October 2000, focusing on production and dealing of processed oil, chemical engineering, chemical fiber andtextile. For the same purpose, in June 2007, Daqing Petrochemical Company and Daqing Petrochemical factory were emerged into PetroChina Ltd Company. Daqing Petrochemical Company, focusing on oil processing, ethylene, plastic, rubber production, extended chemical engineering production, liquid chemical engineering, fertilizer, and chemical fiber production, also providing technical support, equipment manufacturing, and mining services. Second, by transferring the responsibility of community support from state-owned enterprises to local government, these enterprises are less burdened and are able to focus on competing in the market. For example, the educational organizations and the police department were transferred under the jurisdiction of Daqing city Government in 2004. Third, the Daqing Petroleum Administrative Bureau has undertaken specialized integration and grouping operation for service areas except for its main focuses (oil drilling, processing, and selling), such as oil well technical support, engineering construction, administrative support, public services, education, and medical services. Twelve specialized corporations were formed, with a highlighting of oil engineering technical services and equipment manufacturing. Quicker development of Daqing city's non-oil related substituted industries was achieved.

iv) Enhancing independent innovation ability

Enhancing independent innovative capability is fundamental for improving industrial core competitiveness. Daqing has been emphasizing the importance of building an innovation system with a focus of independent innovative capability, hence, provided solid technical support for industrial chain extension. First, Daqing has imported scientific innovation bodies such as colleges and scientific institutions clustering in the "College town" in areas such as modern agriculture, petro-chemistry, and biomedicine. Colleges include Daqing petroleum institute, Heilongjiang August First Agricultural College, and Haerbin Medical School Daqing Campus. Specialized research institutes include Applied Technology Institute, North-Eastern Forestry University, Daqing Biotechnology institute, Heilongjiag Chemical Engineering Academy Daqing Division. To guide and promote the integration of colleges and institutions with enterprises, Daqing has also established industry zones such as Science and Technology Zone, Overseas Returned Students Pioneering Park, and PHD Research Center. This integration has enhanced significantly the scientific research supporting capacity and provided solid human resource support for industrial extension. Second, the city government has guided companies to increase their R&D inputs. A series of R&D organizations with adequate funds and scientifically developing abilities were established, either solely or jointly by companies and colleges. This way, companies' independent innovative capability and core competitiveness is enhanced. The third method was to complete public technology services system, like building up professional incubators. Incubators were built up for areas such as biomedicine, new material, software technology, and petrochemical technology according to their needs. The perfection of the agency services promoted the capitalization of R&D results and technologies, providing complete technical backup and market services (Administratlve Committee of Daqing High-tech Industry Development Zone, 2005).

5. Participants and Functions

The industrial extension process in Daqing is related to the fundamental change in the traditional economic development strategy and redistribution of interests. Thus, it is hardly possible to succeed without the support of higher level of government and willingness to participate from enterprises and relevant research institutes. The industrial extension is undertaken steadily with the central government promoting, the provincial government taking responsibility, the municipal government and companies implementing, and research institutions cooperating actively.

i) Government

As the representation of public interest, the government has played an unreplaceable guidance role in Daqing's industrial chain extension. It is the designer, organizer of the model and the policymaker, as well as the co-operator of stakeholders. Since the implementation of "revitalization of North-Eastern old industrial region", as mentioned above, all levels of governments are providing increasing support to Daqing's industrial chain extension. The steps of designing and implementing policies from the central government, provincial government, and the local government are clear, detailed, complete, and applicable.

First, the central government has provided macro guidance and a series of financial and policy support to Daqing's industrial chain extension; for the historical contribution the city has made to promote balanced regional development. It has significantly helped the city to overcome difficulties in implementing the policies, historical problems, and conflicts in economic development and environmental protection. According to the need for industrial chain extension, since the 1990s, the National Development and Reform Committee has increased its funding for Daqing's oil gas chemistry projects. After the implementation of "revitalizing North-eastern Old Industrial Region" strategy, the central government has also provided subsidies for the process of transferring public facilities from state-owned enterprises to local jurisdiction, to ease off the burden of enterprises. After Daqing was appointed as the pioneering city among all the oil-based cities for economic transition, the nation was also favorable in policy-making for tax, loan, and inter-regional trade. The "Suggestions for promoting sustainability in resource-based cities" by the State Council was regarded as the macro guidance for Daqing's economic transition. It suggested the city to use new technology and process; increase resource drilling efficiency; develop upstream and downstream industries to extend industrial chain; increase resource usage efficiency and convert resource advantage into economic advantage. In 2008, the State Council has established Resource-based Cities Development Center during its structural reform to promote sustainable development in the nation's resource-based cities.

Second, the "suggestions" pointed the provincial government to be responsible. The Heilongjiang provincial government pays a lot of attention to the economic transition: they promptly implemented the policies by central government and provided more detailed guidance, projects, and financial support. The economic transition of resource-based cities has always been a tough task for Heilongjiang province since the "revitalization of North-eastern Old Industrial Region" policy.

A specialized office under the province government was established in 2004 to overlook the transition process. During the same year, the "Heilongjiang Province Old Industrial Base revitalization plan" proposed to build Daqing as a leading petrochemical base in China and also internationally. Since May 2005, the provincial government has been providing support in the usage of land, taxation, financing, technology, and human resource to the development of industrial zone across Haerbin–Daqing–Qiqihaer, choosing the petrochemical industry as the dominant industry in Daqing city and hoping for it to drive the petrochemical industry of the entire province. After Daqing has been appointed as the pioneering city for the economic transition of other national oil-based cities, the provincial government has raised strategies for Daqing's transition. In the "Heilongjiang Petrochemical Industry Transition Strategy" proposal of 2009, 49 major projects were pointed, with an investment of 38.8 billion yuan. It proposed that Daqing would depend on its state-owned enterprises to extend petrochemical industrial chains such as ethylene, propylene, steam cracking C4, and Benzene.

Third, as the practising body of petrochemical industrial chain extension, Daqing municipal government has proposed and implemented industrial chain extension program. Since 1990s, Daqing city government has started to promote economic transition. In 1992, based on the city's competitive advantage and industry condition, the city combined with the UN Development Programme has set the revitalizing of petrochemical industry as one of the seven economic transition projects. In the same year, Daqing's national new high-tech development zone was established, with petrochemical and gas chemical as the dominant industries. Since the implementation of the "revitalizing north-eastern old industrial region", the city has considered the strategy to overcome the issues that is holding back the development of the petrochemical industry and the strategy to gain competitiveness in the international market, and a suggestive strategy has been amended by the government as per the guideline. Furthermore, the city government has also amended the "revitalizing Daqing industrial base plan" and the "strategy for Daqing's economic transition" and other plans, all listed developing petrochemical industry and extending oil industrial chain as the major tasks. With a series of major projects in the petrochemical industry, the city government has also applied for reasonably favorable policies with higher levels of government and PetroChina. Apart from planning and guidance, the city government has also promoted the enhancement of capitalization of R&D results by focusing more on innovative bodies, such as importing scientific researching institutes.

ii) Enterprises

State-owned petroleum and petrochemical enterprises are the main bodies for economic development, fiscal revenue, and technical innovation, thus playing a decisive role in industrial chain extension. To meet the practical need for industrial chain extension, the Daqing Oil Managing Bureau set out the main content of the transition: transformation of concept, system and mechanism, and adjustment of industrial, organizational and technical equipment structure. First, as required by conglomerated and specialized operation, 89 second grade organizations were integrated into 12 corporations, nine specialized companies, and six public institutions. This way, enterprises' working efficiency was enhanced by focusing on their dominant industries. The management model was changed into centralized decision making, hierarchical management mechanism, and specialized operation. At the same time, according to directions from PetroChina on freeing enterprises from performing social functions, Daqing enterprises were released from the burden of social functions. Second, central government controlled enterprises regard independent innovative capability; highly developing core technology was regarded as an important task for long term strategy. The enterprise was highly supportive for the establishment of scientific research bases, its organizational structure, the training of research team and scientific research. During the "11th five-years", the Daqing Oil Managing Bureau, with the objective to extend Daqing oilfield's life to 100 years, supported 632 projects in areas such as oil engineering, technical support, and oilfield operational management. Through extended use of new technologies, technical services, patent exploitation, and new products selling, annual technology-generated revenue was as high as over 2.5 billion yuan. Eleven major research institutions have been founded until now, including Drilling Technology Academy, Chemical Engineering Technology Academy, and Geophysical Prospecting Research Institute (Song, 2009). Third, PetroChina gave more managing authority to Daqing Oil Field in order to enhance its integration with the local economy. PetroChina allowed non-listed companies such as the Daqing Petroleum Administrative Bureau to emerge with local companies. The Bureau has emerged or acquired 10 local companies to develop 17 oilfields in remote areas in joint venture. The produced oil was retained by Daqing to develop its petrochemical industry. Fourth, when facing a situation when oil production was reducing, the central government controlled enterprises took advantage of Mongolian and Russian oil resource and provided oilfield engineering and technical services. They made good use of their regional excess production capability brought by technical and equipment advantages. At the same time, they extended raw material supply channel for industrial chain extension and ultimately promoted the development of related industries such as petroleum and petrochemical equipment manufacturing industry, oil engineering technical services, and outsourcing industry.

iii) Research institutes

Daqing's industrial chain extension was participated and cooperated by the whole nation, international experts and research institutions just like the way, when the oilfield was first built 50 years ago. These experts and research institutes provided strong intellectual backup for setting out Daqing city's macro development strategy, oil drilling, and processing technology innovation, and development of high-tech industry. First, Daqing municipal government hired a group of professors from well-known universities and research institutions as a high tier of consultants. Second, Daqing Oilfield Company has joined with the research institutions to focus on drilling techniques, displacing oil technique for ultra-low oil abundance and ultra-low permeability reservoirs, accumulation and exploitation, and potential of medium–low lithostratigraphic reservoirs (Table 6.3). It became a well-known brand for products such as C5 petroleum resin, super-high molecular weight polyacrylamide and injection installation of polymeric compound. These products contributed towards the maintenance of steady oil production and to the extension of industrial chain. Furthermore,

Table 6.3.   National Award Daqing Oilfield Received During 1990–2010.

Year	Research achievement name	Award
1990	Two-way drilling tool vibration damper	National Invention Award Third Prize
1990	Daqing Ethylene Material Engineering Technique Study	Science and Technology Achievements PrizeThird Prize
1990	DaqingAlpine RegionXingBei type 612 monotube unheated oil Gathering technique	Science and Technology Achievements PrizeThird Prize
1991	High- Resolution Power Earthquake Exploration	Science and Technology Achievements PrizeSecond Prize
1991	Triphase measurement of oil field and oilwell, and gas. Light Hydrocarbon flowing quantity measurement device and Verification system	Science and Technology Achievements PrizeSecond Prize
1991	Management of Sucker-rod pump and electric submersible pump mechanical oil recovery system	Science and Technology Achievements PrizeThird Prize
1992	Reservoir numerical simulation Technology	Science and Technology Achievements Prize Second Prize
1992	Empirical Approach of Precipitation industry standard	Science and Technology Achievements PrizeSecond Prize
1992	Leaking detection, prevention and sealing technology study in Daqing Oilfield with complex structure and Complex Pressure Strata	Science and Technology Achievements PrizeThird Prize
1993	Efficiency study of Oil pumping unit-deep well equipment system	Science and Technology Achievements PrizeSecond Prize
1993	Application of Computer assisted designing in Oil field designing and buiding	Science and Technology Achievements PrizeSecond Prize
1993	Water Stand Device	Science and Technology Achievements PrizeThird Prize
1995	Radio frequency oil water cut analyzer and its verification device	Science and Technology Achievements Prizesecond Prize
1995	Technique and Application of High-Frequency Eiectromagnetic Field-Type Water Treatment for Anti-Scales	Science and Technology Achievements PrizeThird Prize

(Continued)

Table 6.3. *(Continued)*

Year	Research achievement name	Award
1996	"Stabilizing oil output and controlling water content" project in Daqing oilfield high water cut stage	Science and Technology Achievements PrizeSpecial Prize
1996	Oil reserve assessment technique standard for basins and oil traps	Science and Technology Achievements PrizeSecond Prize
1996	Low-permeability and thinly interbed Reservoir discovering study in the Sanzhao Area of Song-Liao Basin	Science and Technology Achievements PrizeSecond Prize
1996	The use of Magnetic Treatment Technique in oilfield	Science and Technology Achievements PrizeThird Prize
1997	Horizontal well drilling technology	Science and Technology Achievements PrizeFirst Prize
1997	Study for Daqing oil total exportation quantity measurement equipment and complimentary computer technology	Science and Technology Achievements PrizeThird Prize
1998	Polymer flooding technology	Science and Technology Achievements PrizeFist Prize
1998	Experiment and study on well-case perforation fracture and its precaution measurements	Science and Technology Achievements PrizeSecond Prize
2000	Production Logging Interpretation workstation system	Science and Technology Achievements PrizeSecond Prize
2003	Bridge typeeccentriclayered exploitation and the study of Complete Sets of Technique of Production Potential	National Invention Award Second Prize
2004	The study and application of liquid-producing profile logging related to impedance	Science and Technology Achievements PrizeSecond Prize
2004	Support technique study of oil drilling engineering in high water-cut stage	Science and Technology Achievements PrizeSecond Prize
2005	Foam Composite Flooding technology	National Invention Award Second Prize
2005	Supporting technology of Cavity Pump Oil Production	Science and Technology Achievements PrizeSecond Prize
2006	Study and application of Effective development of 5 million tons of oil produced by oilfields surrounding Daqing	Science and Technology Achievements PrizeSecond Prize

(Continued)

Table 6.3.   (*Continued*)

Year	Research achievement name	Award
2007	Theories and discoveries in the accumulation and exploitation potential of medium-low lithostratigraphic reservoirs	Science and Technology Achievements PrizeFirst Prize
2008	Explanatory theory, methodology and application of well logging using acid volcanic rocks	Science and Technology Achievements PrizeSecond Prize
2008	Industrial application of polymer flooding technology	Science and Technology Achievements PrizeSecond Prize
2010	High efficient Expoitation technology of Daqing Oilfied in late high water-cut stage to maintain stable production of 40 million tons of oil	Science and Technology Achievements PrizeSpecial Prize

Notes: Summarized based on information at http://energy.people.com.cn/GB/73491/124264/211420/13649071.html.

research institutes have also contributed to the development of Daqing city's IT industry and equipment manufacturing industry. By integrating the R&D forces of research institutions and large enterprises, a series of software products with independent intellectual property rights were developed. These software control education, medication, and logistics, and represent a breakthrough for Daqing's IT industry. Based on the need for Daqing's petroleum and petrochemical industry and the need for city development in the Chinese market, R&D teams have developed petroleum machineries, environmental protection equipment, new energy-saving equipment, electricity generating equipment, and engineering equipment. In summary, by actively importing professions and research institutions, the independent innovative capability was significantly enhanced, and is driving the development of the city's economy. Based on statistics (Xia, 2012), the output value of high-technology industry of Daqing was 150 billion yuan in 2011, with an added value of 46.6 billion yuan, representing an increase of 54% from last year. The contribution of scientific development to the economy was as high as 50%.

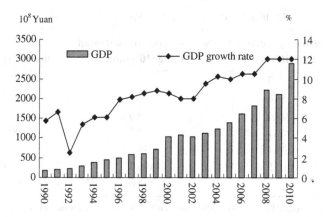

Figure 6.7.   GDP and GDP Growth Rate of Daqing City (1990–2010).

6. Achievements

i) Economic growth speeds up, big progresses achieved in industrial
structure adjustment

Since 1990, based on oil drilling and primary processing, Daqing
city has extended its industrial chain with ethylene, propylene, and
arene, and established the production of deeply processed products
such as light diesel oil, synthetic resins, plastics, fertilizers, and
methanol. This transition has significantly increased the oil gas
industry's added value, which absorbed the impact of reduction in
oil production on the city's economy, leading to a stable but rising
GDP rate (Fig. 6.7). At the same time, larger steps were taken in
the transition of the industry's structure. With petrochemical
industry as the leader and modern agriculture, equipment manufacturing, new material, new energy, and high-ended servicing industries as cornerstone industries, the old oil-dominant industrial
structure was significantly altered (Table 6.4) and the industry was
upgraded. Oil processing quantity changed from 7.57 million tons
in 1990 to 13.06 million tons in 2010. Led by Daqing Petrochemical
Company and Daqing Oil Processing Company, the petrochemical
industry gained added value of 36 billion in 2010, representing
15.5% of city-wide industry added value. Daqing has become an

Table 6.4.   Daqing Industrial Structure Transition.

Year	Oil economy increased value (10^8 yuan)	Non-oil economy increased value (10^8 yuan)	Ratio (oil vs non-oil)
1980	24.5	15.5	61:39
1985	38.8	26.6	59:41
1990	109.4	59.6	65:35
1995	300.1	138.2	68:32
2000	794.1	235.3	77:23
2005	910.5	490.3	65:35
2010	1508.1	1392.0	52:48

Notes: Statistics from reference (Xia, 2011) and (Policy Research Center of CPC Daqing Municipal Party Committee, 2007).

important petrochemical industry base and driving the rapid development of related industries such as petrochemical machinery manufacturing, oil drilling additive, and oilfield engineering services.

ii) Optimized ownership structure and rapid local economic growth

The institutional change is an important factor for ensuring smooth implementation of the industrial chain extension. Through the separation of major and minor business lines, the major business lines of central government controlled enterprises are emphasized, the areas managed by enterprises are largely reduced, thus cnhanced the core competitiveness even though the weight of public-owned economy (state and collective) is less (Table 6.5). With central government controlled enterprises acting as the leading force for oil gas industrial chain extension, non-public-owned economy participate in the city economic development by renting, partnership, and joint venture. Non-public-owned enterprises actively take advantage of the pulling effect and technology radiation of central government controlled enterprises. Many of these companies perform outstandingly well in the areas of petrochemical products deep processing, dairy products processing, and equipment manufacturing industry. Non-public-owned economy is weighing heavier (Table 6.5), which drives the development of non-oil replacing industry, becoming a new force for driving city's economy.

Table 6.5. Daqing Economy Ownership Structure Transition.

Year	1. Added value of public-owned economy (Billion yuan)	2. Added value of non-public-owned economy	Ratio (%) 1:2
1995	394.5	43.8	90.0: 10.0
2000	919.2	110.1	89.3: 10.7
2005	1168.2	232.5	83.4: 16.6
2010	2323.0	577.1	80.1: 19.9

Notes: Data from Refs. Xia (2011) and Zhang *et al.* (2011).

iii) Speeding up the pace of opening up and dynamic inter-regional cooperation

Daqing industrial chain extension needs to establish broad financing and trading/marketing channels. Since 1990s, Daqing has been promoting the opening up of city economy, focusing on attracting investment, and expanding the trading cooperation in superior areas like petroleum, petrochemical, machineries, and service outsourcing. The openness influence of the city has significantly enhanced. Up to now, the city has over 100 companies that have performed international trading, 38 of the top 500 corporations internationally have invested in Daqing; 19 companies are listed on stock exchange. During the "11th five-years", importing and exporting increased from 0.44 billion USD to 2.16 USD. Listed companies have financed 10 billion yuan accumulatively. Overseas communication is becoming more active: Daqing has established stable trading relationship with 104 foreign cities like Tyumen, Russia; the city has become a friend city with 12 foreign and domestic cities like Nanning, Guangxi Province in China, and Zhongzhou in South Korea; it has established trading liaison offices in 16 foreign countries. The city is becoming more dynamic as well: it has founded city tourist alliance; successfully hosted national and regional summits like the China 50 people economic summit and Daqing Cultural expo; it has been listed as top 50 cities in China that has investment potential in 2010 and top 200 attractive cities worldwide in 2011(Xia, 2012).

iv) Urban environment greatly improved

Since the 1990s, Daqing city has been devoted to improving its infrastructure and regional ecological restoration. Hence, the city's environment and functions are significantly improved, thus creating a sound development environment for industrial chain extension. The city's spatial framework was strategically extended and upgraded, based on the purpose of building an "ecological, natural, modern, and livable" city. The city area was expanded from 159 km^2 to 225 km^2 in order to extend the city's strategic frame and secure a long-term development space. For the purpose of building Daqing as a regional center, the city speeded up its pace in building modern traffic network: the Daqing Tusatu Airport was put into use; highways were constructed across the city and are now part of the national highway network; the New Zhaoyuan port connects the river and the sea; the construction of East and West city Train Station and inter-city dedicated passenger railways were speeded up; 39 major traffic projects were accomplished and put into use, such as Road passenger terminal, wetland bridge, and other roads. This upgrade of city transportation provides a broader 3-dimensional channel for the city to integrate into larger economic region. Furthermore, the city's infrastructure is more comprehensive now. During the "11th five-years", 34 infrastructure construction projects were carried out, such as East city Water Supply Station and East city Heat Supply; 2,150 kms of newly built or upgraded water, heat, and gas supply pipes. 15 trash and waste water treatment plants were built, enhancing the detoxification treatment rate of garbage and waste water to 87% and 92%, respectively (Xia, 2012). In addition, the city's public service functions have been significantly upgraded. Large amount of facilities have been built and put into service, for example, the Grand Theatre Center, Conference Center, Ironman (referring to Wang Jinxi, who has devoted himself in the initial building of Daqing Oilfield) Memorial Hall, the city Museum, city West Sports Center and city Hospital of Chinese medicine. Last but not the least the city has been promoting the concept of building an ecological city by improving its water system environment. Actions that were taken included waste clearing, water changing, and revetment and greening of 10 ponds such as the South Lake, Ming Lake, Treasury Lake, and Three-Forever Lake. As a result, the city has been awarded as the National Civilized city, National Hygiene city, and National

Environment Protection city, making Daqing city one of the seven prefecture-level cities with these three awards.

7. Problems and Challenges

i) Institutional barriers remain

Since oil is an important strategic resource for China, the central government takes full control in the allocation of oil resources. Hence, Daqing is still the one resource-based city with the highest proportion of pubic-owned economy in the Northeast region. It is still partially in the planned economic system, with PetroChina Head office controlling the supply of oil and selling of petroleum or chemical materials while the local government has no power over it. Therefore, the market has not yet fully played its role in the resource allocation. Exporting large amount of oil, petroleum and chemical materials stifles the expansion of petrochemical industry of the city. Second, the land management system has influenced the overall plan of the city's "land use" and the development of local substituted industries are limited by land space, since the Ministry of Land and Resources delegated the power of determining the usage of oilfield-purpose land to the Daqing Petroleum Administrative Bureau through authorized procedures. The land is then leased to oil companies by the Bureau (Song, 2009). In addition, the fiscal system of Daqing is rather special. The main taxation revenue is allocated to the central government and the provincial government. The retained part is mainly the insignificant tax types, like the city maintenance tax, goods and services tax, education fees, land using tax, and stamp duty. To give an example, the budgeted fiscal income is 9.59 billion yuan, only representing 3.3% of the regional GDP, much lower than the average of 7.2% in the Heilongjiang Province. As a result, the disposable income of Daqing city is insufficient to provide full support to the industrial structure transition and rapid economic growth.

ii) Low level of industry

During recent years, although the non-oil sector has gained much growth, the oil economy continues to be dominant, representing 52%

of Daqing's GDP in 2010. Oil and gas exploiting industry makes up 64.6% of the entire industry's added value, while as an important substituted industry, petrochemical industry is only 15.5%, making little contribution to driving the local economic growth. Now, among Daqing's three alkene and three benzene products (ethylene, propylene, and butadiene; benzene, toluene, and xylene), only ethylene's productivity maintains a relatively high level, the rest are at a low level in technological sophistication. Petrochemical products are only limited to primary level materials while fewer high added value and high-tech products are produced. The petroleum industry chain is short; deep processing ability is weak and the clustering effect is still insignificant. In addition, stifled by low oil processing amount and chemical material shortage, further development of petrochemical industry is limited. Thus, the extensive production and management methods need to be improved.

iii) Lack of long-term stable national policy support, infant industries face tough competition

The central government's policy is crucial for Daqing to extend its industrial chains through financial aid, projects, and favorable policies. However, most policies from the central government are only short term, not to secure the future financial needs in the industrial chain extension. Now, the "resource exploiting compensation mechanism" and the "deteriorating industries aiding mechanism" proposed in "the suggestions" are still in the discussion phase, without any detailed practicable policies. The oil gas reserve exploration risk fund, and fiscal, and tax reform suggestions raised by the local government have not yet formed into a stable system, since it requires the cooperation of too many other departments. At the same time, substituted industries are facing extensive market competition. Petrochemical, dairy products processing, and pharmaceutical industries are also major developing industries in its neighbor provinces (Liaoning Province and Jilin Province). Task allocations for the same industry in different regions are not clear as they lack cooperation between the governing bodies. Therefore, the industries are not differentiated and over-competition exists. This issue requires urgent overall planning and coordination on macro scale by the central government and PetroChina.

8. Potentials

i) Continuously promote institutional reform, enhance dynamic economic development

When compared with other types of resource-based cities, the institutional problems in China's oil- and gas-based cities are common. Daqing needs to integrate resources of petrochemical enterprises to enhance their market competitiveness by reforming the management system of the central government controlled enterprises, improving corporate governance of these enterprises according to the requirements of modern company system and promoting diversity of investment bodies. Further, the city should promote the development of multiple ownership economy; including central government controlled companies, domestic and overseas strategic investors, local government and private enterprises. By share-holding system, selling, leasing, and technical cooperation, these investment bodies can undertake wider cooperation and achieve revenue sharing (Heilongjiang Provincial Government, 2005). The areas of cooperation should include exploitation of the "four lows" in an oil field (low production, low permeability, low efficiency, and low oil content), exploitation and usage of natural gas, deep processing of petrochemical products and system reform of non-listed companies. The city should also work out the fiscal relationship with the central government and the provincial government to increase the tax benefits and financial aid from these upper levels. This will allow the city government to have sufficient funds for supporting the development of the substituted industries, thus, enabling the city to install a more complete fiscal system. For the optimization of the land management system, the land management power should be transferred to the local government from central government controlled enterprises, in order to improve the local government's functions (Research federation of social sciences in Daqing City, 2007). In addition, the city should accelerate its opening up to the global market and domestic market to improve dynamic local economy and build up management and operation systems that can adapt to the market economy. Measurements to achieve this includes building up of additional export processing zones, inland ports and bonded warehouses to support the growth of the exporting companies, to support private enterprises that can adapt to market change, to attract all types of production factors overseas to participate in Daqing city's industrial transition and encourage key enterprises to discover and take advantage of overseas resources.

ii) Continue to support infant sectors

Industrial restructuring is the key task for Daqing's sustainable development. Non-oil sector in Daqing is still weak and the dominant position of the oil industry is hard to change even in a long period of time. The city should promote diversification of its industrial structure by cultivating the development of non-oil replacing industries to enhance the supportive role of the substituted industries to the city's economy. These industries include modern agricultural, equipment manufacturing, new material and high-end service industries. This requires Daqing to support infant sectors of non-oil industries. For example, the city should remove the barrier of material shortage and raise the weight of petrochemical products that are produced locally. To achieve this, the city should ask for more oil processing quota from PetroChina and increase the processing amount of Russian oil. This will allow the local economy to connect with the oil sectors. In addition, the central government and PetroChina should provide continuous project and financial support to Daqing's local players who are involved more in the petrochemical industry to drive the oil industrial chain extension.

iii) Perfecting the policy support system, further clearing the rights and responsibilities of the interest bodies

The industrial transition of resource-based city touches on the fundamental adjustment of interest sharing structure between all levels of government and resource development companies. Thus, there should be a perfect institutional arrangement to coordinate with all the stakeholders and legislations to standardize the behavior of all stakeholders, which is a common practice internationally in order to promote industrial transition of resource-based cities. The Chinese central government needs to build a long-term aid system to reefed and promote Daqing's industrial transition, in connection with the loss brought by the market failure under the impact of its long-term planned economy. The nation should accelerate the set-up of resource exploiting compensation mechanism, the deteriorating industries aiding mechanism, and the resource-based cities sustainable development reserve fund.

Meanwhile, the pricing system of resource-type products that reflects the relationship between the scarcity of resource and market demand, cost of environmental protection and ecological recovery, generational and inter-generational equity should be formed. This will allow the real value of resource to be realized and fairly allocated between the interest bodies. Reforms in resource taxing systems can also help to resolve debts that should have been compensated. The government should also promote the legislation of sustainable development of resource-based cities, and clearly define the responsibilities and duties of all levels of government and resource exploiting enterprises in fostering substituted industries, ecological improvement and resolving social problems. This is to standardize the working mechanism of Daqing industrial transition at the legislation level.

9. Conclusion and Discussion

Urban transformation of China's resource-based cities is an important strategic issue that initially appeared during its industrialization and urbanization. It is of crucial implication to promoting China's transition toward the economic growth mode, coordinating regional development and building a "harmonious society" (as proposed by the Chinese Chairman Hu Jintao). Looking at the urban transformation practice of resource-based cities globally, industrial transition as the core content of urban transformation has gained intensive attention by their nations, even though these cities significantly differ in background, systematic conditions, growth stage, participating bodies, and strategic measurements. Comparing to these cities, China's resource-based cities face issues such as institutional reformation, completing policy system, and resolving historical problems, except for some common issues present in overseas resource cities: single industrial structure, unemployment, and ecological pollution. Therefore, as a complex systematic project in both theoretical and practicing levels, industrial transition of China's resource-based cities should not only make use of the successful experience of developed countries, but should also take into consideration the specific characteristic of Chinese resource-based cities, to actively seek ideas from industrial transition theory and strategic measurements that are suitable for Chinese resource-based cities. Daqing as a typical oil resource-based city in China intensively reflects many common issues. The city's industrial transition practices through industrial chain extension are at least implicative to resource-based cities in China in the following ways.

i) Timing

Compared with other processing-, service- and knowledge-based industries, the gross output, and net profit of resource-based industries are not always positively correlated: along with the resource reserve reduction and exploitation becoming more difficult, marginal profit of resource-based industries reduces. In addition, the accumulated labor, equipment and capital grow larger, and the accumulated ecological problems of the oilfield become more severe, along with the increase in exploiting intensity and duration. The development characters suggest that the city's industrial transition should be implemented before the region enters its resource draining period. If the process is not started early, not only the sustainable development of city's economy and the social stability are at risk, but also the cost and difficulty of transition are dramatically raised. Daqing started the industrial transition process before its resource draining period, to take full advantage of rich regional resource, superiority of human resource and technology. This has effectively reduced the environmental cost of industrial transition, the withdrawal cost of resource industries, and the development cost of substituted industries, so that it promotes the stable transition into a diversified industrial structure from single resource-based industrial structure. Compared with cities like Fuxin, Fushun, which started industrial transition after entering the resource-draining period, the cost and complications in the industrial transition of Daqing city are significantly lower.

ii) Emphasize the role of resource industries

Extension of industrial chains in resource-based cities does not mean to change the single sector dominant structure into diversified industrial structure, nor replacing the resource sector. For resource-based cities that have not entered the draining period, the dominant place of resource industry is irreplaceable for a relatively long period. Thus, the industrial transition should be carried out step-by-step. Extending resource industrial chain is a practical step for the development of diversified industries. Daqing took advantage of the supporting effect of the resource industry by extending the resource industrial chain, under the situation where non-oil substituted industry was not strong and regional resource supply was sufficient. This measure effectively eased the impact of reduction in oil production in the city's economy, at the same time, it created favorably development environment for non-oil substituted industries. This model will play an important role of reference for other resource-based cities that are not yet at the draining stage. However, it is of worthy attention that industrial extension is a transitional industrial transition model, where the downstream industries are still dependent on the regional resource advantage. So, the city should arrange for reasonable development scale and extension steps, provided that the market demand is considered and regional resource supply is sufficient. This would avoid accumulation of excess labor and capital in resource industries. At the same time, the city should support the development of non-resource-based substituted industries that are suitable for the specific city. Only with all above measurements implemented could the resource-based city achieve sustainable development.

iii) Central government's institutional arrangements are the key
The industrial transition of resource-based city not only faces adjustments in its industrial structure, but also involves institutional reform. The economy of resource-based cities in Northeast China typically owned largely by state and private economy is insufficiently developed. Since the government has long been practicing planned allocation of resources, these resource-based cities have formed unreasonable pricing system, resource taxing system, and compartmentalized administrative management system. Under such a situation, the resource-based city lacks self-accumulation and self-motivated development capacity. Therefore, it is very hard to achieve industrial transition that is entirely dependent on the city's own strengths. The central government has been urged to establish complete institutions to promote the industrial transition. As for Daqing, its industrial chain extension was supported by the central government with favorable policies and projects, which proves that this "top–down" transition motivation model is highly efficient in Daqing's industrial transition. The method rapidly

raises the vitality and intrinsic motivation for Daqing's economic development. But, at the same time, we should notice that the support from central government is only for particular projects or periodical policies, which suggests that the authority, responsibility, and interest allocation is not clearly defined. Furthermore, the resource-based city needs to continuously promote system and mechanism innovation, guide non-public economy and small–medium enterprises to participate in the industrial transition, update the effective cooperative model among governments, enterprises, banks and social groups, and ultimately build up a complete and long-acting institutional arrangement for industrial transition of resource-based cities.

7

Economic Transformation and Continuous Industry Development Model of Fuxin City

1. Introduction

The economic transition of resource-based cities around the world can be summarized into three different approaches. One approach is to extend the traditional industrial chain in order to drive the development of related industries. An example of this approach is Houston in the U.S., the city extended its oil industry chain when the oil drilling industry deteriorated. In addition, related industries such as machinery manufacturing, cement production, electricity production, steel production, and the transportation industry were also expanded when Houston's oil industry was restructured (Liu, 2005). Similar cases can be found in Pittsburgh in the U.S. and the Appalachian Mining area. The Chinese nonferrous metal city of Jinchang, in Gansu province, also followed this approach. The city focused on the development of a new nickel-oriented material industry, this extended the existing industrial chain, expanded industry groups and converted the resource-intensive economy into a technology-intensive economy (Zhang and Zhou, 2007).

The second approach is to make use of new technology to transform the traditional industries. For example, the Ruhr Area of Germany, which hit difficult times, used improved technology with the financial support from the government to convert their traditional industries. At the same time, it imported new industries and became a new industrial zone with an optimized structure and a booming economy (Zheng, 2005). Karamay city, Xinjiang Uygur Autonomous Region, put great effort into the development of continuous industries during the economic transition process, this included the petrochemical industry (Qu *et al.*, 2007). Jinan city, Shandong Province followed its own development model by focusing on deep resource processing industries and growing continuous industries (Zhao *et al.*, 2007).

The third approach is to shut down high-cost, high-consumption, and high-polluting resource oriented enterprises and to develop new industries with financial input from the government. The approach relies on the city developing high-technology industries by importing replacement industries along with the transportation networks and associated infrastructure. The cost of this transformation type is relatively high and time consuming. This type of approach has been implemented in the city of Calais and the Lorraine area in France and the Kyushu area in Japan (Liu, 2005).

The case study presented in this chapter, Fuxin, is a typical coal mining city. Coal reserves are fairly depleted and the economy is suffering from a low economic growth rate. There are growing problems with unemployment, low social security, and increasing poverty, the city urgently needs to find a new sector to replace the coal mining industry and to transform the economy. This chapter explains Fuxin's economic transformation and how and why modern agriculture has now been selected as an alternative to coal mining and is going to be used to stop the city from becoming a ghost town.

2. Background

Fuxin is located in the Northwest of Liaoning Province, with Shenyang city to the East, Jinzhou city to the South, Chaoyang city to the West and Inner Mongolian Autonomous Region to the North. There are two towns and five districts under Fuxin's jurisdiction. In 2003, the ratio of the three levels of industry in Fuxin city was 21:39:40, primary, secondary and tertiary industries, respectively. The primary industry played an important role in the economy, even though the rural area still was far from industrialization. In 2003, even with the deterioration of the coal mining industry, the coal mining and mineral industries still accounted for 31% of Fuxin city's total GDP and the ratio of employees in the industries was 23% of total employees in Fuxin, this was much higher than any other industries.

Within the secondary industries share of 39%, the contribution of heavy industry was higher than that of the light industry. Traditional industry was more prevalent than new industries and the correlation between the different industries was weak. Although the tertiary industry accounted for 40%, this is not automatically a positive sign for industrialization. In the case of Fuxin it is an abnormal situation because of the severe deterioration of the secondary industry and the low degree of tertiary industry. The modern service industries were developing slowly, including the logistics and information technology industries.

In 1774, two coal mines in the Qinghemen area started operating, representing the beginning of coal mining in Fuxin. It has now been operating on a large scale for over 100 years. The Japanese controlled coal mining in Fuxin for the 40 years preceding the end of the World War II, with extensive operation during the 10 years between 1936 and 1945 (Tong, 1999). The Fuxin mining zone coal reserves are now quite low. In the remaining reserve, there is a limited amount of coal that can be mined economically; the costs are high because of the deep coal seam and the complex mining conditions. As a result of the depleted coal resources, Fuxin city has closed 23 mines. In March 2001, the Fuxin Dongliang Mine, Ping'an Mine, and Xinqiu Mine went into liquidation. Then in June 2002, more mines that belonged to Fuxin city went into liquidation. In 2005, the Haizhou Open Coal Mine, which was famous throughout China, went into liquidation. Fuxin is now facing a serious problem.

There are a number of key questions that needed to be raised about Fuxin city's future: How to search for alternative industries? And, what industries can be used as replacements? Before we discuss these issues, it is important to explain the environmental and resource barriers that effected the further development of Fuxin. The city suffers serious water shortages. The annual distribution of precipitation is unbalanced, with rainfall in July to September accounting for on average of 70% of the annual amount and as a result of the summer heat, it easily evaporates. In 2009, the average annual precipitation was only 328 mm and the per capita available water resource was 439 m^3, only half of that of Liaoning Province and 1/5 of that of China (Yin, 2007).

Besides the obvious sectors like agriculture, other high-water-dependent enterprises have suffered from the water shortages, including the coal-fired electricity generation, chemical engineering, and building material industries.

The Western Liaoning mountain area, where Fuxin city is located, also faced severe problems with soil erosion and land desertification. Nearly half of the land was affected by serious soil erosion (Liaoning Province Environmental Protection Bureau, 2005). The fragile ecological environment means that in some areas economic activities and industrialization could not be undertaken at a large scale. Fuxin was facing other social and economic pressures including a very high unemployment rate. The proportion of citizens working in the mining sector was higher than in any other city of this type. Therefore, the closing down of mines has led to volumes of workers being made redundant. By the end of 2001, there were 156,000 unemployed people in the city, many of whom were mining workers who had been made redundant (Liu W. Q., 2003). Through the transition process, from a planned economy to a market economy, the redundant workers were not been able to fully adapt to the market, as it increased the problems of the former two and the unemployed. In addition, there were a large number of surplus workers in the nearby towns and in the rural areas surrounding Fuxin, which increased the pressure of those trying to find employment.

Fuxin city had a large financial debt, as the local expenditure was considerably higher than the local income of the city. The large financial deficit meant it was the only city in the Liaoning Province that required subsidies from the provincial government. Its poor financial condition meant that the city's government was unable to provide financial support to the city's economic transformation. However, Fuxin had several comparative advantages for the development of a modern agricultural sector. The first one was the availability of farm land, with 376,000 km² of farmland or 0.4 km² per capita; Fuxin city has the richest farmland resource in Liaoning Province. This provided the foundation for developing modern agriculture industry. Fuxin also discovered 46 different kinds of minerals, representing 42% of known mineral types in the province. The non-metal mineral resources found were very rich quality, they included silica, silica sand, bentonite, zeolite, and merical stone. There were also large reserves of coal seam gas and coal gangue available for the development of the industry. In addition, Fuxin has a rich forestry resource, as it is an important development base for the "Three-North Shelterbelt" Program.

The second advantage Fuxin has for the development of a modern agricultural sector is its energy resources. Fuxin has a great potential for wind energy. By 2011, the installed wind power capacity reached 1,225,000 kW. Solar energy is also rich in Fuxin with average annual hours of sunshine of over 2,761 hours and total radiation of 138.474 Kcal/cm^2. It is likely that in time Fuxin will develop solar heat and power generation technology, solar water heating technology, and solar energy photovoltaic power techniques. Currently Fuxin city's development and usage of solar energy is still in the early stages. Fuxin also has high-quality, high-salinity geothermal water that is close to the city and conveniently accessible, it has bright development possibilities as well as high economic and social benefits. Finally, Fuxin city has rich biomass energy resources, since it has access to large quantities of bio fuel in the form of crop straws, sweet sorghum, and Jerusalem artichoke that can be burnt to generate power. Fuxin has a relatively good foundation in energy and power production, it has been an important energy base for Liaoning Province for a long time. In addition, the manufacturing of hydraulic equipment, electronic machinery, power equipment, and automobile parts had a good competitive advantage in China.

3. Coal Mining City's Economic Transformation Progress

After the founding of the PRC in 1949, 4 of the 156 national key projects listed in the first five-year plan were located in Fuxin, all of which were large projects in the coal sector. A total of 240 million yuan was invested by the central government for the four projects: Fuxin Ping An vertical shaft, Fuxin Xinqiu first vertical shaft, Fuxin Haizhou open-pit coal mine and Fuxin thermal power station. These projects made Fuxin the first national energy and power industry base and an important player in the Northeast old industrial base. In July 1960, Asia's largest open-pit mine, Fuxin Haizhou was formally opened for production. From 1949 to 2009, Fuxin mined 650 million tonnes of raw coal, which generated 200 billion kW of electricity (Zhang, 2009). This was an important contribution to the national economy. As the exploitation of Fuxin coal continued, the coal resource has gradually dried up. The economic benefit of the coal industry is decreasing, which has resulted in a reduction in the dominance of the coal industry. However, the new leading industries were not yet established, which resulted in Fuxin becoming labelled as "exhausted mining city". Of the 14 cities in the Liaoning province, Fuxin's economic performance has been continuously ranked at the bottom for several years. During the entire 9th five-year period, the city's GDP growth rate stayed at 2.1%, which is two percentage points lower than the average of cities in the Western China. In 2000, the city recorded their lowest growth figure of 0.2% (Wang, 2003).

3.1. *History of Fuxin city's economic transformation*

In 2001, Fuxin city was listed as China's first resource-depleted city to undertake economic transformation. By 2003, 23 key projects, with support from the national government, had been implemented (Table 7.1). A total of 1.79 billion yuan was invested to urban environmental management projects, and construction of new infrastructure (Liu, 2004). Fuxin actively sought out new projects in order to attract further investment into the region. Over the first three years of transition, a further 142 projects, with a total investment of more than 10 billion yuan were agreed upon and have now been completed or are under construction. The projects include pig slaughter

Table 7.1.   Major Economic Transition Timeline.

Year	Important event
2000	First time to raise the idea of economic transition, started to seek pathway for transition.
2001	Fuxin city was appointed as a pilot city for the national economic transition of resource draining cities. In December 2001, the State Council pointed the city as a pilot city of transition in a special meeting.
2003	Fuxin city proposed their strategy for projects to motivate the transition, shifting the emphasis solely onto transition projects.
2005	Fuxin city started large scale reconstruction of squatter settlements to benefit residents by improving living environments and conditions.
2006	Fuxin city identified its goal to develop "a three industry base with six special industries" to gain competitive advantage.
2007	According to the state council's "suggestions for sustainable development of resource-based cities", Fuxin city further developed replacement and continuing industries and reduced social issues like unemployment and social security, and enhanced environmental restoration and ecological protection.
2008	Implemented a strategy for joining the Shenyang economic zone and enhancing cross regional cooperation. Shenzhang new city became an important connection point for Fuxin to integrate into the Shenyang economic zone.
2009	Emphasis on urbanization, with the construction of the "Yulong new city", this improved the cities function and the image of the downtown city.
2010	Determined to develop itself as a demonstration city for the economic transition of national resource-based cities.

enterprises, gangue power plants, Shenyang–Zhangwu and Fuxin–Siping highways, and Fuxin Xinqiu to Eastern Inner Mongolia railway (Wang, 2004). When Liaoning province became China's first pilot area for the development of the circular economy, Fuxin city also began to stimulate circular economy development. In 2008, as a member of the Shenyang economic zone, Fuxin city began to implement a strategy for regional economic integration. Shenyang economic zone was the new national industrialization reform pilot zone, which included Shenyang, Fushun, Anshan, Benxi, Liaoyang, Tieling, and Yingkou. Fuxin had a single industrial structure, and had been dependent on coal and power generation industries for a long time. Therefore, the industrial restructure focused on the upgrading of traditional industries, the optimization of industrial structure and the development of systems to support diversified industries. In the process of transforming the economy there are a number of changes Fuxin city made which includes developing modern agriculture and agro-processing industry, consolidating coal and electricity generation industries, intensifying the development of coal-bed methane, utilizing mineral resources such as coal gangue and fly ash, developing a coal chemical industry and developing electricity from the abundant wind power resources and coal gangue resources. Fuxin city also developed a modern hydraulic equipment industry, leather industry, and furniture industry. The city also provided support for the development of the tourist industry which includes tourism on the regions where industrial history of Haizhou is held, with the open-pit mine as the main attraction, as well as developing eco-tourism in both Daqinggou and Zhanggutai. Fuxin has also started to rely on their agate resource processing facilities. Fuxin city has also sped up the development of the logistics industry and has begun to promote the development of both the transportation and commerce industries. After nearly a decade of development, the Fuxin economic structure has been dominated by the efforts to transform the single-led economic structure to a diversity-oriented economic structure, and gradually advance Fuxin's economic development.

3.2. Development of continuous industries in the economic transition

3.2.1. Modern agricultural sector

Fuxin city has rich arable land resources with 5.6 acres of cultivated land available per capita, the highest in Liaoning province. Fuxin city also has 3.2 acres of woodland per capita and 1.3 acres of grassland per capita.

Around 1 million tonnes of commercial food is produced every year, with per capita production of goods, the highest in the province. There are good conditions for growing both peanuts and cereal crops, which meant there was potential for further development of agricultural resources. Developing an agricultural industry was beneficial to the rural economy and changed the dual structure of urban and rural areas; it also improved the farmers' incomes and employment opportunities. Fuxin region has developed both pollution-free food and specific maize and cereal crops. The city has taken advantage of the characteristics of the drought-resistant peanut and has made itself a major player in the peanut market. The city has also constructed a flower production market, with a good regional advantage. Fuxin has distinctive advantages in the market for meat products, mainly pigs, sheep, donkey, and cattle. However, it should be noted that to be successful in the development of a thriving modern agriculture industry, the construction of an agricultural zone and the construction of transportation network are essential (Zhang, 2005).

The city has also carried out the construction of the Three-North Shelterbelt Forest project, which focused on returning farmland to forest whilst incorporating the processing of forestry products into forestry development. Starting from 2002, Fuxin city initialized the construction of the agriculture zone. Leading enterprises such as the Shanghai Guangming and Henan Shuanghui set up in Fuxin city to develop an agricultural products processing industry (Mu, 2005). By utilizing the high-tech industrial park in Fuxin, the construction of a demonstration district for standardizing agricultural practices and developing a food processing supply base has been completed. Fuxin used advanced agricultural science and technology in developing a modern agricultural system.

3.2.2. Industry development

Fuxin city's industrial structure is still dominated by coal mining, electricity, and heat generation industries. Other competitive industries that have some importance are the dairy products processing industry, general equipment manufacturing industry, food production industry, beverage production industry, ferrous metal mining and dressing industry, non-ferrous metals smelting and pressing industry (Fig. 7.1). Any of these industries could become dominant industries or leading industries for Fuxin city during the economic transformation. The following section highlights how these sectors can develop.

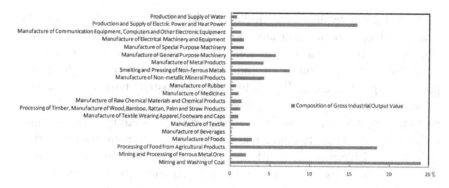

Figure 7.1. The Gross Industrial Output Value of Fuxin in 2007.

Into further development of the energy industry, Fuxin city proposed to build a new energy base. In 2004, the expansion project of the Fuxin Mines Corporation's coal gangue heat and power factory was commenced with an investment of 210 million yuan. In 2005, the Fuxin Jinshan Coal Gangue Heat and Power Factory started its construction as well. The city is also rich in coal bed gas. In 2003, some local residents' gas was switched to gas sourced from the coal mine area. Prior to that, the Jinshan Wind Power Generation Plant was built in 2002. The target of the wind power industry was to build a wind power generation base with 1 million kW installed capacity (He and Wang, 2006). In addition, Fuxin city plans to invest in both solar heating and solar power generation. There are also options for increasing the usage of methane gas as well as developing geothermal energy. In summary, there is a need for secure energy supplies in order to reduce the risk of energy shortages. This could be done by enhancing the usage of clean energy such as wind, solar, and biomass energy and reducing the usage of coal and oil. Second, the city should increase the level of technological input to solve the environmental problems of energy production. Third, it should accelerate the development of coal logistics center so as to ensure the supply of coal resource. Next, the city should develop an electrical machinery industry, building material, and power generating industries that builds on enterprises such as the Fuxin Mines Corporation.

Since the start of the economic transformation, the equipment manufacturing industry of Fuxin city has developed rapidly and has become a dominant industry in the city's industrial economy. In the future, the city can continue to develop the equipment manufacturing industry by drawing on the hydraulic industry, electrical machinery, electricity generating equipment, and automobile parts manufacturing industries. The technical innovative capabilities of enterprises has also been enhanced, the extension of the industrial chain has increased the enterprises' supporting capability. A hydraulic industrial base with national importance can be built by utilizing the strategic positioning of Fuxin as a supporting industrial base for Liaoning Province's equipment manufacturing industry. The city could also support the equipment manufacturing industry of Liaoning city with the steel, iron, and aluminium manufacturing industries, based on Fumeng Town and Xihe District casting industrial base. In time, a unique casting industrial cluster could be developed. In addition, the city has also developed metal mining machinery, automobile parts, engineering machinery, and oil machinery products industries.

The fluoro chemical engineering industry, with an emphasis on products such as inorganic fluorides and macromolecular material has been developed. At the same time, with an enhanced production of florin-containing fine chemicals, Fuxin city could be built into an important fluorine chemicals industrial base. Fuxin city should also develop a new material industry with an emphasis on building materials and mining machinery material. The city should also develop a leather deep processing industry.

To position Fuxin industries in a broader context, we use location quotients to evaluate the position and influence of Fuxin industry in the broader region. By comparing the location quotients of Fuxin's major industries in the nation and the province (Table 7.2), the competitiveness of Fuxin city industries has been separated into three categories and is presented below:

From the aspect of Liaoning Province, Fuxin city's industries that had absolute competitive advantage (location quotient >2) are: coal mining and dressing industry (14.17), water production and supply (3.02), and electricity and heat generation and supply (2.24). Industries with some competitiveness (2>location quotient >1) are textile manufacturing (1.63), food production (1.48), beverage production (1.28) and ferrous metal mining and pressing industry (1.02) and the other industries present in Fuxin lacked competitiveness in the Province.

From the national level, Fuxin city's industries that had absolute competitive advantage (location quotient>2) are: coal mining and dressing industry (7.63), ferrous metal mining and pressing industry (2.94), and

Table 7.2. Comparison of location Quotient of Fuxin City's Major Industries in China and Liaoning Province.

Industry	Country	Province	Industry	Country	Province
Coal mining and dressing	7.63	14.17	Rubber products manufacturing	0.26	0.22
Ferrous metal mines dressing	2.94	1.02	Plastic products	0.21	0.18
Non-metal mines dressing	0.24	0.20	Non-metal mines products	0.57	0.40
Agricultural and non-staple food processing	1.41	0.93	Non-ferrous smelting and pressing	0.66	0.89
Food manufacturing	1.08	1.48	Metal products	0.70	0.54
Beverage manufacturing	1.02	1.28	General machinery manufacturing	0.96	0.46
Textile manufacturing	0.49	1.63	Special machinery manufacturing	0.63	0.39
Clothes, shoes and hats manufacturing	0.38	0.39	Electricity generating machinery, and equipment manufacturing	0.19	0.21
Leather, fur products manufacturing	0.02	0.02	Communication equipment, computers, and other electrical equipment manufacturing	0.15	0.28
Wood processing and wood, bamboo, rattan, and grass products manufacturing	0.60	0.45	Art crafts and other manufacturing	0.04	0.10
Paper manufacturing and paper products manufacturing	0.04	0.08	Electricity, heat generating, and supply	1.85	2.24
Chemical material and chemical products manufacturing	0.16	0.22	Gas production and supply	0.13	0.23
Pharmaceuticals production	0.45	0.59	Water production and supply	2.82	3.02

water production and supply (2.82). Industries with come competitiveness (2>location quotient>1) are: electricity and heat generation and supply industry (1.85), agricultural and non-staple food processing industry (1.41), food production (1.08), and beverage production industry (1.02).

Over all, Fuxin city's five most important industries were coal mining and dressing industry (39.55%), electricity and heat generating and supply industry (18.06%), agricultural and non-staple food processing industry (7.21%), general equipment manufacturing industry (5.39%) and non-ferrous metal smelting and pressing industry (3.29%).

3.2.3. Transportation and tourism development

The city has taken advantage of its location and has accelerated its development in order to build itself as the central logistics spot in Liaoning Province. At the same time, it has reorganized and integrated the existing storage facilities with the newly built storage facilities to form a new structure of the logistics industry.

In August 2002, the Fu-Jin Highway was completed, which increased the regional economic connectivity. Currently, the city has completed and opened the Fu-Jin Highway, Shen-zhang Highway, Tie-Fu-Zhao Highway and Zhang-e Highway; and the Fu-Pan Highway is under construction. The development of new highways could strengthen the connectivity that the city has with the other industrial zones and transportation hubs. Links to Jinzhou city and Taoxian Airport have enhanced the economic connection with the Shenyang economic zone and the coastal Liaoning Province, and has also benefited the development and usage of mining resources, land resources, and human resources of Fuxin city.

Another development has been the tourism projects that highlight the industry heritage and drive religious and nature tourism. Tourism is a supporting sector for Fuxin city's social and economic transformation. The special features of Fuxin city's tourism mainly include:

— Industry heritage tourism with Haizhou Open Mine as the central focus. To initiate the tourism surrounding the open pit, mining machinery, and power generating equipment the city has taken advantage of the unique agate resources and has hosted the Fuxin Agate Festival. Fuxin is the "Agate Capital of China" with 70% of the national agate production. Shijiazi Agate Centre is China's demonstration place for industrial tourism and is the national processing and distribution center of agate.

— Tourism on Buddhism, based on the Haitang Mountain and Ruiying Temple.

— Ecological tourism based on DaqingGou and Zhanggutai. The Daqinggou scenic spot has unique vistas with mountains, water, sand, and forest. The Zhanggutai Sandy National Forest Park is located in Zhanggutai Country, Zhangwu Town; it features scenes of deserts and artificial forests.

3.2.4. *Environmental development*

Water-saving industrial development: Fuxin city lacks a secure water supply, therefore, development of continuous industry must be low-water use. Water use in the agriculture sector should be reduced by promoting water-saving irrigation and rain collection irrigation techniques. Water-saving in industries must be achieved through technical improvements, with an emphasis on developing new techniques and utilizing new equipment to both, circulate cold water and eliminate high water consummation. Out-dated industries and equipment need to be phased out. An industry's water consumption evaluation system and water-saving rewarding mechanism should be set up to motivate reduction in water usage.

Developing a circuit economy: "Reduce, reuse, and recycle" are important principles for a circuit economy to follow. The development of continuous industries needs to comply with the mode of circuit economic development and to take advantage of new technology to build an inter-industrial and intra-industrial chain. This will enable enterprises to combine production, logistics, recycling, and environmental protection, in order to reduce consumption of resources and increase the recycling of waste (Shi and Zhao, 2008). Fuxin city should also develop a recycling industry and try to implement industrial ecological principles by establishing a connection between one enterprise's waste and another enterprise's need for the waste product as a raw material. In addition, mining companies should comply with the principles of "clean production" and re-use and treat waste. Furthermore, in the rural areas, developing an agricultural circuit economy should use scaled livestock and poultry farming industry as the breakthrough point.

Environmental friendly industries are an important way to support regional sustainable development and the development of a circuit economy. The eco-industrial park does not only pursue economic growth, but also aims to stimulate an ecological system with correctly designed logistics and energy system in the industrial park, to form an enterprise symbiosis network, and also achieve closed-circuit circulation and zero emission from the industrial park (Zhang, 2003). The connection of resource-based clusters in the eco-industrial park is the hierarchical usage and value creation of resources (Jiang, 2006). The development of the eco-industrial park is reliant on the existing industrial park, reforming the technology, re-distributing production factors, combining industry innovation, and extending the industrial chain, all of which will support the establishment of waste and energy exchanging relationship amongst enterprises in the park.

The circuit economy industrial chain of Fuxin city is focusing on reusing non-renewable resources such as waste metal and production waste of coal gangue, coal ash, and mine water. In addition, comprehensive usage of non-renewable resources such as coal-electricity-coal ash-new construction material (cement, wall material) and coal-electricity-coal gangue-new building material (burnt clay brick) (see Fig. 7.2).

Low-carbon economic development: The city needs to first, gradually eliminate low efficiency and out-dated industries such as the small cement and glass manufacturing factories. The next step would be to undertake redevelopment of all coal-burning boilers and promote energy-saving projects such as the joint production of heat and power, energy saving for building sites, and energy efficient lighting. Second, the city should promote the usage of new technology to reduce energy consumption and to achieve emission reductions in both the power generating and coal mining industries. Third, the city should accelerate the development of new energy industries such as wind power, solar energy, and biomass

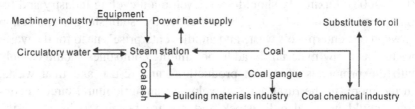

Figure 7.2.   Circuit Economy Industrial Chain.

industries. Lastly, the city should promote the idea of low-carbon development to gain the support of the general public.

3.2.5. Regional task allocation and economic cooperation in the economic transformation of Fuxin city

Economic task allocation between the towns of Fuxin city: In the center of Fuxin city, the emphasis was on developing an ecological industry and modern service industry, mainly for the coal-burning power generation, coal chemical, hydraulic equipment, electronic and mechanical, and agricultural products processing industries. The city has also been focused on developing a financial and commercial area in the center of the city, North of the Xi River. At the same time, this area has put in great efforts to develop the logistics, cultural, and sports industries. Fumeng Town has focused on developing agricultural products processing, fluorine chemical, precision machinery, and casting industries, as well as the agate industrial area in Shijiazi. Zhangwu Town's focus was on furniture production, oil machinery, and agricultural products processing industries as well as building the Shenzhang new city. It also developed "Yulong new city", which focuses on the modern service industry specializing in commercial and residence dwellings, commercial conferences, and businesses. Shenzhang new city is a leader in the furniture industry, and is also focused on logistics, building material, and agricultural products processing, which makes it an important district in the West of the Shanyang economic zone.

Economic Integration of urban and rural areas: Economic integration of urban and rural areas is the trend for regional economic development. Thus, during the process of developing modern agriculture, the city should pay attention to maintaining cooperation between the urban and rural areas. The urban area of Fuxin city should on one hand utilize the advantages of the urban area to develop a modern agriculture and tertiary industry and accept excess labor from the rural area; whilst on the other hand, the city should provide support for town-level enterprises, to drive the economic development. Fumeng Town and Zhangwu Town have rich land resources with farming as the major industry. In the development process, they should take advantage of their rich land resources to plant high quality crops, as well as to improve the development ability of their town-level enterprises.

Strengthened regional economic cooperation: Fuxin city should carry out regional cooperation with the Shenyang Economic Area. On joining the Shenyang Economic Area, it provides a benefit for Fuxin city to cooperatively host investment attraction activities, motivate labor transfer from Northwest Liaoning Province and develop a tourism market. The city should seek to integrate transportation networks by utilizing the Shenzhang new city as transportation and logistics hub for Shenyang city, Fuxin city, and Jilin city. Building a railway line from Shenyang to Beijing through Fuxin as well as extending and reconstructing existing railways from Shenyang to Fuxin and Jinzhou will support the integration. Lastly, the city should leverage support from the leather industry in the central Liaoning Province to develop Fuxin leather industrial base and cooperatively enhance the leather industry.

Fuxin city plans to position itself as the new energy base for the Shenyang economic zone. As a major coal transportation channel between Liaoning Province and Inner Mongolia, the Baxing Railway can secure over 100 million tons of coal resource supply for Shenyang economic zone. Furthermore, the city can utilize its rich wind resources, which Fuxin city has put a great effort into developing. In addition, 4 billion m^3 of natural gas can be supplied to Shenyang economic zone after the completion of Datang Fuxin Coal produced Gas project (Hou, 2010). Fuxin city has also been improving the environment of Fuxin city and Shenyang economic zone through planting trees and creating artificial forests, which provides a natural barrier for the Shenyang economic zone.

The city should also provide support for building a transportation channel to the sea for Eastern Inner Mongolian coal mines. Transportation to surrounding local resource utilization industries should also be developed to enhance cooperation and promote a series of coal power generating projects. Also, the city should accelerate the development of the railways between Bayanwula in Eastern Inner Mongolia and Xinqiu in Fuxin city. The city should also promote the establishment of water-saving high efficiency agricultural and animal husbandry demonstration zones in Eastern Inner Mongolia and Western Liaoning.

Lastly, the city should strengthen regional cooperation with coastal Liaoning Province in order to utilize the port in Jinzhou city to develop Fuxin's logistics industry. A new coordinated relationship could be established between the inland and coastal Liaoning economic zone.

4. Organizational Operation of the Transformation Model

4.1. *Main organizations supporting the development of continuous industry*

The organizations in the Fuxin city which led to the continuous industrial development of the same would be the government, enterprises, universities, research institutes, the market, and the general public. The development of a continuous industry relies on the motivation from the market, the development of enterprises, promotion by the government, and participation by the public — all of these are necessary. The market can efficiently guide the sustainable development of the industry. Enterprises are the main force of regional industrial development. Thus, enterprises should be motivated to participate actively in product development, technology development, and market expansion. The Liaoning Engineering and Technology University has advantages in mining, mechanical design, and hydrodynamics; therefore, can provide intelligent support to regional economic transformation. The government mainly motivates the development of the continuous industry, enhances regulation, reduces barriers for the entry of industries and eliminates outdated production lines, techniques, and products through regulations and policies. Consumers can provide feedback through the democratic system, purchasing power, and the media.

4.2. *Relationship between the main organizations*

During the economic transformation, enterprises are the main organizations involved in the market economy, they are the main strategic bodies driving Fuxin city's transformation, and they are the main source of technical innovation. Enterprises together form the national economy, and the various types of enterprises form the economic system of Fuxin city. Enterprises attract and allocate a range of factors to produce wealth, thus they are the important vessels for developing the production force. The upgrading and transformation of industries need to be achieved through the upgrading and transformation of enterprises.

No economic body will run smoothly without the adjustment within the government. The government under an inefficient market economy can solve problems such as low efficient resource allocation, unemployment and inflation (Fu, 2007). During the economic transformation, the main task of the government is to form a complete framework, make policies, enhance roads and the city's infrastructure and protect the environment.

During the city's transformation, we should make full use of the positive influence that can be utilized. The market can support the prioritization of resource allocation, although we ought to be cautious about market inefficiency. Enterprises are the main body that can eliminate outdated equipment, undertake technical innovation, and adjust the industrial structure to cooperate with the government to achieve industrial transformation. The public should actively participate in the city's transformational practises to gain technical experience, and to support reasonable changes.

4.3. Factors supporting the implementation of the transformation model

4.3.1. Driving force of the projects

The economic transformation of resource depleted cities has to first solve problems of residential living and sustainable development. Economic transformation is carried out through projects: a series of long-term, strong driving force, and high added value projects to drive the regional economic development and employment, and to promote a series of ecological restoration projects. The city should utilize the resource advantage and stock assets to find the connection point between economic transformation and foreign investment.

4.3.2. Fund security

A large number of reasons being said for the transformation and reformation of the resource-based cities and old industrial bases facing serious development problems is that their investments when compared to the national total, is declining. Attractive investments and businesses is the motivation behind project implementation. With attractive investments and expansion in opening-up, the city can cooperate with foreign investors through joint ventures in order to revitalize assets, improve management systems and mechanisms, import advanced technology and ideas and attract skilled management employees, in order to generate high economic benefit and social benefit.

4.3.3. *Policy support*

The continuous development of the resource mining industry depends on strong strategic and financial support from the central government. The government will need to increase its fiscal payments to support resource-based cities' development and make favorable policies to promote economic transformation and development of continuous industries.

4.3.4. *Technology and Human Intelligence strategy*

Economic development and technical innovation can only be achieved with the motivation of outstanding employees. Science, technology, and skilled employees are important to support and develop intellectual security for economic transformation. The city should train high-end workers and skilled laborers, train innovative entrepreneurs who are familiar with the market economy and support universities and scientific institutions to develop new industries.

5. Outcome of Industrial Transformation

5.1. *Major achievements*

The last ten years of effort toward economic transformation have achieved great progress. First, Liaoning city's rate of increase in GDP is second in the country, which represents high potential in the future. The general local budget is almost three times than that of 2001. The per person disposable income for urban residents was three times than that of 2001, the per person disposable income of rural residents was 5.5 times than that of 2001, which implies that the implementation of modern agriculture and agricultural products processing industries have had significant success. Over the past decade, the total number of reemployed people was 614,000 and the number of "zero employed families" assisted was 92,000 and the number of laid-off workers trained was 232,000 (Zhang and Chen, 2011). The registered unemployment rate in the urban area dropped from 7.6% in 2001 to 4.0% in 2010.

After years of effort, the achievement of Fuxin city's industrial structure adjustment was significant and a continuous industry frame was formed. The industrial structure changed from the single coal power generation industry to a diversified industrial structure with agricultural products processing, energy, new material, and equipment manufacturing industries.

The ecological environment has also been improved. Fuxin city implemented environmental protection measurements and implemented the "Three-North Shelterbelt Program", and successfully blocked sand from the North and raised its forest coverage to 32%. With comprehensive restoration to the Haitian Open Mine, it has become a national mine forest park. The ecological environment of the city has also significantly been improved.

5.2. *Features*

Fuxin city was a typical resource-depleting city, and its development was highly dependent on the resource industry; its industrial structure was single and heavy industry's weight was very high. The degree of urbanization in Fuxin city was low, urban and rural areas were significantly differentiated, city's infrastructure was relatively outdated and the ecological environment was putting heavy pressure on the city. During the economic transformation, Fuxin city needed to improve the industrial structure of the three industries and diversify the industries. Also, it needed to develop non-resource oriented industries to disengage from resource dependence.

Fuxin city gave priority to the goal of expanding employment, took advantage of the current industrial foundation to develop continuous industry, put emphasis on diversified industrial development, and developed resource deep processing and high added-value industries. The city also paid attention to its infrastructure and construction, and strengthened ecological environmental resonation. At the same time, it enhanced the economic integration between the rural and the urban areas which brought up the significance of regional cooperation; implemented the market economy and put great effort into scientific and technological innovation and training new employees. Furthermore, adjusting and improving the industrial structure and actually changing the economic development mode cannot be achieved without the support of technical innovation. The Liaoning Engineering and Technology University is a national key university, which can train technical students and enterprise management students. The local government should make preferential policies to encourage and attract new students. In addition, high resource consuming and heavy-pollution enterprises need to pay attention to energy saving and reducing emissions and to raise the resource-use efficiency of the resources.

Fuxin city needs to enhance the restoration of the soft environment, improve transportation networks and pay attention to employment training in order to attract investments by holding a good investment environment and high technology levels. Fuxin city should also continue to improve the city's infrastructure, including implementing projects along the Zhangwu–Tongliao, Fuxin–Panjin Highway, Beijing–Shenyang Railway, Baxin Railway, and other important water conservancy projects.

5.3. *Meanings of the transformation*

Achieving sustainable development within resource-based cities is a sign of revitalization of the Northeast region of China. Fuxin city, as a typical resource-depleting city, has benefited from economic transformation; it has improved the city's comprehensive development level and service functions and ultimately develops the city into a modern city. Economic transformation can improve employment and solve social problems. The economic transformation of Fuxin city is environmental friendly, which means it has changed its extensive development mode. Therefore, the economic transformation of Fuxin city provides an example of how the economic transformation of other resource-depleting cities in China can be redeveloped.

8

Jilin City's Low Carbon Economy

1. Introduction

Cities are moving towards being more environmentally friendly. In post-reform China, urban planners and municipal government officials tend to adopt popular concepts and incorporate them into their urban development planning. For example, after Agenda 21 was accepted in the early 1990s, almost all Chinese government documents and urban planning papers incorporated the ideas of sustainability and sustainable development. The idea of a low carbon city is a relatively new concept, it first appeared in China in 2008 (Yuan and Zhong, 2010). The central government has selected several cities that are low carbon demonstration cities, each with different approaches in moving towards being low carbon, Jilin was one of the first cities to be listed as an experimental site. In 2008, the World Wide Fund for Nature (WWF) established the low carbon city initiative with two pilot sites in Shanghai city and Boading city. Subsequently, the low carbon concept has been adopted by many cities throughout China, including Jilin, Hangzhou, Suzhou, Ganzhou, Wuxi, Chengdu, Dezhou, Guiyang, Yangzhou, Guangyun, and Xiamen. These cities are trying to form a new economic environment where energy savings and emission reductions are aligned with economic growth (Zhuang, 2009; Pu, 2010; Hui, 2009; Wang, 2009; Yuan, 2009; Li, 2009; Zhu, 2009; Wang, 2010; Xu, 2010; Ren, 2009; Nan and Yang, 2009). The details of the projects being implemented in these cities are shown in Table 8.1.

Chinese cities face many challenges during their transition to low carbon cities. On the one hand, they are in the early economic stages of development, with both industrialization and urbanization at peak

Table 8.1.   Summary of China's Major Low Carbon City Programs.

City	Theme	Measures
Shanghai	Construction energy-saving	Increase energy efficiency of large buildings, educate corporate staffs of public buildings on enhancing energy savings
Baoding, Hebei	Becoming China's electricity and electrical valley	Develop 7 industrial parks for manufacturing: i) photovoltaics, ii) wind power generation, iii) power transmission and transformation, iv) new energy storage, v) high efficient energy-saving electrical equipment, vi) automatic electricity and vii) electricity software. Baoding is branded as "China's electricity valley, low-carbon Baoding"
Hangzhou, Zhejiang	Green transportation	First city in China to introduce Public Transport Week and No Car Day. Municipal government's document: "Decision to develop low-carbon Hangzhou" and its six low carbon city targets are: low-carbon economy, low-carbon building, low-carbon transportation, low-carbon living, low-carbon environment and low-carbon society.
Suzhou, Jiangsu	Energy-saving auditing	All enterprises with current energy consumption level over 5,000 tons/year are required to conduct energy-saving audits. Promote tertiary industry development in Taihu Lake areas to reduce industry pollution.
Ganzhou, Jiangxi	low-carbon economy	The municipal government signed energy-saving responsibility contract with 17 high energy consumption enterprises.
Wuxi, Jiangsu	Project 4610	Project 4610 aims to introduce four new supporting mechanisms: i) reward for developing renewable energy, ii) granted central green building, iii) supporting policy for energy saving projects in existing buildings, iv) supporting policies for energy saving in public buildings. Promote six energy saving techniques: i) ground source heat pump, ii) solar energy, iii) rain water tanks, iv) new building materials, v) energy saving doors and windows, vi) underground space. Conduct ten low carbon projects (energy saving projects).

(*Continued*)

Table 8.1. (*Continued*)

City	Theme	Measures
Chengdu, Sichuan	Zero energy consumption and intelligent residential demonstration area	Use light and environmental friendly construction materials and solar energy battery powered indoor lighting and electrical appliances.
Dezhou, Shandong	Million rooftop project and light and power project	To install solar energy panels on the rooftops of 80% of the houses in the metropolitan area and solar hot water in over 100 villages. Install solar energy lamps on new roads.
Guiyang, Guizhou	Ecologically civilized city	Promote energy saving lighting with financial subsidies. Develop the most environmental friendly transportation system. Construct a tree belt around the city and build more energy-efficient houses.
Yangzhou, Jiangsu	Green low-carbon action; low-carbon real estate fund	Encourage the use of low-carbon green construction techniques to reduce CO_2 emissions. Reward real estate enterprises that contribute the most in promoting low-carbon houses.
Guangyuan, Sichuan	Replace coal with gas and electricity	Encourage rural residents to use methane gas, and reduce CO_2 emission by 1.5 million tons annually.
Xiamen, Fujian	Low-carbon transport, production and buildings	Develop low carb on transportation, building and manufacturing (these three sectors accounted for 90% of Xiamen's carbon emission).
Jilin, Jilinw	New Energy and industriwal parks	Develop new energy sources, construct energy saving buildings to reach the target of energy savings of 65%. Set up new industrial parks.

pace. On the other hand, many Chinese cities' economies are reliant on heavy industries, which are predominantly high consumers of energy and have low energy efficiency. The ways in which cities can transfer from heavy industry cities into low carbon cities is a critical topic. This chapter examines how Jilin city has pursued its low carbon dream.

2. Background

2.1. *Low carbon economy*

The Chinese government has responded quickly to the idea of developing low carbon cities, whereas academic research in China has only just started discussing the concept. In December 2009, at the United Nations Framework Convention on Climate Change 15th Conference of Parties in Copenhagen (Cop 15), China committed to reducing carbon emissions per unit of GDP by 40–45% by 2020 compared to 2005. This target puts pressure on Chinese cities to reduce their carbon emissions. In January 2010, almost immediately after Cop 15, the first Low Carbon China Forum was held in Beijing. At the forum, plans were formulated to develop low-carbon cities, low-carbon communities, low-carbon rural areas, low-carbon industries, expand low-carbon trading, promote carbon recycling, and reduce carbon emission. Jilin city was recognized as one of the top 10 cities of China that had the potential to be "a competitive low-carbon industrial city", meaning as a major petrochemical industrial base in China, Jilin was seen as being a good site for low carbon city building.

Work to date on carbon emissions and low carbon cities by Chinese academics has been mainly limited to the introduction of the low carbon concept and definition or summary of low carbon city experiences in western countries (Pan, 2010; Liu *et al.*, 2009; Li and Zheng, 2010). Other research has focused on low carbon urban economics and introduced the idea of having five supporting frameworks for the development of low-carbon cities: low-carbon theory, low-carbon technology, low-carbon finance, low-carbon production and low-carbon consumption (Yuan and Zhong, 2010). Zhang and Zhang (2011) used the Pressure-State-Response model to evaluate the development of Changchun low-carbon city. To date, few studies have been undertaken on Jilin as a low-carbon city. Zhu and Zhuang (2010) used Jilin as a case study in their research, analyzing the measurements of revitalization of the Northeast region under the principles of a low-carbon economy. All these studies were descriptive and focused on developing a definition of a low-carbon economy (Fu *et al.*, 2008), the necessity for developing low carbon cities (Zhang *et al.*, 2008; Zhang, 2009), the relationship between economic growth and carbon emissions (Wu *et al.*, 2005; Xu *et al.*, 2006;), predicted carbon emission growth (Zhu *et al.*, 2009), concepts of carbon trading, low-carbon energy, and low-carbon society (Pan *et al.*, 2004; Qiu, 2009; Liu *et al.*, 2009; Dagoum and Barkerts, 2010; Nader, 2009).

2.2. *Jilin city*

Jilin city is the second largest city in the Jilin Province, with four districts in the metropolitan areas, one national new technology industry development zone and 11 provincial economic development zones. The total population was 4.5 million in 2011. Jilin has become an important heavy industrial city focusing predominantly on the petro-chemical industry. The 2005 Songhua River pollution incident in Jilin affected the environmental safety and security of both China and Russia. This incident not only affected millions of Chinese people's drinking water resources but also became a trigger for potential China–Russia environmental conflict. Jilin is largely responsible for the water pollution in Songhua River; especially its petrochemical industrial park which generates over half of Jilin's industrial wastewater and one quarter of its chemical oxygen demand (COD) in 2008. This was one of the reasons for China to list Jilin city as a pilot low carbon city.

Since the founding of the People's Republic of China (PRC), Jilin has become an important heavy industry city. During the early Mao period, eight of China's so-called "156 priority projects" proposed in the first "five-year plan" (1953–1957) were located in Jilin city, they included projects on chemical fertilizer, fuel, and carbide production and China's first commercial hydroelectric power project, Fengman Dam. The projects provided the preliminary foundation for Jilin city to develop its petro-chemical industries. Now, Jilin has established six pillar industries: petro-chemical, agricultural products, automobiles, pharmaceutical, pulp and paper, production of electricity and gas. Figure 8.1 shows that the top three industries (petro-chemical, agricultural products processing, and automobiles) account for over 65% of the top six industries' output value in 2009.

The petro-chemical industry is the largest sector and produced more than 50% of top six industrial sectors' output value since 2005 (see Fig. 8.1) and the output value continued to increase year by year. The second largest sector is agricultural product processing industry which contributed to about 25% of total output value in 2009. The importance of heavy industry was also reflected in the GDP structure. In 2010, total GDP in Jilin reached 180 billion yuan and the GDP ratio by primary, secondary, and tertiary sectors was 11:50:39, respectively. Both the secondary and tertiary sector's growth rates increased over the last decade. For example, the growth rate of primary industry was only 3.8% but it was 12.5% and 14.4% for the secondary and tertiary industries, respectively.

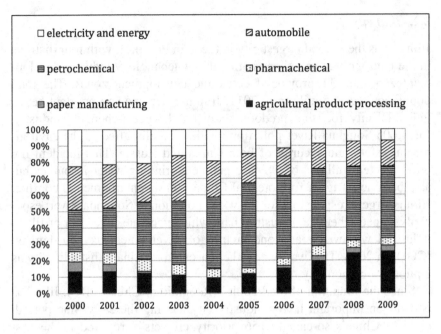

Figure 8.1. The Main Industrial Sectors' Output in Jilin City.

As shown in Fig. 8.2, since 1991, Jilin city's tertiary sector has increased its share in total industrial output value but it is the secondary industry that still produces over 40% of total industrial output value. Figure 8.3 shows that within the secondary sector, heavy industry accounted for 70% of total industrial output value while the light industry accounts for only 30%. The heavy industry share reached a maximum of 89.3% in 2004. Therefore, Jilin city as a heavy industrial city suffers the same common problems as other heavy industrial cities do: high-energy consumption, high CO_2 emission, and industrial pollution. The road towards becoming a low carbon city will be very challenging for Jilin.

The challenge that Jilin has to overcome as a low carbon city is the current energy consumption intensity. Fortunately, Jilin has access to natural resources that can be utilized to support the low carbon city's target. Jilin is rich in hydro-energy resources. There are a total of eighteen rivers including Songhua River, Lalin River, Mudan River, and their tributaries, when combined have the potential of up to 23.5 million kW power resources. Fengman hydropower station with 3 million kW of existing

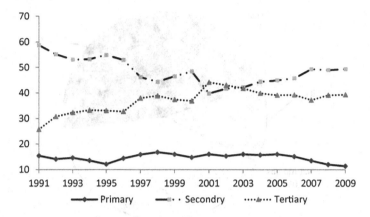

Figure 8.2. Ratio of Three Industries in the Jilin City.

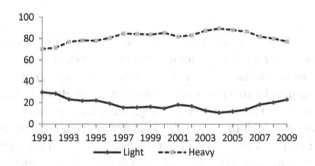

Figure 8.3. Ratio of Light and Heavy Industries in Jilin City.

hydropower capacity accounts for 53% of hydropower installed capacity in Northeast China's power grid. Jilin's hydroelectric power accounted for one-third of its total generated electricity. Even with such a large amount of clean energy (Fig. 8.4), Jilin's current energy consumption still depends on oil (41%) and coal (27%), hydro-power only accounts for 12%. It is obvious that one critically important way to reduce carbon emission in Jilin is to change its energy consumption structure. In the last few years, Jilin city has actively committed to the development of new energy. The major new energy projects include a 4 million kW nuclear power plant, wind power, and a solar photovoltaic project. A wind energy project with 500 wind turbines and a nuclear power project are both part of China's

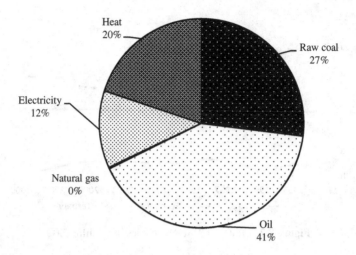

Figure 8.4.   Final Energy Demand in Jilin City in 2010.

national high-tech industrialization project of Jilin. Jilin has also established China's largest bio-ethanol production base, which supplies the
market in the Northeast and Northern China. At present, Jilin city is set to
increase the development of straw fermentation of ethanol. A pilot plant
that supplies 3,000 tons per year has been completed. A carbon fiber wind
blades project, which draws on the knowledge from enterprises such as
Dazu laser and uses raw carbon fiber material from Jilin is under preparation for construction. All these developments will eventually reshape
Jilin's energy consumption structure.

A question that still remains is how Jilin should position itself as a low
carbon city? In 2010, the Chinese Academy of Social Sciences (CASS)
released the government's standard for low carbon cities. It included
12 criteria across the four broad categories of low carbon productivity, low
carbon consumption, low carbon resources, and low carbon policies (see
Table 8.2). According to the government standard, a low carbon city in
China should at a minimum meet the criteria that its low carbon productivity level should be 20% higher than the national average. Against this
criteria, we can see that currently, Jilin has a long way to go to reach its
low carbon city target even though it has nearly reached the CASS standards on a few of the second-level criteria (see Table 8.2). Jilin is about half
way to becoming a low carbon city based on the minimum requirement to
qualify as a low carbon city. This assessment is based on the latest

Table 8.2. China's Evaluation Indexing System for Low-Carbon City and Low Carbon Economy and Jilin's Current Status.

First-level indexes	Second-level indexes	Current status in Jilin city
Low-carbon production output index	Carbon productivity	53% of China average
	Energy consumption per unit of production of key industrial enterprises/ carbon emissions per unit of added value of key industrial enterprises	One of the highest in China
low-carbon consumption index	Carbon emissions per person	2.79 ton/person (China 1.6 ton/person in 2008)
	Carbon emissions per person for domestic energy consumption	0.10 ton/person/year
low-carbon resource index	Zero carbon emissions energy consumption amount per person	0.075 ton/person/year (Jilin's targets: 0.44 ton/person in 2015)
	Forest coverage	10% higher than national average (Jilin region's forest coverage is 55% — equivalent to average level of national environmental/ ecological function zones
	CO_2 emission index per unit of energy consumed	0.01: Lower than national average
Low-carbon policy index	Development plan for low-carbon economy	In place
	Establish carbon emissions monitoring, information gathering, and management system	In place
	Degree of public's knowledge of low-carbon economy	Over 80%
	Implementation rate of buildings reaching the energy saving standard	Over 80%
	Non-commercialized energy development motivation measurements	In place and fully implemented

available data, from 2007. The low carbon productivity in Jilin city was 8,300 yuan per ton of standard coal equivalent, while the national average was 15,600 yuan per carbon ton equivalent. Therefore, we estimated that Jilin city only produced 53% of the national average, which means there was a large gap between Jilin's production and the required level to qualify as a low-carbon economy.

The challenge for Jilin can be better understood by looking at the 2009 carbon emission levels of the key industrial sectors in Jilin city (Table 8.3). The data shows that Jilin's overall industrial carbon emission per unit of added value was over 2.6 times of national average. Jilin province had higher emission levels than the national average in all industrial sectors while Jilin city had higher emission levels than the national average in all but one of the industrial sectors. For example, in Jilin city the carbon

Table 8.3. Carbon Emissions Per unit of Added Value of Key Industrial Sectors for China, Jilin Province and Jilin City.

| Industrial sector | Carbon emission per unit of added value (ton of standard coal/10 thousand yuan) | | | Jilin city as % of China |
	China	Jilin Province	Jilin city	
Industry Total	**1.51**	**2.11**	**3.98**	**263**
Agricultural food processing	0.14	1.28	0.63	45
Mining industry	0.81	1.6	0.47	58
Non-ferrous metal smelting and casting processing	0.32	0.52	0.42	131
Non-metal mineral products manufacturing	1.92	4.82	3.86	201
Power, gas and water production and supply	8.12	14.4	27.05	333
Manufacturing industry	0.84	1.23	3.02	359
Chemical raw material and product manufacturing	1.33	5.24	6.04	454
Beverage manufacturing	0.19	2.04	1.55	816
Chemical fabrics manufacturing	0.56	6.17	7.82	1396
Transportation equipment manufacturing	0.06	0.14	1.28	2113

Source: Zhu and Zhuang, (2010).

emission of transportation equipment manufacturing industry is 21.13 times of the national average, chemical fiber manufacturing industry and beverage manufacturing industry are 13.96 and 8.16 times of the national average, respectively. The remaining industrial sectors (except mining and agricultural product processing) had 2–5 times of the national average carbon emission per unit. It can be discerned that the essential measurements of Jilin city to build low-carbon industries and hence a low-carbon city can adjust to the industrial structure (towards low carbon industries) and the energy supply structure (use more new energy sources and clean energy).

3. The Major Measurements to Lower Carbon Emission

Jilin city is dependent on its carbon-intensive industries, but since the city was listed as China's first pilot low carbon city, it has made a number of key improvements. Jilin's low carbon program is different from other low carbon city programs of China; it is the only city which incorporates their low carbon targets into the five-year plan. The five-year plan is an important political document; it is the most important performance review of the promotion of the local officials. To support the development of a low carbon city, Jilin municipal government was given special policies, privileges, and certain autonomy to work toward the goals of a low carbon city. In addition, the municipal government released a number of policies to improve energy efficiency and lower carbon emission levels. In 2008, Jilin Province published a local Standard for Energy Efficiency of Major Products and Equipment (DB22/T 40, Jil), which set out the energy consumption standards for major products and energy efficiency equipment in Jilin Province. In 2009, Jilin city released a standard for energy consumption level in all public organizations (e.g., government departments, schools, etc.). In 2010, Jilin released its own low carbon development plan and established a new governing body in its municipal government, the Low-Carbon Leading Group. Since then, Jilin city mayor's priority has been to convert Jilin into a low-carbon city and Jilin's economy into low carbon economy. In the Mayor's performance review, these low carbon targets are an important criteria. The transition to the low carbon city may have only started recently but Jilin has mobilized all socioeconomic and political resources in order to reduce its carbon emission. The following sections explain what has been done to Jilin.

3.1. Enterprise decarbonization after entering industrial parks

Jilin's first set new standards for energy efficiency and carbon emissions of different enterprises. Meanwhile, enterprises were encouraged to move to the established industrial parks. For example, Kaidi Low Carbon Circular Economic Industrial Demonstration Zone (KLCCEIDZ), Jilin Chemical Industrial Circular Economy Demonstration Zone (JCICEDZ), and Saudi Industrial Park were all made attractive options for enterprises. Incentives were used to entice the enterprises into the parks, but when they moved they had to agree to invest in a new technology which would support the enterprises in achieving the parks' energy efficiency and carbon emissions criteria. The financial incentives and other special policies for the enterprises that move are very attractive. In addition, the municipal government has stated that all enterprises must relocate out of Jilin's municipal area, either into one of the parks or to another area outside of the municipal zone. To date, over 200 chemical enterprises have relocated from Jilin city to JCICEDZ, 29 of which failed to reach the required environmental targets and were forced to close down. Typically, the enterprises that are being closed down are high polluting and high energy consuming enterprises. Meanwhile, new industrial chains have been formed within the parks. The JCICEDZ was approved by Jilin provincial government and was established on 29 October 2008, it occupies nearly 60 km^2. The enterprises in this zone receive privileges and preferential policies from the government. Enterprises are required to apply low carbon technology and contribute to developing a circular economy. The following slogan reflects the aims of this zone: "to establish low cost, high efficient, and non-polluting or less polluting ecological industrial chain". In JCICEDZ, several new industrial chains have been formed based on the by-products of oil refining such as ethylene, ethylene, fertilizers, and fine chemicals. They are expected to reach an output value of 10 billion yuan within the next 2–3 years. As Fig. 8.5 shows that the industrial park adopted circular economic development principles. Through the implementation of innovative management systems and cooperation from different government bodies, three levels of circular economies were achieved: enterprises' internal circular, circular within park, and inter-park circular.

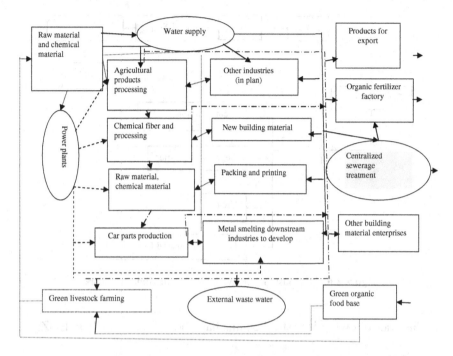

Figure 8.5. Low-Carbon Design of Ecological Industrial Park in Jilin City.
Source: Han (2006).

As Fig. 8.5 shows, the interdependency of some of the upstream and downstream industrial chains highlights the circular nature of the industrial production in the park. For example, there are inputs that are necessary for all industries including raw materials, water and power, and chemical material supply materials. And, the downstream products include organic fertilizer and building materials. The factories' raw material mainly comes from the sewerage of the upstream industries; the material can be used efficiently to realize the ideals of low-carbon production.

In the middle of the industrial chains there are four key nodes: agriculture product processing, chemical fiber and processing, raw material and chemical material, and car parts production. For example, the downstream of the car part production is metal smelting and other building materials. These industries can use the waste from the car parts industry as raw materials to produce new products. The aim is to reuse the materials totally through the lengthening of the industrial chains.

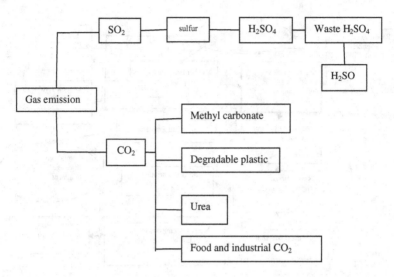

Figure 8.6. Exhaust Gas Recycle Used in the Industrial Park.

So far, the following industrial chains have been formed in JCICEDZ:

* Acrylonitrile industrial chain: Acrylonitrile is used to produce acrylic, acrylamide, polyacrylamide, carbon fiber and ABS. The byproduct, hydrocyanic acid can be used to produce Acetone cyanohydrin, methyl ester, polymer with methyl ester and waste liquid which are then used to produce acetonitrile and ammonium sulphate.
* Reuse of waste gas emissions: gas emissions are reused as shown in Fig. 8.6.
* Reuse of solid waste: The industrial park firstly recycles the waste from the power plants and the fly ash, according to the "regulation for developing new wall materials in Jilin Province". The waste-residues and fly-ash recycling enterprises have been established: "Dadi Environmental Friendly Building Material", "Jihua Northern Building Material" and "Jire Building Material". The daily waste treatment capacity has reached 2 million tons with zero discharge.
* The biochemical industrial chain has been formed. The industrial chain is illustrated below:
    * Corn $\rightarrow$ CO_2 $\rightarrow$ industrial and food deep processing.
    * Corn $\rightarrow$ Starch, fuel ethanol, butanol, glucose and vitamin $\rightarrow$ Ethyl acetate, DDGS feed and corn oil.

3.2. *Low carbon industry and energy policies*

As stipulated by both the central and Jilin provincial governments, Jilin city released its own policies and regulations, including the "Basic Policies to Attract Foreign Investment to Jilin city" and "Jilin Municipal Government's Land Transfer Fee Policy". These regulations offer various incentives for foreigners to invest in Jilin, especially in the low-carbon parks. To attract investors, all government bodies, especially the Development Zone Management Council are required to provide services 24/7 to all investors. The municipal government also guarantees the option for companies to borrow from the banks with discounted fees and lower rates. Both the provincial and municipal governments have instructed that the banks must support these borrowing terms. The regulations require:

i)   Financial support and tax reductions are used to attract foreign funds. The land-transfer fee is usually retained by the city government but for foreign funded projects that are developing new or high technology products it is returned to the local government, specifically to be used for factory infrastructure development. The local government will also return a proportion of the land transfer fee relative to the level achieved by the industry above the designated investment standard; this will be assessed after the completion of the project and will be verified by the city's investment administrative departments. The entire city's land transfer fee could be returned to the investors.

ii) External investors who provide fixed asset investments over 500,000 yuan will be eligible for local urban citizenship along with their spouses, children, and parents.

iii) The Development Zone Management Council will listen to new ideas from the business community whilst supporting daily business operations and providing comprehensive services for all processes. The council adheres to the laws, regulations, and policies made by the state and provincial governments. Being actively supervised by local government departments, the council grants permission and enforces law within the zone.

iv) Financial investment to the Jilin Chemical Industrial Park that is usually given to the local and provincial government will be re-invested into the industrial park for infrastructure development. Public projects and large infrastructure construction in the Park were not only listed as priority projects but were allocated the necessary support. During the 12th five-year plan, the policy which supports the "returning of incremental income from the basic level" will be implemented in certain development zones (including industrial clustering zones) in central cities. The returned funds will have specific uses — for the infrastructure development of the developed zone.

v)   The banks must give priority loans with lower interest rates to the industrial parks. Any special equipment purchased by enterprises in the industrial park that is used for energy saving, water saving, safe production and environmental protection purposes and are listed on the discount list for company tax, can be used for income tax deduction up to 10% of the total investment amount.

vii) Encourage leaders to communicate with Jilin Chemical Industry Circular Economy Pilot Park and encourage expert technical staff to provide technical consultation and services to the enterprises in this park. Support the development of training for staffs and list the training of employees into the Province and city Employees Strategy.

Clean energy is an important component of Jilin's attempt at building a low carbon city. Jilin has invested heavily into developing low-carbon and zero-carbon energy, including solar energy, wind energy, biomass energy, hydro energy, nuclear energy, and natural gas water compound. In April 2010, the Jilin Yulin 220 KV (Thousand Volts) power transformation plant was successfully put to use. This represents a significant improvement to the Jilin electricity network. Kaidi Low Carbon Circular Economic Industrial Demonstration Park in Jiaohe set up a combined heat-gas-steam biomass power plant with a production capacity of 4×15 MW per annum. It is also associated with the production of bio-organic fertilizer factory, with a production capacity of over 1 million tons from the residue plant ash of the biomass power plant. The forestry residue and crop straws are used by the biomass petroleum and as well as diesel processing factory with an annual production ability of 0.3–0.5 million tons.

Rapid development of the new energy sector in Jilin has enabled the government to commit to providing reliable power over the 12th five-year plan period. In the next five years, Jilin metropolitan area plans to build three more 220 KV electricity transformations plants. Together with the existing seven 220 KV transformation plant, these ten plants can provide a relatively independent power supply for Jilin and will help Jilin to realize its low carbon city dream.

3.3. *Industrial structural adjustment and industrial technology improvement*

To become a low-carbon city, Jilin needs to eliminate any outdated production lines, and to upgrade and import more environmental friendly equipment. The electricity, petrochemical, steel, paper manufacturing, automobile, and transportation industries all need to remove low-efficiency products, then upgrade equipment on a large scale and import environmental friendly devices. The Jilin Petrochemical Company Fertilizer Factory upgraded the water pump and optimized the water supply, which saved 440,000 kW/hour of electricity per annum. As set out in the low-carbon economic plan, from 2010 to 2030, the total investment required by Jilin city to develop 10 million kW of clean electricity is 110 billion yuan. The total investment required to increase ethylene production capacity is 55 billion yuan and the total investment required to increase the steel production capacity is 9 billion yuan.

Jilin city has focused on eliminating outdated production processes, equipment and products in high energy consuming, and high polluting industries such as steel, ferrous metal, chemical engineering, building materials, and power generation industries. Jilin has achieved significant progress by eliminating 1 million tons of steel production capacity from small furnaces and electric-arc furnace and 1.5 million tons of cement production capacity from hollow, wet rotary, and shaft kilns. Jilin Chemical Company shut down around 100 sets of devices with outdated technology, high pollution levels and weak competitiveness; they included ethanol production devices, aromatics extraction units, organic silicon devices, and alkyl benzene sulfonic acid devices. The energy consumption per 10,000 of the production value reduced from 5.03 tons of standard coal in 2000 to 0.53 tons of standard coal in 2008.

4. Discussion

As the central Government's experimental site for the low carbon city, Jilin as a heavy industrial city, has implemented a city-wide carbon reduction campaign. The carbon reduction actions are still in the early stage of its process. This chapter has shown that Jilin has managed to reduce its industrial energy consumption and increase development of clean energy so as to reduce carbon emission levels.

The development of the circular economy is an important measure in the construction of a low carbon city, because it supports the increase in the efficiency of material reuse and reduces carbon emissions. The core of the circular economy is in Jilin's industrial park where one enterprise's waste is used as the raw materials for another. This means that the materials are completely utilized and there is an overall reduction in carbon emissions.

Another action taken by Jilin during the process of building a low-carbon city is to push the industry structural adjustment. Jilin municipal government first targeted the big energy industries and enterprises, offering them incentives and support, rather than a penalty, to be energy efficient. Forty enterprises in the petrochemical, metallurgy, electricity, and building material industries were selected as energy reduction targets because they were large energy consumers and large contributors of carbon emission. They were encouraged to apply for energy-saving and low-carbon technology. Rewards and incentives were available for low-carbon businesses that implemented energy-saving and emission reductions. For example, the 12 major energy-saving projects saved 215,000 tons of standard coal equivalent energy. At the same time, enterprises that entered into the low-carbon economy industrial parks are being rewarded some tax relief incentives.

Jilin has established an energy consumption and carbon emission assessment system for all key industrial products. If enterprises fail to meet the standard, they are first given an extended deadline by which to reach the standards. Then if they still do not reach the target after the deadline, they receive a financial penalty and they also face the possibility of being closed down.

Jilin has done a lot in a very short period of time in order to reduce energy consumption levels. They were supported by strong government leadership. Developing a low carbon city is a long-term task and the key players for the transition that have been identified through the Jilin case are municipal government and the enterprises.

9

Regional Integration Development in Central Liaoning Urban Agglomeration

1. Introduction

Liaoning central urban agglomeration is a core region of the Northeast old industrial base including the eight prefectural-level cities such as Shenyang, Fushun, Benxi, Liaoyang, Tieling, Yingkou, and Fuxin. This region was the model for Chinese industrialization and urbanization during the planned economy; it made important contributions to the development of new China (Fan and Sheng, 2004). However, the long-term planned economic structure and the dominance of the heavy and chemical industries accelerated the systematic and structural problems. This resulted in the region being hit harder by the "Northeastern phenomenon". The duplication of dominant industries, the deepening of administrative separation, lack of inter-city economic cooperation, and weak industry associations constrained the region from capitalizing on their overall advantage. As a result, the regional economy fell far behind the coastal regions like Yangtze River delta region and Pearl River delta region. In 2003, the central government introduced a strategy for the rejuvenation of the old industrial base of Northeast China and as the center of the economic region, the Central Liaoning urban region aimed to lead by example. The Liaoning provincial government and the party committee rolled out the developmental strategy, "Building Big Shenyang Economic Zone" which aimed to better utilize the knowledge in Shenyang and the advantages of the Central Liaoning urban agglomeration in order to improvise the integrated regional development. Promoted by the Liaoning provincial government, the strategy was designed to support policy advantages, establish cooperative systems and structures, and guide the "One core-Five stripes" spatial development strategy. It should act as a catalyst for integrating and increasing the prosperity of Liaoning's central urban agglomeration. This Chapter discusses the main processes and the effects of Liaoning's central urban agglomeration.

2. Establishing Mayor and Secretary Joint Meeting System, and Forming Regional Integral Government Aid Mechanism

In 2003, the Liaoning provincial party committee promoted the integration of central urban agglomeration of Liaoning and the building up of big Shenyang economic zone, and treated it as a key strategic component in the rejuvenation of the Liaoning's old industrial base. In 2005, the Liaoning government work report explicitly proposed the strategic plan, "building Shenyang economic zone which not only leads all Northeast area, but also become competitive in China and abroad" (Lin, 2007). With the strategic support of the Liaoning provincial government and the party committee, Shenyang, Anshan, Fushun, Benxi, Yingkou, Liaoyang, and Tieling officially signed the "Central Liaoning urban agglomeration (Shenyang economic zone) cooperation agreement" with the aim of forming a regional economic community surrounding Shenyang. This agreement established cooperative principles — equality and voluntary compliance, market-orientation, complementary sharing of advantages, resource sharing, mutual development, simple tasks prioritization, and result focused — which set up more than ten cooperative sectors, such as transport, industry development, financial servicing, commercial circulation, attracting foreign investments, human capital, education and culture, tourism development, eco-environment, and communication. The mayor and secretary joint conference system was officially established.

The mayor and party secretary joint conference system was a cooperative platform for party secretaries and mayors of each city and was designed to enhance communication and cooperation, seek consensus, and fulfill mutual agreements on the ten cooperative sectors as outlined in the "cooperation agreement" and achieve cross-regional development. The integrated development of Central Liaoning urban agglomeration followed the routine government promotion mechanism of the mayor and secretary joint conference system. First, the lead group, headed by the governor of the province for the Central Liaoning urban agglomeration was set up, with the main duty of integrating leadership, decision-making, and arrangements and deliberating on the development strategy and planning. Second, the administrative body was formed known as the Central Liaoning urban agglomeration leading office, headed by the key leaders of the Liaoning development and reform committee. The office's duty is to study and write the developmental strategy of the Central Liaoning's urban agglomeration and take charge of coordination and implementation; propose government policies that promote the development of Shenyang economic zone; coordinate the planning and implementation of major projects; coordinate key problems in the development of Shenyang economic zone; manage the organization's information and statistics, and media promotion and inspections. At the municipal level, each city in the Central Liaoning's urban agglomeration set up a corresponding lead and administrative body to ensure successful implementation of the cooperative agreement. For the leading and administrative bodies at both the provincial and municipal levels, top officers were appointed at the head offices, i.e., the provincial governor and mayor were there to guarantee the authority and successful implementation of the integrated plan. Authority is a vital political resource and acts as a key influence in the regional development. If there is lack of authority in the promotion mechanism of regional integration, it is harder to integrate the interests of each city and province and the development is less likely to be achieved.

Since 2005, the mayor and secretary joint conference has been hosted annually (Table 9.1). The meetings focused on regional cooperation, evolving from single issues to integrated topics. The conference themes were usually determined in the conference working group which is comprised of the eight mayors during the previous mayor and secretary joint meeting and were based on the key issues, the Central Liaoning's urban agglomeration was facing. The choice of the themes also took into account the strategy and intention of the Liaoning provincial government and party committee.

Over the past seven years, as a result of the mayor and secretary joint conference, Central Liaoning's urban agglomeration has signed more

Table 9.1. Previous Mayor and Secretary Joint Conference Themes.

Year	Location	Themes
2005	Shenyang	"Cooperative agreement" signed, integrated development and initiated
2006	Anshan	Central Liaoning urban agglomeration — green economic zone
2007	Shenyang	Innovate on regional cooperation, promote integrated development
2008	Shenyang	Industry modernization, establishment of globally competitive equipment manufacturing base
2009	Shenyang	Promote comprehensive and coordinated reform of modern industry in Shenyang economic zone, build new Northeastern economic growth engine.
2010	Shenyang	Initiate and trial, promote comprehensive and coordinated reform, Work together in harmony, accelerate economic development
2011	Fushun	Exploration and innovation, promoting thorough implementation of the comprehensive and coordinated reform Win–win cooperation, seeking new breakthrough for modern industrial development

than 70 bilateral and multilateral cooperative agreements (Table 9.2). A comprehensive evaluation of the effect of the cooperative agreement showed that improvements in the development of infrastructure promoted the flow of economic elements and the establishment of the mutual market (Feng, 2011). First, the development of the public transport infrastructure enforced connection between the cities, and promoted the development of the integrated transport corridor which consists of a high-speed railway, inter-city railway, and hi-speed highways. The new 440 km highway surrounding Shenyang economic zone was built and put into service. All five "KaiFa (development) roads" were built and are open to traffic, and many bus routes between Shenyang–Fushun, Shenyang–Tieling, Shenyang–Anshan were incorporated into the public bus network. These developments contributed to the integration of the eight cities. The second major development was the improvement and integration of information infrastructure facilities. High-speed, efficiency, and barrier-free communication are important factors for integration.

Table 9.2.   Major Cooperative Agreements.

Cooperative fields	Major agreements	Date signed
Transport	The cooperative agreement on Central Liaoning urban agglomeration transport integration.	11 May 2015
	The framework agreement on integral development of Shenyang economic zone.	12 November 2011
Financial service	The letter of intent on city commercial banks (city credit cooperatives).	14 October 2005
	The framework agreement on financial cooperation and development in Shenyang economic zone.	12 November 2011
Human resources	The letter of intent on labor security cooperation of seven Central Liaoning cities.	19 October 2004
	The agreement on employment service resource sharing in seven Central Liaoning cities.	27 April 2005
	The framework agreement on sharing employment information and "one-card pass" medical care in Shenyang economic zone.	12 December 2011
Education and culture	The framework agreement on intellectual property cooperation in Shenyang economic zone.	21 April 2006
	The framework agreement on education integration in Shenyang economic zone.	12 November 2011
Tourism development	Cooperation program for further promotion of Shenyang economic zone tourism circle.	26 April 2005
	The agreement on tourists exchange in Shenyang economic zone's market integration.	19 May 2012
Information and communication	The framework agreement on Central Liaoning cities' information industry.	21 July 2005

Sharing the area code of 024 was always the main aim of the information integration of the Central Liaoning's urban agglomeration. On 28 August 2011, the networks in Shenyang, Fushun, and Tieling were successfully upgraded and combined to share the new area code "024". According to the plan, this change is predicted to save up to 700 million yuan for all residences and enterprises of these three cities.

3. Establishment of Shenyang City's Position of Leadership

The central city is the engine for the integration of regional development; and fully utilizing the driving effect of the central city is the key to success in the development of Central Liaoning urban agglomeration. By the time the "Central Liaoning urban agglomeration cooperative agreement" was signed in 2005, Shenyang had been established as the leader in the integral development of Central Liaoning urban agglomeration, and this boosted the progress of regional integration.

Shenyang was the economic center of the Central Liaoning urban agglomeration and had the economic foundations to lead the development of the region, with both economies of scale and financial income accounting for more than 40% of the total urban agglomeration, retail sales of consumer goods accounting for over 50%, and direct foreign investment accounting for more than 60%. By comparing Table 9.3 with Table 9.4, it is evident that since "Central Liaoning urban agglomeration cooperative agreement", Central Liaoning cities have all experienced rapid development, meanwhile, Shenyang's share of GDP and retail sales of consumer goods increased by less than 1%, the weight of Shenyang's financial income dropped by more than 5%, and actual foreign investments slumped by more than 25%. These changes demonstrated that Shenyang fully exerted its leading and driving skills as the central city and other cities embraced the much-needed opportunities to develop and consequently all the cities benefited from the development of the urban agglomeration.

Shenyang municipal government voluntarily took on the duty of coordinating and leading the regional cooperation. Shenyang municipal party committee and municipal government saw the value in utilizing the Shenyang center in the development of the Shenyang economic zone. Since the very start of integrating development, Shenyang municipal party committee and municipal government have made the promise that "Shenyang will initially lead the work and then cities that collaborate can be pulled together with the mutual goal" (Zhang, 2005). Shenyang

Table 9.3. Economy Level of Each City in Central Liaoning Urban Agglomeration and Shenyang's Weight on Total (2005).

	Total population at end of 2005('000)	GDP (billions Yuan)	Financial income (billions Yuan)	Retail sales of consumer goods (billions Yuan)	Actual foreign investments (billions $)
Shenyang	6986	208.41	13.81	91.51	2.122
Anshan	3476	101.8	5.52	22.15	0.069
Fushun	2244	39.02	2.23	17.78	0.042
Benxi	1564	34.33	2.18	8.76	0.039
Yingkou	2305	37.96	1.64	10.7	0.078
Fuxin	1927	14.26	0.74	6.56	0.013
Liaoyang	1820	33.01	1.74	9.05	0.033
Tieling	3026	26.42	1.09	9.69	0.016
Total	23348	495.21	28.96	176.19	2.413
Shenyang's share (%)	29.92	42.09	47.69	51.94	87.97

Table 9.4. Economy Level of Each City in Central Liaoning Urban Agglomeration and Shenyang's Weight on Total (2010).

	Total population at end of 2010 ('000)	GDP (billions Yuan)	Financial income (billions Yuan)	Retail sales of consumer goods (billions Yuan)	Actual foreign investments (billions $)
Shenyang	719.6	501.75	46.55	206.59	5.054
Anshan	351.8	212.50	18.00	51.42	0.905
Fushun	220.9	89.52	8.13	333.90	0.442
Benxi	154.6	86.04	7.46	192.35	0.301
Yingkou	235.5	100.25	10.01	249.75	0.860
Fuxin	192.4	37.89	3.01	149.03	0.110
Liaoyang	183.4	73.54	7.65	208.61	0.334
Tieling	305.1	72.21	8.01	22.73	0.263
Total	2363.3	1173.7	108.8	394.10	8.268
Shenyang's share (%)	30.45	42.75	42.77	52.42	61.12

initiated the formation of the regional cooperative body, the office of Shenyang economic zone development, where each department actively communicates with corresponding departments in each of the seven cities. After eight years' of integrating development, Shenyang's cohesive and driving forces have significantly improved. In 2011, at the mayor and secretary joint conference, Benxi municipal party secretary declared that "As Shenyang is marching South, Benxi has to head North. This is the very symbol of Benxi to promote the Shenyang–Benxi integration process and the only choice to build a new Benxi, and achieve sustainable development" (Jiang, 2011). Tieling municipal party committee and government also proposed, "Sticking with the principles of active involvement, willing acceptance of supporting role, promotion of advantages, comprehensive revitalization, win–win result-oriented, and accepting the benefits of Shenyang in all aspects" (Li, 2010).

4. Joint Planning in the Implementation Region

Regional planning is an important factor for good governance in urban and integrated development. Since 2005, planning for many regional decisions has been carried out, led by the Liaoning provincial government and participated by municipal governments of all eight cities. The plans promoted the development of Central Liaoning urban agglomeration, the most important regional plans are:

— Overall planning outline for the development of Central Liaoning urban agglomeration.
— Overall plan for comprehensive reform experiment of new industrialization in Shenyang economic zone.

They were organized and drafted by the Liaoning provincial development and reform committee and were authorized by Liaoning provincial people's government on 26 February 2008. The plans explicitly proposed the principle of "reciprocity and sharing of benefits" and clearly identified each city's functional position, surrounding industrial specialization and co-operation; promote the adjustment in the industrial structure and space reformation to realize "win–win" and "multilateral win" and profit sharing. The plans also proposed the establishment of the "one core, five stripes" regional industrial spatial development structure. "One-core" refers to the development of the Shenyang mega economic core zone. The one core recognizes the advantages of the driving and radiation effect Shenyang had and integrates developmental space and expands the urban function, with the aim of building a global leading equipment manufacturing base, research and development, and innovation base. It also aims to build a regional commerce logistics and finance center, science, education, and culture service center, new high-technology industry center, and establish a competitive regional center with a view to gradually develop into an international center of Northeast Asia. "Five stripes" refers to building five economic development stripes.

i). "Tonghai industry road" economic stripe was based on the Shen-Xi industry corridor and the road that was also built starting from Shenyang, going through Anshan and Yingkou and into Shen-Xi. It was designed to smoothly connect the industry structure and leading industry development of the four cities and promote the positive development interaction between hinterland and coastal areas of Liaoning, thus becoming the economic artery and important growth corridor which can lead Central Liaoning urban agglomeration to achieve high-speed growth and the development of the economic booming stripe with an expansion from Shenyang to the North and Yingkou to the South.

ii). Shenyang–Tieling industry economic stripe is based on the axis of the No. 102 national highway and expanded from Puhe new city to the South and into the Maojiadian village. This economic stripe was established to support the development of modern industry base led by new high-technology and based on mega industry projects, with a view to Tieling be the major recipient for regional industry transfer and major industry concentration, and evolve to be an important regional economic growth polar.

iii). Shenyang–Benxi industry economic stripe starts from Shenyang–Hunnan high-tech development zone to the North, and expands to Benxi economic and technology development zone, Benxi industry manufacturing zone, and Nanfen circular economic zone. This economic stripe focuses on the further processing of steel products, modern Chinese medicine and tourism, with the aim of building a

high-quality steel plate production base, supportive manufacturing
base for Shenyang equipment production industry, modern Chinese
patent medicine manufacturing base and tourism, and service industry
base. The major role of this economic stripe is to connect Shenyang,
also with a view to expand to the direction of Liaoyang, Anshang, and
Dandong.

iv). Shenyang–Fushun industrial economic stripe according to the "Shenyang
East priority — Fushun West alliance" cooperation strategy, is designed
to achieve resource sharing, bio-environment co-development, strategy
co-planning and functional co-upgrading, with the aim of developing
Shenyang–Fushun industry bio-environment ecological landscape belt
with the axis of Hun river, the mother river shared by the two cities,
Shenyang–Fushun new hi-technology concentration and build developed service industry zone and international residential, leisure, ecological tourism resorts area.

v). Shenyang–Fusxin industrial economy stripe, with the axis of No. 120
national highway (Shenyang–Xinmin section) and No. 304 national
highway (Xinmin–Fuxin section), it is built to become an important
growth polar driving Western areas of Shenyang economic zone and
the bridging tie for Shenyang–Fusxin economic cooperation and
development.

The overall proposal of the Shenyang economic zone new industrial
comprehensive reform trial was established by Liaoning provincial government following the authorization of the Shenyang economic zone
(Central Liaoning urban agglomeration) becoming a new national industrial comprehensive trial reform zone on 6 April 2010 and it was signed
by the state council of China on 16 September 2011.

The comprehensive proposal specifically set the goal of reform, building the Shenyang economic zone to be internationally competitive
advanced equipment manufacturing base, a crucial raw material supplier
and new hi-technology industry, energized regional economic center and
a national model for industrialization. By the year 2015, it is planned to
achieve regional economic integration status; by the year 2020, the
proposal aims to evolve Shenyang's economic zone into an important
economic center of Northeastern Asia. The main content of the proposal
covers structural innovation in the ten areas that drive regionally

integrated development, namely developing modern industrial structure, promoting the development of various market subjects, leading in new technology, sustaining resources, protecting the environment, exerting advantages of human resources, coordinating urban–rural development, equalizing basic public services, tax and finance, administration and openness to outside. Amongst the cities, Shenyang took charge of the fusion of industrialization and collaboration of information. Anshan continued focusing on the low-carbon economy, Fushun developed Shenyang–Fushun integration, Benxi conducted urban–rural coordination, Yingkou reenergized the port, Fuxin deepened economic transition, Liaoyang performed urban–rural integration, Tieling built eco-city etc., with a total of eight special fields.

5. Strengthening Industry Specialization

Industry integration is the major driving force for regional integration. Industry integration is based on the regional industry differentiation, and can be in the form of vertical integration by means of vertical specialization in industry development, or horizontal integration through restructuring, merging and acquisition in industry development. The underlying drive for integration is to build a mutual market, in order to optimize regional industry structure, and lift the overall competitiveness of regional industry (Wang, 2009).

5.1. *Promoting cities' industrial features, strengthening specialization and cooperation*

The eight cities in Central Liaoning urban agglomeration share a similar resource base as well as operate under the rigid region planning economy structure, which has resulted in the cities having identical pillar industries and competition outweighing cooperation. As a result, the advantage of the old industrial base was limited. From the start of regional integration in 2005, Central Liaoning urban agglomeration focused on developing six industry chains, and clarifying each city's advantage and function.

Equipment manufacturing industrial chain. The chain was built to support the center of Shenyang as the regional equipment manufacturing and R&D integrated headquarters, and the parts processing was shifted to radiant neighboring cities. Anshan developed metallurgy full-set equipment production base, which was improved by the supporting ability of Fushun and Benxi's equipment manufacturing, Liaoyang established specialized equipment production base, and Yingkou built up a ship production base.

Petrochemical industrial chain. For the center of Fushun, the aim was to develop an industry base for refined petroleum, ethylene, catalysts, and to build refinery for fine chemicals; for the center of Liaoyang, the aim was to develop three product lines including refined petroleum, ethylene and aromatics, and establish nationally important aromatics and chemical fiber raw material base. Shenyang focused on fine chemicals and chlorine alkali chemical industry. Anshan and Benxi utilized their coking by-product resources and Tieling took advantage of its coal resources by focusing on the coal chemical industry.

Steel industrial chain. With the center of Anshan Steel Co. and support from Benxi Steel Co, Yingkou's new Anshan Steel Co. branch, and Fushun Special-purpose Steel Co., the aim was to build a steel industry and to support the steel products deep processing and extend the steel industry chain.

New material chain. With the nanotechnology center in Shenyang, the aim was to turn Anshan and Benxi into new steel material industry centers, and agglomeration of new materials with Fushun, Liaoyang, and Yingkou.

New high-tech industrial chain. For the center of Shenyang, the focus was on developing key industries including integrated circuits and software, and building the national biology project, telecommunication electronics, and civilian aerial hi-tech industrial base.

Pharmaceutical manufacturing chain. For the center of Shenyang the aim was to build a platform for national new medical research and development and involve Benxi into the international production and trading standard making.

5.2. *Transforming the organization of the industries*

Developing industry agglomeration is an important method to achieve new industrialization. By building up the industrial cluster, expanding the industry chain and integrating technological and innovative resources, the aim is to enrich the depth of industries and overall competitiveness and secure the industrial base of Central Liaoning urban agglomeration. Central Liaoning urban agglomeration is focused on ten industries, and strives to move from being an "industry base" to an "industry cluster" and finally to achieve the industry specialization (Zhao, 2010).

Shenyang–Tiexi advanced equipment manufacturing industry cluster. The cluster was designed to develop equipment and support product developments based on each city's advantage and ultimately form an optimized and coordinated industry structure in the equipment manufacturing industry. The cluster focused on six competitive industries including computer numerical control machines, general petro-chemical equipment, heavy mining machinery, power transmission equipment, engineering machinery, and automobile parts and motorcars.

Shenyang aerial industry cluster. With support from the Shenyang economic zone, enterprises such as the Shenyang aircraft, Liming aircraft and the GE engine repair constitute the Shenyang aerial national hi-tech industry base. Shenyang is utilizing its equipment manufacturing and research and development skills and productivity advantage as a platform to connect to the international aerial industry.

Shenyang–Hunnan electronics and information industry cluster. The cluster focuses on developing core products such as electronic circuits and software, and establishing digital medical equipment, digital consumer goods, automobile electronics, new display parts, and embedded software.

Anshan Dadaowan Steel deep processing industry cluster. Utilizing Anshan steel resources, the cluster aims to build a world-class steel company and steel product processing base.

Fushun new material industry cluster. Based on the project of "ten million tons of refined petroleum, ten million tons of ethylene", the cluster focused on developing a new material industry that builds carbon fiber projects, especially new chemical materials, new metallic materials, and carbon fiber.

Benxi biomedicine production industry cluster. Benxi has an historic advantage in the medicine industry, and has a solid industry base of 37 pharmaceutical companies and 369 approved drugs, including 44 sole-manufacturer categories. The cluster was developed as a national level

R&D platform for new medicine, and strives to be involved in the making of standards in the international Chinese medicine production and trading, and builds the Liaoning (Benxi) biomedicine production base.

Yingkou Xianren Island petrochemical industry cluster. The cluster took full advantage of the port and imported crude oil from overseas to build the chemical-refining integrated project and to plan the development of a large shipbuilding base. Furthermore, based on the development of deep water oil port, the cluster was to become the logistic center for oil and chemical products, to promote energy and oil chemical industries and the adjacent port area's petrochemical industry.

Liaoyang aromatics and chemical fiber industry cluster. Liaoyang's chemical fiber industry is one of the national key chemical fiber bases and developed three product lines including the petrochemical industry represented by refined oil, ethylene and aromatics, fine chemicals and new chemical materials, and it is an important raw material base nationally for aromatics and chemical fiber.

Tieling special automobile industry cluster. With the aid of Shenyang and Changchun automobile industry's advantage, the cluster was to promote the merging and acquisition of car manufacturers and build the cluster to become the sole producer of Liaoning, the largest in China, and a world-famous special automobile manufacturing base, with the aim of producing special cars accounting for one quarter of the national total, and industry output of special cars accounting for one quarter of the national total.

Fuxin Zhangwu forest product processing cluster. Fuxin is rich in forest resources. As the trial location of a resource-independent city, the cluster was to be based on the regions of forestry resource advantage with the aim of developing a product deep processing chain and building the biggest forest product distribution center and forest product commerce center.

The plan for industry clustering achieved positive economic effects (Liu, 2012). Until May 2010, 2,229 companies had registered in one of the ten industrial clusters. There were 650 large companies in Shenyang–Tiexi advanced equipment manufacturing industry cluster. In 2010, the gross industry output and the growth in the cluster accounted for 67% of Shenyang–Tiexi's total output and preliminarily established the area as a globally competitive equipment-manufacturing base. In the Shenyang aerial production cluster, key projects such as Q400 airplane large parts sub-contracting project, ARJ21 engine assembly project, and Southern China airline maintenance are still under development. Shenyang–Hunnan electronics and information industry cluster had registered 300 companies, and accounted for 70% of the total software companies in Shenyang. Anshan Dadaowan steel deep processing industry cluster had been registered by 754 companies with a total investment of 66.5 billion yuan, spread across 366 projects. In the Fushun new material cluster, 24 big projects funded by 1 billion yuan investment progressed quickly, such as carbon fiber and HHPE fiber production which are leading hi-technology projects in China. Benxi biomedicine production cluster had registered 150 companies and invested 20 billion yuan in total. The 47 projects of Xinren Island petrochemical cluster have been put into production in Yingkou, with a total investment of 5,450 million yuan. Liaoyang aromatics and chemical fiber raw material industry cluster has invested in about 9.2 million yuan and achieved the output of 60 million yuan. Tieling special automobile industry cluster has registered 116 projects, of which 53 are under construction, and 11 projects have been put into production with investment of 1.4 billion Yuan. For Fuxin Zhangwu forest products processing industry cluster, 27 companies had started construction and 10 companies had been put into production with a total output of 1.2 billion yuan.

6. Establishing New Growth Space, Promoting Space Integration Development

Space integration is a vehicle for economic integration. Central Liaoning urban agglomeration's space structure was formed in the planned economy period, and reflected the situation of economic and social development (Fan and Sheng, 2004). With the implementation of reform and opening-up of policy and the transition to the market-orientated economy, the existing space structure was out of pace for the needs of regional development. In the process of promoting the integration of Central Liaoning urban agglomeration, Liaoning provincial government and local governments aimed to reshape the urban agglomeration space structure and exert space structural potential through urban integration and development of new cities and towns. At the same time, they strove to achieve an intercity connection belt accumulation effect through putting effort in to developing "five stripes", namely Shenyang–Fushun intercity belt, Shenyang–Benxi intercity belt, Shenyang–Liaoyang–Anshan–Yingkou intercity belt, Shenyang–Fuxin intercity belt and Shenyang–Tieling intercity belt. Based on 37 new cities and towns and 56 leading industry parks, the goal was to develop new growth space for the Central Liaoning urban agglomeration.

6.1. *Focusing on Shenyang–Fushun integration development, promoting intercity integral development*

Urban integration usually refers to the phenomenon of two or more cities adjacent in space and with close ties in economic and social development and sharing the characteristics of space adjacency, function connection, transport convenience, and strong belongingness. It does this through integral allocation of intercity economic elements, intercity industry allocation, infrastructure development, land development and government administration forming high-level coordination and unity, with residents softening the belongingness and mutually enjoying the fruit of development (Xing, 2007).

In recent years, through the development of intercity integrated development, Central Liaoning promoted the rational flow of (economic) elements and optimized regional space allocation and improved the competitiveness. A good case is the integrated development of Shenyang and Fushun (Sang *et al.*, 2009; Peng and Qu, 2011). The current development of Shenyang was influenced by the limitation factors such as the landscape, including the river, transport conditions, developmental base and administrative fringe, and showed obvious single-centered circular pattern. Currently, the city is strangled by urban traffic congestion, unorganized construction of the fringe area; weakening of the old urban industry parks, urgently needed upgrade and restructuring; constraints by existing urban space conditions, compared with the urgent demand and support from outer areas. Shenyang and Fushun's industry are highly correlated, very complementary, closest in terms of location, and the development focus of Shenyang–Fushun new industry district has shifted to the West. Thus, Liaoning province drew out the intercity co-development area at the boundary of Shenyang and Fushun and utilized the advantageous conditions of the area, such as eco-environment resources, land cost, existing industry base and road and other transport networks. By planning the development of functional districts such as the technology industry district, business office district, tourism and sightseeing district, leisure and holiday district, logistic district, Shenyang and Fushun's intercity space development would gradually fuse and form regional coordinated and new urban space development structure.

6.2. *Developing new cities and towns, promoting the development of intercity connection belts*

One key starting point of the integration of Shenyang economic zone and the urban integration development is the connection between Shenyang and the seven other cities. By developing a set of small cities to achieve closely-connected urban agglomeration, the region can establish important support from industry aid and also double the flow of urban and rural resources. On 10 February 2010, Liaoning provincial government issued "the notice for Shenyang economic zone intercity connection belt development and building new cities and towns" (Liaoning Provincial Government Office, 2010) and issued "The planning range of Shenyang economic zone intercity connection belt of new cities and new towns", included 37 new cities and towns, and pointed out the working focus of economic integration and urban integration development.

Liaoning provincial government also brought up specific requirements for the development of new cities and new towns: break all limitations and barriers against integration, strive for the integration of Shenyang economic zone in the areas of transportation, production elements, communication, market, households, social security, employment, and infrastructure. Innovate new structures and systems, issue and improve the policies and measures on administrative structure, land, finance and loans, subsidized loan projects, regional adjustments etc., and provide strong power for acceleration of development and good outer environment. New cities and towns should specify their leading industries, take charge of industry agglomeration development, and form the industry base for urbanization.

In the aspect of planning, each new city and town in the Shenyang economic zone should scientifically form a comprehensive plan by focusing on shaping city features and protection of the natural environment, identifying leading industries, establishing measures for sustainable development, and following the principles of "new city" and building elite model of new cities and towns. The plan also pointed out that the city should specify its overall function, coordinate the planning of new cities and towns' residence, commerce, industry, public service facilities, road and transport, urban gardening and landscaping system and city infrastructure development, with the view to forming rationally functioning, economically bonded, and newly integrated urban development.

Each city in the Shenyang economic zone is required to accelerate the planning and development of new cities and towns. According to the requirements of Shenyang economic zone's integration, urban integration and urban–rural coordinated development, each city must consider and coordinate population clustering, land consolidation, industry clustering, and equality of urban–rural public service to improvise the overall bearing capacity of new cities and towns, establish framework of new cities and towns and achieve the preliminary breakthrough of farmers by concentrating on the new establishments and industrial districts and use new methods to promote development of new cities and towns in Shenyang economic zones.

In the aspect of reform and innovation, each city in the Shenyang economic zone was required to support reform in the new cities and towns, and strengthen innovative administrative structures and systems, with a focus on facility allocation, function, administrative space division, skilled worker identification and allocation, and wages and distribution etc. Apart from that, strengthening the security of land and increasing the development of rural residential land and making use of related land exchange policies; deepening the reform of investment and finance system, tackling the problem of lack of investment, encouraging private capital investment in public service production, building new platforms for investments and finance for new cities towns; improvise the industrial upgrade, increasing the support of advantageous new industries; developing new industrial clusters with local features; deepening reform in public service structure, building livable ecological cities, and promoting the integrated development of education, health, culture, and social security systems; strengthening protection mechanisms of farmers' interests, focusing on farmers' reallocation of work and improving the service function of farmers' transferred employment. Promoting public infrastructure and support facilities, increasing input of investment and accelerating the development of new cities and towns.

In the aspect of leading structure and coordination mechanism, new cities and towns were requested to set up leading structures and organize strong working structures, specify their areas of specialization, carefully organize, thoroughly plan, and facilitate the efficient and orderly progress of every task. It was also required that all key projects are actively organized through all stages, plan the authorization of land expropriation and land requisition regarding infrastructure development and bank loans for its implementation, in order to ensure all the preliminary work for the development of new cities and towns is carried out. Also the cities and towns must make efficient and practical preferential policies to attract population and foster enterprises. The provincial government's various departments and units must improve communication and cooperation, identify and make related supportive policies and measures. They must make every effort to support the development of new cities and towns in Shenyang economic zone.

6.3. *Planning layout-oriented industry parks, strengthening space integrated industry support*

Liaoning provincial government proposed that new cities and towns must take charge of developing industry clusters, every new city or new town must plan a leading industry park with a minimum of 10 billion yuan in sales volume; develop new industry with local features, achieve innovation in administrative structure, human resource structure, government service structure, investment and finance structure and land management etc., and make it a model city or town for the comprehensive and support reform. The leading industry park for the new city or town will lead the integrated optimized allocation of resources, which will support the new industrialization and urbanization and interactive development.

According to the economic base and industrial features, Liaoning provincial government planned 56 leading industry parks, focused on different industry areas to avoid the structure and industry convergence among new cities and thus the problems of over-heated and blind competition arises. For example, Shenyang–Tiexi industry new city chose the equipment industry as its leading industry, comparing to new material industry for Fushun–Shenfu new city, biomedicine for Benxi–Shenxi new city. With a view to location and layout, Shenyang has 26, Anshan has 5, Fushun has 2, Benxi has 6, Fuxin has 1, Liaoyang has 12, and Tieling has 4. Among those, Benxi biomedicine, Fushun advanced energy equipment, Fuxin hydraulic equipment, Liaoning aromatics and fine chemicals were all approved to be national new high-technology industrial bases.

In order to promote the projects of the leading industry parks, Liaoning provincial government issued "Administrative measures for subsidized loan for industry park projects of new cities and towns in Shenyang economic zone intercity connection belt" (Department of Finance, Liaoning Provincial Government, 2010) and Liaoning Provincial Development and Reform Committee and Liaoning Financial Bureau mutually approved and issued the subsidies. In 2010, Liaoning province for the first time issued subsidies for projects in the leading industry parks of Shenyang economic zone, with 65 projects in total listed in the first subsidy plan, with a total subsidy amount of 121.7873 million yuan. Regarding financial support, in 2011 Liaoning provincial government made payments of 500 million yuan to support project development in the leading industries of the Shenyang economic zone. As a whole, Liaoning provincial government's financial support acted as an important engine for the development of industry parks, promoted the development of new cities and towns, and accelerated the integrated development of Central Liaoning agglomeration.

7. The Inspiration on Regional Integration Development

Regional development is a sophisticated and systematic project, a development process from low to high levels. Regional integration is also a dynamic process of integrating regional markets involving the free flow of products, elements, labor and capital, between geo-related provinces, areas inside provinces and cities seeking development and implementation of economic unity and adjustments of different degrees in the social reproduction. Its goal is to carry out rational specialization in the region, optimize allocation of space for resources, improve efficiency in resource usage and promote mutual prosperity (Liang, 2009). Over the past eight years, it shows that accelerating regional integration processes must rely on fully exerting government's function, building active regional coordination mechanisms and structured plans, making practical regional plans and accomplishing tasks in the sequence of difficulty (Easy first, hard next) and advancing to perfect order.

7.1. Fully taking advantage of every level of government's promotion effect

Throughout the development history of Central Liaoning urban agglomeration, the top–down approach of policies has always been critical in shaping the area (Zhang *et al.*, 2010). After the establishment of new China, Central Liaoning region had the potential to become an advanced heavy industry where cities and towns are focused upon and this could not be achieved without the national industry policy support and regional policy support. Since the implementation of the strategy for revitalization of Northeastern China, the fast development of Central Liaoning area integration also relied on polices that are being carried out and promoted by each level of governments.

Central government level: From 2003, the central party and State Council complemented the strategy of revitalizing the Northeastern old industrial base and made special polices to support the revitalization. In 2010, the Shenyang economic zone (central Shenyang urban agglomeration) was upgraded to be a national strategy and became a trial zone for new industrialization. In 2011, the "overall plan for comprehensive and support reform trial of Shenyang economic zone's new industrialization" was issued and provided strategic guidance for the integrated development of the Central Liaoning urban agglomeration.

The provincial government level: Liaoning provincial government actively promoted the coordination and cooperation of the strategy. One example is building the key cities' combined conference system for the economic zone, by discussing critical problems in cooperation with the economic zone at the annual conference; establishing coordination and communication systems and enhancing the exchange of intercity political work information; building follow-up and process checking systems and ensuring the solid application of the economic cooperation agreement. To realize these goals, investment in infrastructure has been given higher priority, such as regional transport infrastructure (including constructing highways surrounding the economic zone and intercity railways) and it is expected to consolidate the physical base for the integration between cities in the economic zone.

Municipal government level: Each city actively moved to become integrated within the region whilst at the same time sticking with the focus of self-functional enhancement and structural adjustment. Shenyang, as the central city of Shenyang economic zone, achieved urban space expansion and created a new industrial layout. This was achieved through four big space development and structural adjustments including the redevelopment of Tiexi district. Shenyang upgraded the urban functions through the "Golden gallery project" and the restructuring of urban space. Surrounding cities also followed the pathway of the center city. Shenyang–Fushun, Shenyang–Benxi, Shenyang–Tieling strove for overall integration and city-to-city integration by developing infrastructure in the connection belt and the fusion of urban land and space.

7.2. Establishing a leading body with authority for regional coordination

Currently, most Chinese urban agglomeration area's developments are facing problems such as administrative barriers, identical industry structure and unhealthy competition, and more are showing the feature of "administrative regional economy" instead of "regional economy" with the aim of promoting the development of regional integration. A coordinating body with some authority must be established, and focused on the bigger picture in dealing with problems. When conflicts of interest occur between cities, it is the higher level of government that was sought for support and judgment. Liaoning provincial government became the working leader in the Central Liaoning agglomeration development, with the provincial governor being the group leader meaning the group had authority. This facilitated the coordination of conflicts between cities and had the advantages of promoting cooperation between provincial departments and each city. The provincial level coordination system ensures the progress of Central Liaoning agglomeration development.

7.3. Focusing on the instructional role of the regional plan

In the process of regional integration, each city in the urban agglomeration must identify its development goals, industrial features, and functional location, and then plan first before action by way of issuing and then implementing a practically achievable development plan. Also, each city needs to overcome the insufficiency of market self-generated power and use administrative power tailored for the situation and to promote urban agglomeration. Central Liaoning urban agglomeration had a focus on the instructive role of planning at the beginning of the integrated development, and made the "Central Liaoning urban agglomeration development plan", "Outline for overall planning of Central Liaoning urban agglomeration economic zone development", "Plan for Shenyang economic zone intercity connection space development", the regional level overall plan and special plan, which largely accelerated the establishment of urban agglomeration integration.

7.4. *Easy tasks first and hard tasks next, promoting regional integrated processes in order*

The integration of Central Liaoning urban agglomeration is a sophisticated project, involving interest adjustments in every district and department. The agglomeration implemented the working principles of easy tasks first and hard tasks next, with a gradual advancement in the order. Focusing on important and breakthrough points, starting with the easiest task first and then moving on to the harder ones as per the difficulty in the level of cooperation in each industry and field. First, breakthrough was achieved in easy public transport integration and brought real benefits to each city in the Central Liaoning agglomeration and won general support in the region. The next step extended to fields such as commerce, finance, information, tourism, and human resources and improved the power for the development of urban agglomeration as well as building the network structure for integrated development. Furthermore, bilateral cooperation was based on the fact that the region had a good base and integrated development could be implemented.

10

Towards a Northeast China Model?

The cities of Northeast China had two major problems to overcome during their economic development and transition period: the prospect of becoming ghost towns and the economic and social burden of that the dysfunctional state-owned enterprises (SOEs) had placed on the cities. Over the last decade, through the implementation of various different policy changes not only have the major cities not become ghost towns, they have all managed to survive, revitalize, and further develop their local economies. After more than two decades since the start of the opening-up reform the "planning mentality" inherited from the Mao era has almost faded away, and the market mentality is now more prevalent and is having a greater influence on economic decision making. When the NCRP was first introduced in the early 2000s, there was little resistance or dissidence to the implementation of increasingly market-oriented economic practices. The NCRP has been viewed as a positive development and a good opportunity for the local economy to develop. Big demonstrations by laid-off workers have been relatively rare since the early 2000s.

The previous chapters have demonstrated how cities in Northeast China have used different methods to achieve revitalization. It should be noted from our discussions that the official title of the revitalization program reflects an incomplete definition of the actual processes and outcomes; in other words, the term "revitalization" implies that the existing industrial bases were to be maintained and regenerated. This term, therefore, does not fully capture and may even obscure the nature and dynamics of these innovative economic activities that are not only adapted to the characteristics of existing local industry but also go beyond the traditional boundaries of the local industry.

Most industrial bases in Northeast China were initially built as part of the colonial industrialization undertaken by Russians and Japanese since the 1900s and then were maintained as part of the big push for industrialization after the foundation of socialist China. The revitalization of some cities in the West China has focused on their long-standing and traditional industrial sectors. Comparatively, our case studies show that the cities in Northeast China have looked for various ways to revitalize their economies specific to their circumstances, such as utilizing existing industrial structures and comparative geographical and economic advantages. For example, Fuxin has almost totally closed down its coal mining and associated sectors which it relied on as a resource-dependent city. In addition, in many cases in Northeast China, the post-transformation urban industries are characterized by a mixture of old and new elements and sectors. For example, the petrochemical industry in Dalian, the machinery industry in Tiexi machinery, and the oil drilling industry in Daqing were the traditional industries of these cities. They have all been successfully restructured and repacked through various approaches such as industrial upgrades (in all cities studied), extension of the industrial chain (in Daqing), and the de-carbonization of the industrial sector to pursue a greener and more sustainable economy (in Jilin). Meanwhile, an information technology (IT) industry has been newly developed in Dalian and the old, traditional industries have been replaced by a modern agricultural industry in Fuxin. Therefore, the term revitalization merely tells a part of the full story (e.g., some old sectors were upgraded) but it reveals less about the fact that there have been new aspects integrated into the new wave of (re)development.

These cities in Northeast China share some common characteristics during the implementation of the NCRP. First, the development pattern under the NCRP, which is a lower policy priority, is different from those under the GWDP and the coastal development. Compared to the provinces in the western region and the hot spots of development in the coastal provinces, the cities in Northeast China (except Dalian) were not on the central government's priority list before the implementation of NCRP. The actual financial support of 60 billion yuan supplied by the NCRP to the SOEs was inadequate to solve the problem once and for all. The western region did not face the same difficulty as the central government made more funding available to the western provinces under the so-called "four seventy-percent" policy. This policy was designed for the GWDP (i.e., the central government promised to provided no less than 70% of multilateral funds, 70% of fiscally supported projects, 70% of policy loans, and 70% of development bonds), implying that the central government supplied at least 70% of the funds. As a result, substantial capital inflow largely driven by the central government has been piped into the western region to invest in the infrastructure and other key projects. These favorable policies were unavailable to provinces in Northeast China. Although the NCRP has been financially supported by the central government, the scale of capital inflow from the central government was much smaller than that obtained by West China. The case studies show that although the funding from the central government was limited for the Northeast region, the local governments managed to secure funding for the restructuring programs from other sources. In fact, these cities successfully applied an approach that combined institutional opportunities and market forces rather than waiting for a central funding scheme.

The second common characteristic across the cities in Northeast China is that they have changed their economic portfolios from a single industrial sector to an industrial chain including a number of follow-up industries. Most economic centers in Northeast China were developed on the basis of a single, predominant economic sector, such as coal mining, steel making, forestry or oil exploitation. But many of them have experienced resource depletion and environmental degradation. After the revitalization, industrial chains (e.g., from oil drilling to oil processing) have been established in the region and have created new opportunities for laid-off workers and new workers joining the labor force.

Third, Northeast China's rapid urban transformation over the past decade, as empirical studies prove, has been the result of the combined effects of domestic and global forces, as well as the national and locality-specific factors of the cities. Such forces and factors have affected China's multiple and simultaneous transformations. Most importantly, the party-state's presence at the central and local levels is strong and persistent. This is exemplified by its decisive role in urban economic transformation and its dual identities both as a regulator and participant in economic production, industrial restructuring, and urban development. Walder (1997) argues that the Chinese state is essentially an ensemble of economic actors, and he points out that government officials behave as entrepreneurs, corporate management teams, silent partners, and investors in the private economy. The long arms and (in)visible hands of the state, in their various practical forms, have played a critical role in the urban restructuring.

Fourth, the revitalization of the Northeast China features a model of "incubation from inside". Unlike the coastal cities, global forces have not always had a strong presence in the restructuring of urban industries of Northeast China. This is changing as shown by the increase in foreign investments in the area of automobile industry. It is predicted that the economy of scale, once fully built, will attract more attention from global investors in the near future. This "inside" transformation experience indicates that sustainable economic growth can also be achieved by supporting old urban economic sectors and does not necessarily need to be led by newly introduced economic sectors. In addition, SOEs which have been portrayed as negative to China's modernization by the literature and media are in fact not always a burden but can be the key factors for urban economic transformation.

The economic future of cities in Northeast China will be, however, determined by a large extent of their abilities to reestablish traditional links with neighboring economies including Japan, South Korea, North Korea, Russia, and Mongolia. The scope for cross-border economic development is huge. Although further economic cooperation between the economies is challenging, it will be rewarding for the region as a whole. Establishment of various types of economic cooperation among the countries of North East Asia are already underway. It is expected that Northeast China will significantly benefit from the cooperation, when it comes into full operation.

Finally, Northeast China's urban revitalization experience should be considered as an integral part of the China Model — China's economic success under an authoritarian political system in the over past 30 years, if the model does exist. This rust-belt transition is not uncommon in industrialized economies. Chinese coastal cities transformation which has been predominantly driven by the external forces and the private sectors does not uncover much about the transition of an urban economy which was dominated by the state sector. Transition in Northeast China was mainly led by the government and the SOEs. These features should be considered as a part of the China Model.

Of the Northeast China's GDP, the majority was being produced by SOEs, many of which were actually loss-making. Therefore, revitalizing Northeast China was an ambitious project for a region that had few of the advantages of the fast-growing coastal areas like the Pearl River and Yangzi deltas, with their better access to investment, strong private sectors, and know-how from abroad. There is much work still to be done, including furthering the reform of SOEs and improving social-security provisions for ageing and laid-off workers. But a decade on, the Northeast's revival is regarded as one of the recent successes of the Party and the Hu–Wen administration. Since the mid 1990s, Northeast China's GDP has grown faster than the other three main economic regions of China (namely the East, Center and the West). These regions have outpaced national GDP growth every year since the late 1990s, with a markedly wider lead since 2008.

This leaves us thinking about some broader questions: to what extent does Northeast China offer a distinctive way of re-industrialization in a state sector dominated region? To what degree does Northeast China's experience contribute to China Model, which is characterized by success-ful co-existence of free market and an authoritarian state in order to main-tain economic growth and political stability? And, what are the appeals and limitations of the Northeast China transformation?

References

Administrative Committee of Daqing High-tech Industry Development Zone (2005). *Daqing gaoxin jishu chanye kaifaqu guanweihui. Laolao bawo xin chuangye zhuti zai 'erci chuangyi' zhong zaizhu huihuang* (Firmly grasp the theme of innovation and entrepreneurship and achieve new progress in the "second pioneering development"). Available at http://www.most.gov.cn/ztzl/gjgxjskfq/gxd-fjlcl/200508/t20050826_24237.htm. Accessed on 26 June, 2013 (in Chinese).

Bao, ZD, XF Cao and Q Chang, *et al.*, (2006). *2006 nian Zhongguo dongbei diqu fazhan baogao, Beijing: Shehui kexue chubanshe* (2006 Development Report of China's Northeast Region), Beijing: Social Sciences Academic Press (in Chinese).

Bradbury, JH and I St.-Martin (1983). Winding down in a Quebec mining town: A case study of Schefferville. *The Canadian Geographer*, 27(2), pp.128–144.

Breslin, S (2011). Rethinking the "China model". Available at http://www.eastasia-forum.org/2011/12/29/rethinking-the-china-model/ Accessed on 26 June, 2013.

Case summary of old industrial bases in Ruhr of Germany and Lorraine of France (2011). *Deguo luer he faguo luolin laogongye jidi gaizao de anli zongjie.* Available at http://wenku.baidu.com/view/e9fda21514791711cc7917f7. html. Accessed on 26 June, 2013 (in Chinese).

Cai, Y (2005). *State and Laid-Off Workers in Reform China: The Silence and Collective Action of the Retrenched.* London and New York: Routledge.

Chai, N and MJ Choi (2012). The utilization planning of historic and cultural buildings in declined region: In the case of Gongrencun region in Shenyang city of China. *Advanced Materials Research*, 361–363, pp. 1109–1116.

Chang, H-J (2002). *Kicking Away the Ladder: Development Strategy in Historical Perspective*. London, UK: Anthem Press.

Chen, C, GQ Li and XH Yang (2004). *Dongbei laogongyejidi xinxing gongyehua zhilu: zenyang renshi dongbei. Changchun: Dongbei, shifandaxue chubanshe (Path for New Industrialization of Northeast Region-How to know the Northeast Region)*. Changchun: Northeast Normal University Press (in Chinese).

Chen, P (2011). *Qudong weilai xinyinqing-dalian laogongyejidi banian zhuanxing zhilu. Dalian ribao* (Driving the future of the new engine — the road of eight-year restructuring and development in the old industrial bases of Dalian). Dalian Daily on 25 May 2011 (in Chinese).

Chen, XS (2009). *Shenyang tiexi jiugongyequ gengxin celue. Harbin: Harbin gongyi daxue (Shenyang City Tiexi District Old IndustriL Base Revitalising Strategy Study)*. Harbin: Harbin Institute of Technology (in Chinese).

Chen, Y (1993). *Zhongguo laogongye zhongxin de xinshuai fenxi. Zhongguo jingji wenti* (Rising and fall of Chinese old and new industrial centres). *Economic Issues in China*, (2), pp. 18–26 (in Chinese).

Chen, Y (2006). *Dongbudiqu shuaixianfazhan de kexue neihan. Wenhuibao* (Scientific connotation of eastern region to lead the development). *Wenhui News*. On 16 June 2006 (in Chinese).

Chen, YF (2004). *Cong bijao youshi kan zhusanjaodiqu de chanye jiegou zhuanxing*. The industrial restructuring in the Pearl River Delta region from the perspective of comparative advantage. *Pearl River, Economics*, (5) pp. 12–19. (in Chinese).

Chen, YJ (2003). *Dongbei liaogongyejidi jiben qingkuang diaocha baogao. Jingji yanjiu cankao* (Research report of basic conditions of Northeast old industrial base). *Review of Economic Research*, (77), pp. 2–13 (in Chinese).

Chinese Communist Party Shenyang City Tiexi District Party School (2008). *Zhonggong Shenyang Tiexi quwei dangxiao, tiexi "gongyewenhua" tansuozhilu. Shenyang ganbu xuekan* (Searching for the Tiexi culture). *Shenyang Cadres Journal*, (10) 4, pp. 47–49 (in Chinese).

Cohen, B (2006). Urbanization in developing countries: Current trends, future projections, and key challenges for sustainability. *Technology in Society*, 28(1–2), pp. 63–80.

Cui, WT (2008). *Dongbei laogongye jidi zhenxing yu quyu jingji chuangxin (Northeast Old Industrial Base Revitalization and Regional Economic Innovation)*. Beijing: Economic Management Publishing House (in Chinese).

Dagoum, AS and AS Barkerts (2010). Pathways to low-carbon economy for the UK with the macro econometric E3MG model. *Energy Policy*, (38), pp. 3067–3077.

Dalian City Bureau of Statistics and National Bureau of Statistics Dalian Investigation Team (2005). *Dalian tongjiju, guojia tongjiju, Dalian diaochadui. Dalian tongji nianjian. Beijing: zhongguo tongjiju chubanshe.* (*Dalian Statistics Yearbook, 2004*). Beijing: China Statistics Publishing (in Chinese).

Dalian City Bureau of Statistics and National Bureau of Statistics Dalian Investigation Team (2011). *Dalian tongjiju, guojia tongjiju, Dalian diaochaduei, Dalian tongji nianjian. Beijing: zhongguo tongjiju chubanshe* (*Dalian Statistics Yearbook, 2011*). Beijing: China Statistics Publishing (in Chinese).

Dallas, S (1985). *Colorado Ghost Towns and Mining Camps.* Norman: University of Oklaboma Press.

Daniel, RD and LH Stuart (1987). *Revival in the Rust Belt.* Michigan: University of Michigan Press.

Department of Finance, Liaoning Provincial Government, 2010. "*Shengyang jingjiqu chengji lianjiedai xincheng xinshizhen zhudao chanye xiangmu tiexi zijin guanli banfa*" (Administrative measures for subsidized loan for industry park projects of new cities and towns in Shenyang economic zone intercity connection belt), Department of Finance, Liaoning Provincial Government, Document file No. 605 (in Chinese).

Diao, CB (2001). *Dalian xiandaihua guoji chengshi jianshe fanglue. Dalian: Dalian chubanshe* (*The Building Strategy of Modern International City in Dalian*). Dalian: Dalian Press (in Chinese).

Din, D and J Zhou (2008). *Woguo ditan jingji fazhan moshi dei shixian tujeng he zhengce jianyi "Huanjingbaohu yu xvnhuan jingji* (Realization approach and policy recommendations of low-carbon economic development model in China). *Environmental Protection and Recycling Economy*, 28(3), pp. 4–5 (in Chinese).

Ding, SB (2003). *Dongbei "xianxiang" zhengjie fenxi yu chulu de tantao. Xiandai chengshi yanjiu* (The problem of the northeast China: Why and the way out). *Urban Research*, (6), pp. 6–9 (in Chinese).

Dong, GX (2012). *Dalian dongbei hangyun zhongxin jianshe jiasu benpao. Dalian ribao.* (Accelerated run for construction of Dalian international shipping center in Northeast Asia). Dalian Daily on 5 July 2012 (in Chinese).

Dong, F (2007a). *Dongbanxinjian- Shenyang tiexi liaogongyejidi zhenxing de moshi xuanze. Guotuziyuan* (Moving out from the East and revitalising the

Tiexi, Shenyang old industrial base). *National Land Resource*, (5), pp. 23–27 (in Chinese).

Dong, F (2007b). *Zhenxing Shenyang tiexi gongyequ de lujing xuanzhe he jiben jingyan* (Path selection and basic experiences of revitalising Tiexi district, Shenyang City industrial base). *Macro Economic Management*, (7), pp. 67–69 (in Chinese).

Dong, S, Z Li, B Li and M Xue (2007). Problems and strategies of industrial transformation of China's resource-based cities. *China Population, Resources and Environment*, 17(5), pp. 12–17.

Dong, ZK (1999). *Guanyu "156 xiang" di queli. Zhongguo jingjishi yanjiu* (About the Establishing of the 156 Projects). *Researches in Chinese Economic History*, (4), pp. 93–107 (in Chinese).

Dong, ZK (2004). *Cong ershishiji houbanye dongbai jijian touzi di tezheng kan liaogongyijidi de zhenxing. Zhonggong dangshi yanjiu* (From the features of infrastructure construction investment of Northeast region in second half of 20th century to study the revitalization of the old industrial base). *Journal of Chinese Communist Party History Studies*, (5), pp. 50–56 (in Chinese).

Economist (2011). *Rustbelt Recovery*. Available at http://www.economist.com/node/18332894. Access on 26 June 2012.

Engel, B (2006). Public space in the Blue Cities in Russia. *Progress in Planning*, 66(3), pp. 147–239.

Fan, J, W Sun and X-F Fu (2005). *Woguo kuangye chengshi chixufazhan de wen-tichengyin yu celue. Ziranziyuan xuebao* (Sustainable development of mining cities in China: problems, causes and policies). *Journal of Natural Resources*, 20(1), pp. 68–77 (in Chinese).

Fan, F and M Sun (2008). Regional Inequality in China, 1978–2006. *Eurasian Geography and Economics*, 49(1), pp. 1–20.

Fan, J and K Sheng (2004). *Liaoning zhongbu chengshiqun fazhan de jingji jichu fenxi. Chengshi guihua* (Analysis on economic base of the city cluster in central Liaoning Province). *City Planning Review*, 28(1), pp. 37–41 (in Chinese).

Fasenfest, D and J James (2003). An anatomy of change and transition: The automobile industry of Southeast Michigan. *Small Business Economics*, 21(2), pp. 153–172.

Feng, GS (2011). *Shenyang jingjiqu xinxing gongyehua he quyu yitihua jinzhan yu chengxiao. Liaoning jingji* (New industrialization in Shenyang economic zone and progress of regional integration and effectiveness). *Liaoning Economy*, (11), pp. 28–30 (in Chinese).

Feng, GS and GF Long (2000). *Jingji jiegou zhuanxing yu Liaoning laogongye jidifuxing. Shehuikexuejikan* (Economic structural transformation and revitalisationg of Liaoning Province old industrial base). *Social Science Magazine*, (6), pp. 77–80 (in Chinese).

Florida, R (2010). *The Great Reset: How New Ways of Living and Working Drive Post-Crash Prosperity*. New York: Harpper.

Fu, XD (2007). *Xunhuan jingji yu quyujingji. Beijing: Jingjiribao chubanshe* (*Cyclic Economy and Regional Economy*). Beijing: Economy Daily Publishing (in Chinese).

Fu, Y, YH Ma and YJ Wu, *et al.*, (2008). *Ditan jingji defazhanmoshi yanjiu Zhongguo renkou, ziyuan yu huanjing* (Study of low-carbon economic development model). *Chinese Population, Resource and Environment*, 18(3), pp. 14–19 (in Chinese).

Grabher, G (1993). The weakness of strong ties: the lock-in of regional development in the Ruhr area. In *The Embedded Firm: On the Socioeconomics of Industrial Networks*, G Grabher (ed.), pp. 255–277. London: Routledge.

Greg, RG and R Palmer (2010). *Eventful Cities-Cultural Management and Urban Revitalisation*. Oxford: Butterworth-Heinemann Ltd.

Guo, XY and JJ Xu (2011). *Guanyu shiyou ziyuanxing chengshi xiandaihua zhuanxing de sikao. Chongqing kejixueyuan xuebao (shehueikexueban)* (Reflections on the transformation of the oil resources of urban modernization). *Journal of Chongqing Institute of Technology (Social Science Edition)*, (13) (in Chinese).

Han, L (2006). *Jilinsheng laogongyejidi de shengtai fazhan moshi yanjiu*. (Study for Jilin Province old industrial base ecological industrial development model), Changchun: Northeast Institute of Geography and Agroecology, Chinese Academy of Sciences, PhD dissertation (in Chinese).

Han, Y (2004). *Shenyang zhuangbei zhizaoye chongjian yanjiu, Beijing: Qinghuadaxue* (Study for reforming equipment manufacturing industry of Shenyang City). Beijing: Qinghua University Press, (in Chinese).

He, L, Z Ping and Q, C. Ye (2009). Economic vulnerability of mining city — A case study of Fuxin city, Liaoning Province, China. *Chinese Geographical Science*, 19(3), pp. 211–218.

He, R (2007). *Shenyang tiexi qu yizuo zhengshi nenggou yi zenyang de sudu bianqian shidaijianzhu* (How soon can Shenyang Tiexi district transform). *Conventional Architecture*, (1), pp. 128–131 (in Chinese).

Heilongjiang economic development, Editorial Board (1999). *Heilongjiang jingji-fazhan wushinian. Harbin: Heilongjiang renmin chubanshe* (Fifty years of Heilongjiang economic development). Harbin: Heilongjiang People's Publishing House (in Chinese).

Heilongjiang Provincial Government (2005). *Heilongjiangsheng zhengfu daqing ziyuanxing zhengshi ke chixu fazhan shidian fangan* (The pilot program of Daqing's sustainable development). Available at http://www.daqing.gov.cn/ztrd/gzkcxfz/gndt/10/19298.shtml. Accessed on 25 Oct 2005 (in Chinese).

He, ZH and XR Wang (2006). *Fuxin zhuanxing mubiao: jianshe xinxing nengyuan jidi. Jingji ribao* (Aim for Fuxin City's transformation: Building new energy base). Economy Daily, 18 Oct 2006 (in Chinese).

High, SC (2003). *Industrial Sunset*. Toronto: University of Toronto Press.

Hospers, G-J (2004). Restructuring Europe's rustbelt. *Intereconomics*, 39(3), pp. 147–156.

Hou, Q (2007). *Ziyuan kujiexing chengshi chanye zhuangxing de pingjia- Fuxin jingji zhuangxing pingjia fenxi. "Ziyuan yu chanyi"* (Evaluation on industrial transformation of the resource-exhausted cities — Evaluation and analysis of economical transition in Fuxin). *Resources and industry*, 9(2), pp. 1–4. (in Chinese).

Hou, ZQ (2010). *Zhuazhu fazhan lishixing xinjiyu jiakuai fuxinjingji zhuangxing zhenxing. Dongbeixinwenwang* (Grasping the Historical Opportunity to Accelerate Fuxin City Economic Transformation and Revitalisation). Northeast News Website. Available at http://liaoning.nen.com.cn/liaoning/492/3483992. shtml (in Chinese).

Hu, C. and X Liu (2011). Deepening the reform of state-owned enterprises and accelerating the revitalization of old industrial bases. *Applied Mechanics and Materials*, (58–60), pp. 642–646.

Hu, CL (2011). *Zhusanjiao diqu chanye jiegou zhuanxing yanjiu. "Dangdaijingji"* (Industrial restructuring in the Pearl River Delta region). *Modern Economy*, (10), pp. 73–77 (in Chinese).

Huang, ZH (2002). *Dalian jingying chengshi di linian he shijian. Dongbei caijing daxuexuebao* (The urban management philosophy and practice in Dalian operation city). *Journal of Dongbei University of Finance and Economics*, (2), pp. 23–25 (in Chinese).

Hudong Document of Tiexi District (2011). *Tiexiqu. Hudobaike* [Online] Available at http://www.hudong.com/wiki/%E9%93%81%E8%A5%BF% E5%8C%BA. Accessed on 22 Mar 2011 (in Chinese).

Hui, WL (2009). *Yangzhou fangdichanye yao "ditan" liao. Yangzhou shibao* (Real Estate Industry of Yangzhou City going Low carbon). Yangzhou Daily, 29 Dec 2009 (in Chinese).

Inayatullah, S (2011). City futures in transformation: Emerging issues and case studies. *Futures*, 43(7), pp. 654–661.

James, JH (1999). *Images of the Rust Belt.* Kent, OH: State University Press.

Jiang, GG (2006). *Dongbeidiqu xunhuan jingji fazhan yanjiu. Dongbeilinye daxue* (Northeast region cyclic economy development study). Northeast Forestry University (in Chinese).

Jiang, R (2011). *Jiakuai jianshe zhongguo yaodu tuijin shenben yitihua- zai 2011 nian Shenyang jingjiqu shuji shizhang lianxi huiyishang de fayan. Benxi xinwenwang* (Accelerate the development of Chinese medicine metropolis and promote Shenyang–Benxi integration). Benxi News Net. Available at http:// bx.nen.com.cn/82483163292499968/20111114/2537185.shtml. Accessed on 25 June 2013 (in Chinese).

Jin, FJ, PY Zhang and J Fan (2006). *Dongbeidiqu zhenxing yu kechixu fazhan zhanlve yanjiu* (Revitalisation and sustainable development strategy study) Beijing: The Commercial Press. (in Chinese).

Knox PL (1991). The restless urban landscape: Economic and sociocultural change and the transformation of metropolitan Washington, DC. *Annals of the Association of American Geographers*, 81(2), pp. 181–209.

Knox, PL (1993). *The Restless Urban Landscape.* Englewood Cliffs: Prentice Hall.

Lan, Y (2003). *Yao cheng dongbei, xian cheng dongbeiren. Fenghuangzhoukan* (Change the residents of Northeast region before revitalizing the Northeast region). *Phoenix Weekly*, (26), pp. 58–61 (in Chinese).

Li, CG and ZQ Li (1996). *"Dongbei xianxiang" tezheng ji xingcheng yinsu. Jingjidili* (The features and causes of Northeast Phenomenon). *Economic Geology*, 16(1), pp. 34–38 (in Chinese).

Li, H (2000). *"Dongbei xianxiang": wenti de shizhi yu genyuan. Guanlishijie* (The northeast Phenomenon: fundamentals and causes of the problem). *Management World*, (4), pp. 206–207 (216) (in Chinese).

Li, HY (1993). *Guanyu Shenyang tiexi gongyequ zongti gaizao de diaochabaogao Zhongguo gongyi jingji* (Investigation report about the reformation of Tiexi district, Shenyang City industrial zone). *China Industrial Economy*, (4), pp. 60–65 (in Chinese).

Li, JY (2001). *Guanyu Dalianshi jingji fazhan moxing de zhanlve sikao, Dongbeiya luntan* (Strategic thinking of Dalian City economic development model). *Northeastern Summit*, (3), pp. 12–16 (in Chinese).

Li, SL (2010). *2010 nian tiexiqu zhengfu gongzuobaogao. Shenyang: Shenyang tiexiqu zhengfu* (Year 2010, Tiexi Government Report). Shenyang: Shenyang City Tiexi District Government (in Chinese).

Li, TB and SB Wang (2011). *Dalian zizhu chuangxin shixian laogongyejidi zhanlve zhuanxing. Jingjiribao* (Independent innovation for achieving the strategic transformation of the old industrial bases in Dalian) Economy Daily, 17 June 2011 (in Chinese).

Li, WK (2010). *Jiasu shentie tongchenghua bufa. Shangyang renbao* (Accelerate the pace of Shenyang railway), Shenyang Daily, 7 April 2010 (in Chinese).

Li, XL and JF Nan (2011). *Shiyou ziyuanxing chengshi de xunhuan jingji jianshe yu xinnengyuan fazhan* (Recycling economy construction and development of new energy in oil resources cities). *Yunnan Social Sciences*, (1), pp. 101–105 (in Chinese).

Li, XX, GZ Tian and CH Miao (2010). *Quyv zhongxin chengshi jingji zhuanxing: Jizhi yu moshi.* Chengshifazhan yanjiu (Economic Transformation of Regional Centre cities' mechanisms and models). *Urban Development*, 17(4): 26–32 (in Chinese).

Li, Y (2009). *Chengdu jiangjian quanguo shouge lingnengyuan zhineng zhuzhai shifanqu. Chengdu shangbao* (Chengdu City will build the first in China zero energy consumption intelligent houses demonstration area). Chengdu Commercial Paper, 27 Dec 2009 (in Chinese).

Li, ZF and YH Zheng (2010). *"Ditanchengshi" de shixian jizhi yanjiu. Jingjidili* (Implementation mechanism of low-carbon city). *Economic Geography*, 30(6), pp. 949–954 (in Chinese).

Liang, Q (2009). *Oumeng yitihua guocheng gei women naxie qishi. Xueshuyanjiu* (Enlightenments from the integrating process of the European union upon us). *Academic Research*, (8), pp. 14–16 (in Chinese).

Liaoning Province Bureau of Statistics (1999). *Liaoning dongjiju bian, lishi di kuayue — Liaoning 50 nian huimou. Beijing: Zhongguo tongji chubanshe (Historical Jump — Looking Back at 50 years of Liaoning)*. Beijing: China Statistics Publishing (in Chinese).

Liaoning Province Bureau of Statistics (2009). *Huihuang de suiyue-liaoning 60 nian huimou*. Beijing: Zhongguo tongji chubanshe (*Historical Jump — Looking Back at 60 years of Liaoning*). Beijing: China Statistics Publishing (in Chinese).

Liaoning Province Environmental Protection Bureau (2005). *Liaoning huanjing baohuju. Liaoning huanjing baohuquzhi. Shenyang: Wanjuan chubanshe* (Liaoning Province Environmental Protection Record). Shenyang: Wanjuan Publishing (in Chinese).

Liaoning Provincial Government, 2010 "*Guanyu zai shengyang jingjiqu chengji lianjiedai guihua jianshe xincheng xinshizhen de tongzhi*" (The notice for Shenyang economic zone intercity connection belt development and building new cities and towns), Liaoning provincial government document number #8 [2010] (in Chinese).

Lin, CSG and YHD Wei (2002). China's restless urban landscapes 1: New challenges for theoretical reconstruction. *Environment and Planning A*, 34(9), pp. 1535–1544.

Lin, MX (2007). *Liaozhong chengshiqun di qishi. Juece* (Inspiration of urban agglomeration in Central of Liaoning). *Policy Decision*, (9), pp. 38–39 (in Chinese).

Liu, SL (2004). *Zhuazhu lishi jiyu maichu jianshi yibu-guanyu Fuxin shishi jingji zhuanxing shidian gongzuo de diaocha yu sikao. Liaoning jingji tongji* (Grasp the historical opportunity to take a step further — investigation and thinking of economic transformation of Fuxin City). *Liaoning Economic Statistics*, (2), pp. 14–15 (28) (in Chinese).

Liu, WB (2003). *Jingji zhuanxingqi guoyouqiye de ruogan wenti. "Shenhua guoyouqiyi gaige, zhenxing dongbei liaogongyejidi" guoyoujingji. Changchun luntian wenji* (A number of issues for the state-owned enterprise restructuring of the economies in transition: Deepen the reform of state-owned enterprises; Revitalization of the northeast old industrial base, State-owned economy) Changchun Forum (in Chinese).

Liu, WQ (2003). *Fuxin jingji zhuanxing liangnianlai de huigu yu zhanwang. Ziyuan chanye* (Review and outlook of two-years of Fuxin economic transformation). *Resource Industry*, 5(6), pp. 29–31 (in Chinese).

Liu, XD (2012). *"Shiyiwu" shiqi Shenyang jingjiqu zonghe shili xianzhu tigao. Liaoning jingji tongji* (Comprehensive strength of Shenyang economic zone in the "Eleventh Five-Year" period improved significantly). *Liaoning Economic Statistics*, (1), pp. 17–18 (in Chinese).

Liu, XL and HR Chang (2005). *"Dongbeixianxiang" de wenhua toushi yu qidi. Xingzheng yu fa* ("The Northeast Phenomenon": Its perspective and its enlightment). *Public Administration and Law*, (9), pp. 51–52 (in Chinese).

Liu, Y (2006). *Tudi duanque poshi changsanjiao jingji zhuanxing. "Zhongguogaige."* (The Yangtze River Delta economic transformation forced by the shortage of land). *China's Reform*, (7), 57–59 (in Chinese).

Liu, YB (2005). *Ziyuanxing chengshi chanye zhuanxing de guojijingyan jiqi duei woguo de qishi. Shijedili yanjiu* (International experience of resource-based city industrial transformation and their implications). *International Geographic Study*, 14(4), pp. 57–63 (in Chinese).

Liu, YG (2002). *Xinshiqi dongbeidiqu ziyuanxing chengshi de fazhan yu zhuanxing. Jingjidili* (Development and transformation of resource-based cities for Northeast in new era). *Economic Geography*, 22(5), pp. 594–597 (in Chinese).

Liu, YJ (2009). *Cong Shenyang tiexiqu gongye fazhan de lishi kan laogongyejidi gaizao yu zhenxing. Changchun: Dongbei shifan daxue* (From the history of Shenyang Tiexi industrial development to analyse old industrial base reformation and revitalisation). Changchun: Northeast Normal University (in Chinese).

Liu, ZH and LC Li (2003). *Guoyou qiye guodu fuzhai: binggen ji dueice Shenhua guoyouqiye gaige, zhenxing dongbe liaogongye jidi. Changchun luntan wenji* (Over-liabilities of the state-owned enterprises: The causes and countermeasures). Conference paper presented at Deepen the reform of state-owned enterprises; Revitalization of the northeast old industrial base, State-owned economy. Changchun Forum, Changchun, Jilin, China, 20–21 December, 2003 (in Chinese).

Liu, ZL, YX Dai, CG Dong and H Qi (2009). *Ditan chengshi linian yu guojijingyan. Chengshi fazhan yanjiu* (Low-carbon city theory and internationa experiences). *City Development Study*, (6), pp. 1–7 (in Chinese).

Lopez, SH (2004). *Reorganizing the Rust Belt*. Berkley: University of California Press.

Lu, DD and WD Liu (2003). *"Xinxihua yu shehui jingji kojian chongzu"* (Information Technology and Socio-Economic Space Reorganization) in

DD Lu, edited Zhongguo quyu fazhan di Lilun yu shijian (*Theory and Practice of China's regional development*). Beijing: Science Press, pp. 493–520 (in Chinese).

Lu, DD (2009). *Guanyu woguo quyu fazhan zhanlve yu fangzhen wenti. Jingjidili* (A number of issues on China's regional development strategy and policy). *Economic Geography*, 29(1), pp. 2–7 (in Chinese).

Lu, M and E Wang (2002). Forging ahead and falling behind: Changing regional inequalities in post-reform China. *Growth and Change*, 33(1), pp. 42–71.

Lubove, R (1996). *Twentieth-Century Pittsburgh*. Pittsburgh: University of Pittsburgh Press.

Luo, J (2004). *Lun jingying chengshi ji jingying chengshi tudi yu yingxiao chengshi. Ziyuan diaocha yu pingjia* (The management and operation of urban and its land with marketing city). *Resources Survey and Evaluation*, 21(3), pp. 53–56 (in Chinese).

Marton, MA (2013). *China's Spatial Economic Development: Regional Transformation in the Lower Yangzi Delta*. London: Routledge.

Mao, ZD (1976). *Lunshida guanxi. Renmin Ribao* (On ten relationships). People's Daily, 26 Dec 1976 (in Chinese).

Meng, C (2006). *Dongbeidiqu ziyuanxing chengshi chanye zhuanxing wentiyanjiu Changchun: jilindaxue* (Studies on industrial transformation of resource-based cities of Northeast). Master Thesis, Chang Chun: Jilin University (in Chinese).

Meyer, DR (1989). Midwestern industrialization and the American manufacturing belt in the nineteenth century. *The Journal of Economic History*, 49(4), pp. 921–937.

Moe, R and C Wilkie (1997). *Changing Places: Rebuilding Community in the Age of Sprawl*. New York: Henry Holt & Co.

Mu, Y (2005). *Fuxin: zhuanxing shiyan. Zhongguojingjizhoukan* (Fuxin: Transformation Test). *China Economic Weekly*, (2), pp. 26–27 (in Chinese).

Nader, S (2009). Pathway to low-carbon economy-The Master example. *Energy Procedia*, (1), pp. 3951–3958.

Nan, BF and RY Yang (2009). *Zhongguo dazao "ditanchengshi" chengshi fazhan xingainian bei guangwei jieshou. Renminribao* (The new concept of developing low-carbon city in China was widely accepted). People's Daily, 12 Oct 2009 (in Chinese).

Northeast Revitalisation Committee (2006). *Dongbei zhenxingban tiexigongyequ tiaozheng gaizao de lichen ji chengxiao* (Process and progress of reforming in

Tiexi industrial zone). Available at http://chinaneast.xinhuanet.com/200607/26/content_7618346.htm. Accessed on 26 July 2006 (in Chinese).

Pallagst, K (2009). The future of shrinking cities: Problems, patterns and strategies of urban transformation in global context. University of California, 8, pp. 1–88.

Pan, XD (2010). *Zhongguo ditanchengshi fazhan luxiantu yanjiu. Zhongguo renkou, ziyuan yu huanjing* (Path map study of Chinese low-carbon city development). *Chinese Population, Resource and Environment*, 20(10), pp. 13–18 (in Chinese).

Pan, JH, T Teng and YX Zheng (2004). *Ditan fazhan de shehuijingji yu jishufenxi: Kejixufazhan di linian, zhidu yu zhengce. Beijing Shehuikexue wenxian chubanshe (Social Economic and Technological Analysis of Low-carbon Development). Theory System and Policy for Sustainable Development.* Beijing: Social Science Academic Publishing (in Chinese).

Peerenboom, R (2008). *China Modernizes: Threat to the West or Model for the Rest?* Oxford: Oxford University Press.

Pei, P and Yang, F (2008). Study on revitalizing Northeast China through a new road of industrialization. *Canadian Social Science*, 4(2), pp. 74–80.

Peng, CG (2006). *Si da lin moshi zai zhongguo di lishi kaocha. Wuhan ligong daxue xuewei lunwen* (Historical study of Stalin Model in China). Masters Dissertation, Wuhan: Science and Engineering University of Wuhan (in Chinese).

Peng, HA and Yang, D (2004). *Dalian ruanjianyuan kuaisu chao guojihua fangxiang fazhan Zhongguo gaoxin jishu keji daobao* (Fast Development of software towards international direction in Dalian). Chinese High-tech technology, Herald, 21 July 2004 (in Chinese).

Peng, HA (2008). *Nuli dazao juyou shijie jingzhingli di zhuangbei zhizaoye jidi. Zhongguo gaojishu chanye daobao* (Develop equipment manufacturing base with international competitiveness). China New High Technology Industry Paper, 8 December 2008 (in Chinese).

Peng, Z and N Qu (2011). *Woguo tongchenghua fazhan yu quyu xietiao guihua duice yanjiu. Xiandai chengshi yanjiu* (Study on integrative development and regional coordinated planning strategies in China). *Modern Urban Research*, (6), pp. 20–24 (in Chinese).

Policy Research Center of CPC Daqing Municipal Party Committee (2007). *Zhonggong Daqing shiwei zhengce yanjiushi. Daqing kechixufazhan tansuo yu shijian — 2000–2006 quanshi youxiu diaoyan chengguo xuanbian*

Harbin: Heilongjiang kexuejishu chubanshe (Exploration and practice of sustainable development of Daqing: Selected outstanding researches from 2000 to 2006). Harbin: Heilongjiang Science and Technology Press (in Chinese).

Pu, MQ (2010). *Wuxi shishi lvse jianzhu ditanjihua. Xinhua ribao* (Wuxi City implemented low-carbon buildings plan). Xinhua Daily, 11 Jan 2010 (in Chinese).

Qi, YY (2003). *Tigao guoyou ziben xiaolv shi zhenxing dongbei liaogongye jidi de guanjian. "Shenhua guoyou qiye gaige, zhenxing dongbei liaogongye jidi" guoyou jingji. Changchun luntian wenji* (Improving the efficiency of state-owned capital is the key for the revitalization of old industrial bases in Northeast China. Deepen the reform of state-owned enterprises; Revitalization the northeast old industrial base, State-owned economy). Changchun Forum, Changchun, Jilin, China, 20–21 December, 2003 (in Chinese).

Qian, WJ and Y Li (2009). *Zhishi chengshi: zhongxin chengshi fazhan yu zhuanxing de xuanze. Chengshi guancha* (City of knowledge: The choice of development and transition for central cities). *Urban Watch*, (2), pp. 155–162 (in Chinese).

Qiao, M (2004). *Zhenxing dongbei- Zhongguo jingji "di si ji" zhanlve yu shijian. Beijing: Zhongguo gongren chubanshe.* (*The Strategy and Practices of Revitalising Northeast Region — The Fourth Polar of Chinese Economy*). Beijing: Chinese Workers Press (in Chinese).

Qin, W (2010). *Tiexi, bainian gongyewenhua de chuancheng. Zhuangbei zhizao* (Tiexi: Heritage of Hundred Years Industrial Culture). *Equipment Manufacturing*, (6), pp. 94–99 (in Chinese).

Qiu, BX (2009). *Woguo chengshi fazhan moshi zhuanxing qvshi — ditan shengtai chengshi. Chengshi fazhan yanjiu* (Trend for Chinese City development model transition — Low-carbon ecological city). *City Development Study*, 16(8), pp. 1–6 (in Chinese).

Qu, JS, F Gao, WF Zhang, *et al.*, (2007). *Butong ziyuan leixing de ziyuanxing chengshi jingji zhuanxing jichu yu moshi bijao — yi dianxing ziyuanxing chengshi weili. Ganhanqu ziyuan yu huanjing.* (Comparison of economic transformation foundation and transformation mode for different types of resource based cities — using typical resource-based city as example). *Drought Area Resource and Environment*, 21(2), pp. 12–16 (in Chinese).

Ren, XC (2009). *Guojia fagaiwei lingdao chongfen kending guangyuan ditan chongjian he fazhan zhilu* (Directors of the national development and reform committee admired the Guangyuan low-carbon reformation and development path). Available at http://www.scwmw.org. Accessed on 28 Dec 2009 (in Chinese).

Research Federation of Social Sciences in Daqing City (2007). *Daqingshi shehuikexuejie lianhehui ketizu. Guanyu tuijin Daqing shiyou ziyuanxing chengshi jingji zhuanxing di yanjiubaogao. Daqing shehuikexue* (Research report on advancing the economic transformation of Daqing City). *Daqing Social Sciences*, (1), pp. 10–18 (in Chinese).

Revitalising Northeast Region Committee (2007). *Zhenxing dongbeiban. Liaoqiye huanfa qingchun: Shenyang tiexiqu tiaozheng gaizao chenggong anli* (Old enterprises Revitalised: Successful Case of Tiexi Industrial District Reformation). Available at http://2007.changchun.gov.cn/other/wenku/wk_detail.jsp?ID=31704160000000000,1699. Accessed on 16 Nov 2005 (in Chinese).

Sang, Q, HP Zhang and Y Luo (2009). *Shengfu tongchenghua de shengcheng jizhi he dueice yangjiu. Renwendili* (Formation mechanism and countermeasures of cohesion of Shenyang and Fushun). *Human Geography*, 24(3), pp. 32–36 (in Chinese).

Shan, L and J Zhao (2011). *Liaoning yanhai jingjidai shehui jiuye yali fenxi ji jiejue tujin. Haiyang ji guanli* (Analysis on job pressure and its solution in coastal Liaoning). *Ocean Development and Management*, (7), pp. 104–108 (in Chinese).

Shen, J and F Wu (2012). Restless urban landscapes in china: A case study of three projects in shanghai. *Journal of Urban Affairs*, 34(3), pp. 255–277.

Shenyang City Plan Committee (2001). *Shenyangshi shiwu jihua huibian.* (*Shenyang City Tenth Five-Years Plan Collection*). Shenyang: Shenyang Beiling Press (in Chinese).

Shenyang Statistical Bureau (2011): *Shenyang tonjiju. Shenyang tonji nianjan (2002–2010). Beijing: Zhongguo tonjiju chubanshe* (*Shenyang Statistical Year Book 2002–2010*). Beijing: China Statistic Press (in Chinese).

Shenyang Tiexi District Plan Museum (2011). *Shenyangtiexiqu guihuazhanlanguan. Tiexiquzhanlanguan ziliao* (Tiexi District Museum Documents) (in Chinese).

Shi, JH and LJ Zhao (2008). *Ziyuanxingquyu chanyezhuanxing yu k echixufazhan yanjiu. Ganhanqu ziyuan yu huanjing* (Resource based districts industrial transition and sustainable development study). *Drought Area Resource and Environment*, 22(3), pp. 47–50 (in Chinese).

Song, GX (2009). *Guanyu daqing zai zhenxing dongbei liaogongyejidi zhong chanye jeigou tiaozheng de zhanlve sikao. Weilai yu fazhan* (Strategic thinking about daqing industrial structure adjustment in revitalizing the northeast old industrial base). *Future & Development*, 30(9), pp. 33–38 (in Chinese).

Song, XW (2009). *Zhongzhi qiye yu defang jingji xietiao fazhan yanjiu- yi Daqing, Jilin, Anshan, Benxi sichengshi weili. Jingjiyanjiu cankao.* (Coordinated development of state owned enterprises and local economy: Case study of Daqing, Jilin, Anshan, Benxi). *Review of Economic Research*, (47), pp. 3–14 (in Chinese).

Su, M (2004). *Fengsheng shuiqi kan tiexi- caizi zhenxingdongbei liaogongyejidi qianyan de baogao. Guotuziyuan* (Revitalised Tiexi District — Report from the frontline of revitalising Northeast old industrial base). *National Land Resource*, (1), pp. 4–15 (in Chinese).

Sun, YT and FC Liu (2010). A regional perspective on the structural transformation of China's national innovation system since 1999. *Technological Forecasting and Social Change*, 77(8), pp. 1311–1321.

Tang, WZ and HM Jiang (2001). *Sulianmoshi yu xinzhongguo de shehuizhuyi jianshe. Lilun yuekan* (The Soviet model and new China's socialism development). *Theory Monthly*, (9), pp. 22–24 (in Chinese).

Tapela, TN (2002). Planning for economic diversification and sustainable communities in mining towns: Towards a development planning framework. In Planning Africa 2002 International Conference, regenerating Africa through planning. Durban: ICC.

Tian, XW (2001). Deng Xiaoping's nanxun: Impact on China's regional development. In *The Nanxun Legacy and China's Development in the Post-Deng Era*, J Wong and Y Zheng (eds.). Singapore: Singapore University Press, pp. 75–94.

Tiexi District History Editing Committee (1998). *Tiexiquzhi bianweihui. Tiexiquzhi. Shenyangshi tiexiqu renminzhengfu difangzhi bangongshi* (*Tiexi District History*), pp. 29–30. Tiexi District, Shenyang: City Government Local History Office (in Chinese).

Tiexi District Government (2010). *Tiexiqu renminzhengfu. Jieyue jiyue liyong tudiziyuan cujin tiexi liaogongyejidi gaizaozhenxing. Guotuziyuan* (Save land resource to promote revitalisation of Tiexi old industrial district). *National Land Resource*, (12), pp. 18–19 (in Chinese).

Tiexi Local History Editing Office (1987). *Tiexiqu difangzhi bianzhuan bangong-shi. Tiexigongye di xingcheng yu fazhan de sange lichengbei. Tiexiqu difangzhi bianzhuan bangongshi* (*Three Milestones of the Formation and Development of Tiexi District Industry*). 1987 Shenyang: Shenyang Beiling Press (in Chinese).

Tong, BS (1999). *Fuxinshi. Beijing: Dongfang chubuanshe* (*Fuxin City History*). Beijing: Eastern Publishing (in Chinese).

Wan, T, JQ Zhang and J Dong (2011). *Ditan jingji beijingxia meitan kujie cheng-shi zhuanxing de sikao-yi fushun chengshi zhuanxing weili. "Meitan jishu"* (Reflections on the transformation of Coal-exhausted cities in the back-ground of a low carbon economy — Fushun City in transition as an example). *Coal Technology*, 30(5), pp. 1–3 (in Chinese).

Wang, DD (2009). *Ditanshidai jiasu daolai. Guiyang ribao* (Guiyang: Low-Carbon Era Coming Soon). Guiyang Daily, 25 Aug 2009 (in Chinese).

Wang, H (2005). *Tiexi liaogongyejidi gaizaozhenxing de celve yanjiu. Shenyang: Dongbeidaxue* (*Study for Tiexi Old Industrial Base Revitalisation Strategy*). Shenyang: Northeast University (in Chinese).

Wang, HQ (ed.) (1995). *Dalian wushinian. Dalian: Dalian chubanshe* (*Dalian 50 Years*). Dalian: Dalian Publishing (in Chinese).

Wang, JJ and MC Cheng (2010). From a hub port city to a global supply chain management center: A case study of Hong Kong. *Journal of Transport Geography*, 18(1), pp. 104–115.

Wang, LL and L Tan (2000). *Zhaizhuangu shi shenyang jichuang qingzhuang shangzhen. Jidian chanpin shichang* (Debt to share conversion has eased burden for Shenyang City machine tool industry). *Mechanical and Electrical Equipment Market*, (7), pp. 18 (in Chinese).

Wang, LL and MN Li (2004). *Laogongyejidi gaizao yu tizhi chuangxin. Beijing: Jingjikexue chubanshe* (*Reform and Systematic Innovation of Old Industrial Base*). Beijing: Economy Science Press (in Chinese).

Wang, LS and P Li (2002). *Dalian "chengjian jingji" fazhanmoshi yanjiu. Chengshi kaifa* (Dalian "City construction economic" development model). *City Development*, (2), pp. 25–28 (in Chinese).

Wang, Q (2004). *Tansuo zhongguo tese de ziyuanxingchengshi jingji zhuanxing zhilu-yi Liaoning Fuxin de shijian weili. Kejidaobao* (Search for economic transformation path of resource-based cities with Chinese features using Fuxin City, Liaoning Province as an example). *Scientific and Technological Paper*, (10), pp. 7–9 (in Chinese).

Wang, QY (2003). *Ziyuanxingchengshi zhuanxing yanjiu. Beijing: Zhongguo jingji chubanshe* (*Study for Resource Based Cities Transformation*). Beijing: China Economy Publishing (in Chinese).

Wang, SL (2010). *Xiamen xianxing xianshi tansuo ditan fazhan xiangguan guihua gangyao wancheng bianzhi. Xiamen wanbao* (Xiamen City leads the trail for low-carbon development, relative planning and frameworks completed). Xiamen Evening Paper, 07 Jan 2010 (in Chinese).

Wang, W (2011). *Xibu ziyuanxing chengshi fazhan dueice tanxi Zhongguo xibu keji*. (Countermeasures for Western resource-based urban development). *Science and Technology of West China*, 10(17), pp. 68–70 (in Chinese).

Wang, Z and YL Li (2009). *Huanbohai quyu jingji cujin zhengce yanjiu. Haiyangkaifa yu guanli*. (Studies on economic promotion policies in Bohai Sea rim Regional). *Ocean Development and Management*, 26(4), 112–115 (in Chinese).

Wang, XJ (2009). *Changjiang sanjiaozhou diqu chanyeyitihua de neihan, zhuti, yu tujing. Nanton daxue xuebao* (*shehui kexueban*) (Industry Integration in Yangzi River Delta: Connotation, Subject and Path). *Journal of Nantong University* (*Social Sciences Edition*), 25(4), pp. 26–30 (in Chinese).

Wang, ZH (2003). *Cong "xioudai fuxing" kan meiguo laogongyequ jiegou tiaozheng. Kejixinxi* (Old industrial structural adjustment from the "rust belt revival"). *Science and Technology Information*, (9), pp. 8–9 (in Chinese).

Wang, ZH and ZQ He (2003). *Kuangqu kechixufazhanzhong de jishuchuangxin yu chanyelian yanshen. Meitan xuebao*. (Technological innovation and industrial chain extension of sustainable development in mining area). *Journal of China Coal Society*, 28(4), pp. 348–352 (in Chinese).

Wei, F and HX Xing (2007). *Qiantan woguo kuangye chengshi kechixufazhan cunzai de wenti yu duice. Ziyuan yu chanye*. (Problems and countermeasures of sustainable development of mining cities in China). *Resources and industry*, 9(2), pp. 9–12 (in Chinese).

Wei, HK (2010). *Lun zhongguo chengshi zhuanxing zhanlve. Chengshi yu quyu guihua yanjiu*. (China's urban transformation strategy). *Urban and Regional Planning*, (1), pp. 1–19 (in Chinese).

Wei, X (2006). *Dongbei liaogongyejidi tizhi jizhi bianqianzhong de lujing yilai yu suoding xiaoying fenxi. Shangye yanjiu* (Path-depending and lock-in effect of institutional innovation in the Northeast old Industrial Base). *Commercial Research*, (23), pp. 188–191 (in Chinese).

Weisz, H. and K Steinberger (2010). Reducing energy and material flows in cities. *Current Opinion in Environmental Sustainability*, 2(3), pp. 185–192.

Weng, XQ (2010). *Chang sanjiao diqu chukou maoyi zengzhang fangshi zhuanxing. Tequjingji.* (Growth mode transformation of region export trading in Yangtze River Delta). *Special Zone Economy*, (4), pp. 44–46 (in Chinese).

Won, J (2004). Withering away of the iron rice bowl? The reemployment project of post-socialist China. *Studies in Comparative International Development*, 39(2), pp. 71–93.

Won, J (2005). The making of the post-proletariat in China. *Development and Society*, 34(2), pp. 191–215.

Wong, CYL, CCJM Millar, CJ Choi (2006). Singapore in transition: From technology to culture hub. *Journal of Knowledge Management*, 10(5), pp. 79–91.

Wu, WJ and XS Cheng (2009). *Ziyuanxingchengshi kechixvfazhan pingjia zhibiao tixi goujian yanjiu. Meitan jingji yanjiu.* (Research on evaluation index system for the resource-based sustainable urban development). *Coal Economic Research*, (2) (in Chinese).

Wu, L, S Kaneko and S Matsuoka (2005). Driving forces behind the stagnancy of China's energy related CO_2 emissions from 1996 to 1999: The relative importance of structural change, intensity change and scale change. *Energy Policy*, 33(3), pp. 319–335.

Xia, LH (2011). *Daqing 2011 nian zhengfu gongzuo baogao* (2011 report on government work of Daqing City). Available at http://www.daqing.gov.cn/zfgz/zfgzbg/135766.shtml. Accessed on 17 Jan 2011 (in Chinese).

Xia, LH (2012). *Daqing 2012 nian zhengfu gongzuo baogao* (2012 report on government work of Daqing City). Available at http://www.daqing.gov.cn/zfgz/zfgzbg/232354_2.shtml. Accessed on 21 Jan 2012 (in Chinese).

Xiang, W, QL Qian and KR Sheng (2006). *Xibu dakaifa yu dongbei zhenxing dongbei liaogongyejidi zhanlve de bijiao yu sikao. Jingjidili* (Comparison and ponder of the strategies between "the development of the western" and the "revitalizing the northeast old industrial base"). *Economic Geography*, 26(6), pp. 902–918 (in Chinese).

Xia, YZ and M Wang (2010). *Qianxi maozedong zai gongyehua daolushang weineng chaoyue sulian moshi de yuanyin ji qishi. Hubeishing shehuizhuyi xueyuan xuebao* (Analysis of the reason and implications of Mao Zedong's Unsuccessful breakthrough of the Soviet Model). *Journal of Hubei Institute of Socialism*, (4), pp. 62–64 (in Chinese).

Xiao, PC (2010). *Riben beijiuzhou shengtaicheng fazhan xvnhuan jingji de jing-yan ji qishi. Xinan kejidaxue xuebao.* (Experience and enlightenment of eco-city development of circular economy in Kitakyushu of Japan). *The Southwest University of Science and Technology Journal (Philosophy and Social Science Edition),* 27(1), 29–34 (in Chinese).

Xing, HF and GF Gu (2007). *Dongbei diqu chanye xietiao jizhi yanjiu. Jingji zongheng.* (Studies on coordination mechanism in Northeast region). *Economic Aspect,* (3) (in Chinese).

Xing, M (2007). *Shengfu tongchenghua jianshe de ruogan sikao. Chengshi gui-hua.* (Thoughts over integration of Shenyang–Fushun metropolitan area). *City Planning Review,* 31(10), pp. 52–56 (in Chinese).

Xu, BY, X Yun and JH Zhang (2011). *Zhenxing lushang hulu zhuan-dalian laogongyejidi banian zhuanxing fazgan zhilu. Dalian ribao* (On the revitalization way the peak "back" and road "turn" — The road in eight years transformation and development of Dalian old industrial bases. Dalian Daily, 23 May 2011 (in Chinese).

Xu, J (2009). The revitalization of Northeast China economy must start with institutional innovations. *Chinese Business Review,* 8(2), pp. 28–30.

Xu, F (2010). *Suzhou dazao chang sanjao ditan chengshi. Gusu wanbao* (Suzhou City building low-carbon city in the triangular Chang river area). Gusu Evening News, 11 Jan 2010 (in Chinese).

Xu, GY (2006). *Dongbei liaogongyejidi gaizao moshi yanjiu. Harbin: Harbin gongye daxue* (Studies on transformation model of Northeast old industrial base). Harbin: Harbin Institute of Technology (in Chinese).

Xu, GQ, ZY Liu and ZH Jiang (2006). *Zhongguo tanpaifang de yinsu fenxi moxing ji shizheng fenxi: 1995–2004. Zhongguo renkou, ziyuan yu huanjing* (Causes analysing model of Chinese carbon emission and empirical study: 1995–2004). *China Population, Resource and Environment,* 16(6), pp. 158–161 (in Chinese).

Yang, D (1990). Patterns of China's Regional Development Strategy. *The China Quarterly,* (122), pp. 230–257.

Yang, G and LH Rong (2001). *Xiandaihua chengshihuanjing youshi de dingwei fenxi- jiyu dalianchengshi jingji fazhan de gean yanjiu. Daliandaxue xuebao* (Positioning analysis of modern civilised city economic advantages — case study of Dalian City economic development model). *Dalian University Paper,* 22(3), pp. 7–11 (in Chinese).

Yigitcanlar, T (2010). Making space and place for the knowledge economy: Knowledge-based development of Australian cities. *European Planning Studies*, 18(11), pp. 1769–1786.

Yigitcanlar, T, K O'Connor and C Westerman (2008): The making of knowledge cities: Melbourne's knowledge-based urban development experience. *Cities*, 25(2), pp. 63–72.

Yin, YQ (2007). *Fuxinshi shuihuanjing xianzhuang yu weilai fazhan. Nongye yu jishu* (Water resource condition and future development in Fuxin City). *Agriculture and Technology*, 27(5), pp. 101–103 (in Chinese).

Yuan, JB (2009). *Shangdong Dezhou jianxing ditanchengshi, shishi "baiwan wuding gongcheng"*. *Bohai zaobao* (Dezhou City, Shangdong Province practising low-carbon city, implementing 1 million rooftop project). Bohai Morning News, 27 Dec 2009 (in Chinese).

Yuan, XL and YY Zhong (2010). *Zhongguo ditan chengshi de shijian yu tixi goujian*. Chengshi fazhan yanjiu (Practices and systematic formation of Chinese low-carbon city). *City Development Study*, 17(5), pp. 42–47 (in Chinese).

Yun, X (2007). *Yinling dongbei kaifang de longtou, quanmian zhenxing zhongyao di yinqing. Dalian ribao* (A leading city of northeast China open and an important engine of all-round revitalization). Dalian Daily, 15 Sep 2007 (in Chinese).

Zhang, DH (2004). *Dongbei laogongyejidi shenhua guoyou qiyegaige de nandian yu duice. Changchun: Jilin daxue* (Difficulties and countermeasures of deepening the reform of state-owned enterprises in the northeast old industrial base). Changchun: Jilin University (in Chinese).

Zhang j. inli, Lin H. ui. (2006). *Dalian feigongyouzhi qiye tiaoqi jingji fazhan daliang. Liaoning jingji tongji* (Non state-owned enterprises play important role in Dalian). *Liaoning Economic Statistics*, (12), pp. 9–11 (in Chinese).

Zhang, KM (2009). *Ditan zhongguo: diwei, tiaozhan yu zhanlve. Zhongguo renkou, ziyuan yu huanjing* (China in low-carbon: Position, challenges and strategy). *China Polulation, Resource and Environment*, 18(3), pp. 1–7 (in Chinese).

Zhang, KM, JH Pan and DP Cui (2008). *Ditan jingjilun. Beijing: Zhongguo huanjing chubanshe (Low-Carbon Economy Theory)*. Beijing: China Environment Publishing (in Chinese).

Zhang, LZ (1993). *Daqingshi guotu kaifa zhengti guihua. Harbin: Heilongjiang kexuejishu chubanzhe* (Overall Planning of Land Development Regulation in Daqing City). Harbin: Heilongjiang Science and Technology Press (in Chinese).

Zhang, ME and CY Wu (2001). *Ziyuanxing chengshi chanye zhuanxing zhangai yu duice yanjiu* (Industrial restructuring obstacles and countermeasures research of resource-based cities). *Economic Theory and Economic Management*, (2), 35–37 (in Chinese).

Zhang, PF, YM Fu, ZP Xiong and M Liu (2011). *Tiexiqu jianzhu jingguan shikong bianhua tezheng ji yingxiangyinshu. Shengtaixue zazhi* (Change in Tiexi district building landscape and its influencing factor). *Ecology Magazine*, 3(2), pp. 335–342 (in Chinese).

Zhang, PY (2008). Revitalizing old industrial base of Northeast China: Process, policy and challenge. *Chinese Geographical Science*, 18(2), pp. 109–118.

Zhang, PY (2005). *Fuxin jingji zhuanxing de zhanlue wenti ji duice. Kuangyeyanjiu yu kaifa* (Strategic Problems and Responds for Fuxin City Economic Transformation). *Mining Industry Study and Development*, 25(1), pp. 1–5 (in Chinese).

Zhang, PY, H Li and LJ Tong, *et al.*, (2011). *Dongbeidiqu Kuangyechengshi rendi xitong cuiruoxing- lilun, fangfa, shijian. Beijing: Kexue chubanshe* (Vulnerability of Man-land System of Mining Cities in Northeast China: Theory, Method and Case studies). Beijing: Science Press (in Chinese).

Zhang, PY (2006). *Shenyang tiexigongyequ gaizao de zhidu he wenhua yinsue Renwen dili* (System and cultural factors in reforming the Tiexi industrial zone of Shenyang City). *Humanity Geography*, 21(2), pp. 45–49 (in Chinese).

Zhang, WQ (2007). *Maozedong zhongguo shehuizhuyi gongyehua sixiangzhong de sulian yinsu. Lilunyuekan* (Soviet Union factor in the Chinese socialism industrialisation theory of Mao Zedong). *Theory Monthly*, (5) 1 pp. 1–14 (in Chinese).

Zhang, X (2003). *Dui jianli xiandai chengshi xunhuan jingji tixi de sikao. Xueshu jiaoliu* (Thinking of developing modern city's cyclic economic system). *Academic Communication*, (10), pp. 54–57 (in Chinese).

Zhang, XY, X Li and J Yin (2010). *Cong chengshiqun dao dadushiqu- xinzhengce yujingxia de Shenyang jingjiqu kujian fazhan yanjiu. Chengshi gueihua* (From urban cluster to metropolitan area: Spatial development of Shenyang economic region in the new policy context). *City Planning Review*, 34(3), pp. 60–64 (in Chinese).

Zhang, XX (2005). *Jingcheng hezuo gongdong zhenxing kaichuang Shenyang jingjiqu weilai. Shenyang ribao* (Sincere cooperation, collusion development to create a better future of the Shenyang economic zone). Shenyang Daily, 8 April 2005 (in Chinese).

Zhang, Y (2009). *Fuxin "tuwei"- zhongguo diyige ziyuanxing chengshi jingji zhuanxing shidianshi fuxin diaocha. Renmin ribao* (Fuxin City's breakthrough — the first pivot city for resource-based cities economic transition). People's Daily, 6 Mar 2009 (10) (in Chinese).

Zhang, Y and WJ Chen (2011). *Chuangjian zhuanxing shifanshi fuxin xinqidian zaichufa. Jinri liaoning* (Building transition model, Fuxin City on the road at new start). *Liaoning Today* (2), pp. 7–17 (in Chinese).

Zhang, YH and Zhang, PY (2011). *Changchun ditan shengtai chengshi fazhan ceping yanjiu. Dongbei shida xuebao (zirankexueban)* (Changchun City low-carbon ecological city development evaluation). *Journal of Northeast Normal University (Natural Science Edition)*, 43(2), pp. 151–156 (in Chinese).

Zhang, YK and YX Zhou (2007). *Hexi zoulang ziyuanxingchengshi kechixufazhan yu zhuanxing tantao. Ganhanqu ziyuan yu huanjing.* (Discussion of sustainable development and transformation of resource-based cities in the Hexi corridor). *Drought Zone Resource and Environment*, 21(9), 6–9 (in Chinese).

Zhang, YX and L Tong (2011). The serious problems and countermeasures of Northeastern China's resource-dependent cities' transformation and development. *Energy Procedia*, (5), pp. 1631–1635.

Zheng, QS (2005). *Deguo luer meitanjidi de chenggong gaizao dui Shanxi meitan ziyuanxing chengshi kechixu fazhan de jiejian yiyi. Shengchanli yanjiu* (Implications to sustainable development of coal-oriented cities in Shanxi Province from successful experience of Ruhr district Germany coal base reformation). *Productivity Study*, 12(4), pp. 166–168 (in Chinese).

Zhao, XJ, DR Wu and X Rong, *et al.*, (2007). *Chengshuqi ziyuanxing chengshi chanye zhuanxing fazhan moshi yanjiu-yi Jiningshi weili. Dili yu dilixinxi kexue* (Study of industrial transformation model of resource-based cities at maturity stage — using Jining City as example). *Geography and Geographic Information Science*, 23(6), pp. 87–91 (in Chinese).

Zhao, XN and X Liu (2007). *Zhidu lujing yilai lilun de fazhan, luojijichu he fenxi kuangjia. Dangdai caijing* (Development, logics and analyzing frameworks of systematic path dependency theory). *Contemporary Finance & Economics*, (7), pp. 118–122 (in Chinese).

Zhao, Y (2010). *Chanye jiqunhua fazhan de gean yanjiu- yi Shenyang jingjiqu weili. Jingji zonghing* (The research on industrial cluster development — take Shenyang economic district as example). *Economic Review*, (7), pp. 101–106 (in Chinese).

Zhou, LQ and XR Deng (2009). *huanbohai quyu jingji fazhan baogao. Shehui kexue chubanshe* (*Economic Development Report of Bohai Sea Rim Region*). Beijing: Social Sciences Academic Press (in Chinese).

Zhu, SX and GY Zhuang (2010). *Jiyu ditanhua shijiao de dongbeidiqu zhenxing- yi Jilinshi weili. Ziyuankexue.* (Revitalising Northeast region from low-carbon perspective — using Jilin City as an example). *Resource Science*, 32(2), pp. 230–234 (in Chinese).

Zhu, SX (2009). *Changxian "ditanjingji". 21 shiji licai* (Jilin City: Low-carbon Economy Trail). *21st Century Financial Management*, (9), 37–38 (in Chinese).

Zhu, YB, Z Wang and L Pang, *et al.*, (2009). *Jiyu jingjimoni de zhoguo nengyuan xiaofei yu tanpaifang gaofeng yuce. Dilixuebao.* (Chinese energy consumption and carbon emission peak estimation based on economic stimulation). *Journal of Geographical Science*, 64(8), pp. 935–944 (in Chinese).

Zhuang, GY (2009). *Yi ditan chengshi wei zhuxian, dazao lvse zhongguo. Lvye* (Develop green China relying on low-carbon cities). *Green Leaf*, (1), pp. 62–64 (in Chinese).

Index

235